MODERN HISTORIANS AND THE
STUDY OF HISTORY

MODERN HISTORIANS AND THE STUDY OF HISTORY

*

ESSAYS AND PAPERS
BY
F. M. POWICKE

ODHAMS PRESS LIMITED
LONG ACRE, LONDON

First Published 1955
Reprinted 1956

Copyright T.756.1R.G.

MADE AND PRINTED IN
GREAT BRITAIN BY ODHAMS (WATFORD) LTD.
WATFORD, HERTS

CONTENTS

PART I
MEMOIRS AND NOTICES

	PREFACE	*Page* 7
Chapter I	Sir Paul Vinogradoff	9
II	The Manchester History School: T. F. Tout, 21; J. Tait, 44; A. G. Little, 73	19
III	Henri Pirenne	96
IV	Charles Homer Haskins	109
V	H. W. C. Davis	118
VI	Three Cambridge Scholars: C. W. Previté-Orton, Z. N. Brooke, and G. G. Coulton	127
VII	Leopold Delisle and Anglo-French History	142
VIII	Sir Charles Firth	150
IX	Reginald Lane Poole	154
X	James F. Willard	156

PART II
HISTORICAL STUDY

XI	History Lessons and the League	159
XII	Historical Study in Oxford	164
XIII	The Collection and Criticism of Original Texts	184

CONTENTS

Chapter			Page	
XIV	Modern Methods of Medieval Research			193
XV	The Limits of Effective Co-operation in the Synthesis of History			200
XVI	A Presidential Address			206
XVII	Recent Work on the Origin of the English Parliament			217
XVIII	After Fifty Years			225
XIX	The Economic Motive in Politics			240
	INDEX			252

PREFACE

The memoirs, lectures and papers collected in this volume reflect some of the influences which have given life and direction to historical activities, particularly in England, during the last sixty or seventy years. I have felt no desire to make them the basis of a "study," still less to give them an autobiographical setting. They speak for themselves. Their value would have been impaired if I had tried to bring them up-to-date. I have made a few changes in them, but have not altered their character.

References to the originals are given in footnotes to the various articles. I thank those who have allowed me to reprint them, the Council of the British Academy, the Council of the Royal Historical Society, the Director of the Institute of Historical Research, the University of Louvain, the delegates of the Clarendon Press, the Editors and Publishers of the *English Historical Review*, the Editors and Editorial Board of *History*, the Editors of the *Cambridge Historical Journal*, the *Economic History Review*, the *Oxford Magazine*, the *Times*, and *History Today*. I am also indebted to the house of John Murray for permission to reprint some pages about Leopold Delisle from a joint article which appeared anonymously in the *Quarterly Review* in 1911, and to the Editor of the *Manchester Guardian* for permission to reprint an article, also anonymous, from its issue of 12 March, 1921.

F. M. P.

CHAPTER I

SIR PAUL VINOGRADOFF[1]

Paul Vinogradoff was born in Kostroma, Central Russia, on 1 December, 1854. His father was the director of a school in Moscow, his mother was a daughter of one of the veterans of the war of 1812—General P. Kobeleff. At the age of sixteen he entered the university of Moscow, then at the height of its fame, as a student of history. After graduation he spent a year (1875-6) in Germany, and studied at Berlin where he was admitted to the seminars of Mommsen and Brunner. His first published paper appeared in 1876 in the *Forschungen zur Deutschen Geschichte,* and its theme—the legal aspect of manumission—shows that he had already chosen the ground from which he was never to move during his ever-widening survey of history and politics. His first book, a treatise on the origins of the feudal system in Italy, was begun after his return to Moscow as a lecturer, and was published in 1881 as a thesis for the degree of master. Not long afterwards, in 1883, he made his first visit to England, where he worked for fifteen months or so in the Public Record Office, the British Museum, the Bodleian, and the Cambridge University Library. There have been some memorable visits to England by foreign scholars since Master Vacarius came and taught law in the twelfth century, and the visit of this young Russian was to be as memorable and fruitful as any. He gave even more than he received. Of what he received he said something in the preface to *Villainage in England,* where we meet the names of Pollock, York Powell, Seebohm, Maitland. "Henry Bradshaw was the first to lay an English MS. cartulary before me in the Cambridge University Library; and in all my travels through

---

[1] Reprinted, with corrections, from *The English Historical Review,* xli (1926), 236-43. For a more detailed and intimate appreciation, see H. A. L. Fisher's memoir, prefaced to Vinogradoff's *Collected Papers* (1928).

European libraries and archives I never again met such a guide." He gave to medieval scholars Bracton's Note Book, the discovery of which in the British Museum he announced in a letter to the *Athenaeum* in July, 1884, and he was a real stimulus to Maitland who in a few years published his brilliant edition of the newly noted manuscript. The two men had first met in January of this year, and in April Maitland, in the end of a note about his own studies in Bracton, anticipates a meeting in Oxford on 11 May. The result of this meeting was described by the late warden of New College:

> The day was fine and the two scholars strolled into the Parks, and lying full length on the grass took up the thread of their historical discourse. Maitland has spoken to me of that Sunday talk; how from the lips of a foreigner he first received a full consciousness of that matchless collection of documents for the legal and social history of the middle ages, which England had continuously preserved and continuously neglected, of an unbroken stream of authentic testimony, flowing for seven hundred years, of tons of plea rolls from which it would be possible to restore an image of long-vanished life with a degree of fidelity which could never be won from chronicles and professed histories.[1]

A few months later Maitland's edition of the earliest Gloucestershire plea roll appeared with a dedication to Vinogradoff. As Mr. Fisher said, the slim volume marks an epoch. *Villainage in England*, which appeared in Russian in 1887, the year of his appointment as professor of history, and in English in 1892, was the result of Vinogradoff's own investigations in England. It was hardly less significant than the work which Maitland was now rapidly pouring out.

[1] Fisher, *Frederick William Maitland* (Cambridge, 1910), pp. 24-5. The story that Maitland first visited the Public Record Office after the talk at Oxford is not correct. It is true that he was there on 13 May; but he had previously consulted records there on 25 February, 30 April and 5 May of this year 1884. Mr. H. C. Johnson of the Public Record Office has kindly noted the dates of Maitland's visits in the Literary Search Room Register. As Professor T. F. T. Plucknett shows in his lecture on Maitland's view of law and history (*Law Quarterly Review*, lxvii (1951), 185-7). Maitland must have been at work on the Gloucestershire plea roll for some time before 11 May, 1884.

SIR PAUL VINOGRADOFF

Villainage in England is the best of Vinogradoff's books, because it is the freshest, the most finished in style and plan, with its parts duly subordinated to the exposition of definite "questions of social history connected with the period of the formation of Common Law". It was the work of a young man, who had been trained by the best masters in Russia and Germany, and whose encyclopaedic outlook and practical interests were sharpened and given a new significance by work upon the richest collection of medieval historical material in the world. What he terms the glorious vista of comparative study was revealed to him; he found here an exhilarating confirmation of his belief in the inner validity of his interests and in the value of historical inquiry to the Russian patriot. His attempts, in his introduction, to relate the more somnolent course of historical inquiry in England to the great movement begun by Savigny and Ihering, provoked his friend Maitland to gentle and humorous criticism; and later developments in Russia made books of this kind sadly irrelevant to the "one main question: how far legislation can and should act upon the social development of the agrarian world". But when Vinogradoff became professor in Moscow the prospect was fair. The leaders of liberal opinion in Russia, like those in Germany earlier in the century, were tending, in a more hopeful atmosphere, to give a more constructive bias to ideals which had been almost too cosmopolitan. "No writer of any standing [in Russia]", Vinogradoff wrote in the first year of the late war, "would dream of building up a theory of violence in vindication of a claim to culture",[1] but the culture, which had so generously comprehended the claims of literature, music, and art—claims never neglected by Vinogradoff throughout his life—might now find scope for practical influence. Vinogradoff has himself described his aims as professor of history.

He endeavoured not only to form a school of historians, trained in the methods of western scholarship, but also to

[1] In the remarkable contribution to *The Times*, 14 September, 1914, reprinted in *Oxford Pamphlets*, 1914, no. 12: "Russia, the Psychology of a Nation."

influence the progress of general education in Russia. . . . He was elected councillor of the municipal Duma and became chairman of the educational committee. This gave him an opportunity to promote an extension of the network of elementary schools that made it possible for every child living in Moscow to go through a course of primary education. In 1896 he founded a paedagogical society in which teachers of all grades could meet to discuss problems and conditions of education.[1]

Activities of this kind naturally affected his historical work; and, apart from his English edition of *Villainage in England,* his main publications were a manual of universal history in three parts for use in secondary schools, and a collection of essays on medieval history in four volumes, to which his pupils and colleagues contributed. Yet several striking essays and reviews belong to these years, including a paper on the text of Bracton in the *Law Quarterly Review* (1885), articles in German periodicals on kinship in old Norwegian law, and on wergeld, and, in the pages of the *English Historical Review* (1893), the famous little paper in which Sir Henry Spelman's concise definition of "folcland" was rehabilitated.

We in England find it hard to regret the unhappy and anxious circumstances which led to Vinogradoff's withdrawal from this life of social influence and administration and gave us for a quarter of a century one of our most illustrious teachers and scholars. As time went on both the spirit of reaction and revolutionary discontent become more intense, and the professors who tried to follow a middle course were placed, to use Vinogradoff's own phrase, between two fires. Held responsible by the government for disorder and accused by their pupils of treachery to their own principles, their position was impossible. As chairman of a professorial committee, Vinogradoff devised, during one of the frequent crises, a form of understanding between the university authorities and the students.

[1] I am much indebted to Lady Vinogradoff for the use of an autobiographical sketch prepared for the new Académie Internationale de Droit Comparé; and to Miss M. F. Moor, Professor Stenton, and other friends of Sir Paul for helpful information.

The minister of public instruction came to Moscow in person to destroy the arrangement. The professor resigned in despair and came to England (December, 1901). For a time he settled with his family at Tunbridge Wells, then at the end of 1903 he was elected Corpus professor of jurisprudence at Oxford in succession to Sir Frederick Pollock.

The new professor added a cosmopolitan element to the academic life of Oxford. He spoke, I suppose, more than a dozen languages and wrote in at least five. It was characteristic of him that, when he took up the study of early English history, he felt it necessary to master not only the history of Scandinavian institutions but also the Scandinavian tongues; and it was during a long visit to Norway that he met the lady whom in 1897 he married. After his settlement in England he made frequent visits to France, where his particular friends were Paul Viollet, R. Dareste, and Charles Bémont. He thrice visited the United States—in 1907, 1923, 1924—and his lectures in the chief American universities, especially on his later visits, give very interesting indications of the way in which his mind was directed towards the juristic discussion of current problems. In 1913–14 he delivered a course of lectures in Calcutta, in 1922 in Leiden, in 1924 in Oslo. He was foreign or corresponding member of at least ten learned academies in various European countries and was given as many honorary degrees. He died in Paris in December, 1925, just after he had received an honorary degree at the Sorbonne. Yet, throughout all these years Vinogradoff's main interests were in Russia. Only in 1918, to use his own words, did he give up "all hope of a healthy national development in Russia", and obtain naturalization as a British subject. The preceding years had been years of high hope shattered by constant disillusionment. He was much moved and uplifted, for example, by the summoning of the Duma. In 1910 and 1911 he gave courses of lectures as supernumerary professor in Moscow, but renounced the pleasant task when in 1911 a number of progressive professors in the university were dismissed by the minister of public instruction. The last opportunity for service came during the war. In 1915 he was elected a member of the Imperial Academy of Sciences in Petrograd, and he made several visits to Russia in the cause of the allies and their solidarity. He was knighted in 1917.

The constant recurrence of saddening disappointments might well have weakened the energy of a strong man; but Vinogradoff was always faithful to his wide intellectual interests, and, while his outlook as a scholar and as a student of politics may have shifted somewhat, his vigour was unabated to the end. It has been suggested that the productivity of his later years was restless and that his spirit lost its old buoyancy. This judgement is not confirmed by an examination of his writings, nor by the impressions of his closest friends. His writings are scattered and numerous, and we may regret that he gave up social history for historical jurisprudence, but no one can read the published lectures of the last few years without seeing that his mind was deliberately and alertly occupied upon what he considered to be the fundamental issues in the study of jurisprudence. In the old Moscow days he had lectured on Greek and medieval history; and the possibility of a two-fold development is indicated clearly in his earliest writings. His impatience with abstractions and "general statements not based on any real investigation into facts" might drive him on to still more elaborate researches into the social conditions of medieval England. His strong interest in law as an applied science, providing "a rational background for a vast body of practical precepts", might force him to display the general principles of historical jurisprudence. For some years after he settled in Oxford he followed the former course, and such admirable little books as his *Roman Law in the Middle Ages* (1909) and his *Common Sense in Law* (1914) seem, when set beside *The Growth of the Manor* (1905), *English Society in the Eleventh Century* (1908), and the seminar study and text of the *Survey of Denbigh* (1914), to be slight concessions, as it were, to less specialized expectations. But the absorption in legal principles, or rather in the circumstances under which they found expression, was probably at all times present. It appeared constantly in his teaching and gives meaning to many a page in his most minute investigations. It has been observed that Vinogradoff used fourteenth-century legal terms as though he were a practising lawyer of the time rather than an historical student living centuries later.

The Growth of the Manor, better than any of his books, reveals Vinogradoff's great gifts as a teacher. It is based upon lectures, and abounds in those steady, broad-based generalizations which are so useful as correctives to the ready speculations of quick-minded students revelling in a store of unsolved problems. The range of learning is immense, the temper somewhat conservative, showing a distinct, though not very far-reaching, reaction against the teaching of Maitland. In his seminar, to which so many younger medieval students are deeply indebted, he would always lay stress on the significance of the salient texts. He would permit no inaccurate facility, no shoddiness of thought or expression. *English Society in the Eleventh Century*, on the other hand, is an elaborate treatise hard to read. The exact bearing of the argument is not always clear, and one suspects that Vinogradoff was rather too inclined to regard Domesday Book as a treasury of facts and not sufficiently alive to the necessity of understanding the structure of the record. As was also natural, he never became familiar with the details of medieval English topography. But as a study of Domesday terminology the book will maintain its position until detailed work on the twelfth century has led to a clearer understanding of the differences between the organization of the various regions of England than was possible when Vinogradoff wrote. In it he fulfilled a promise, made in *Villainage in England,* to carry his work back to earlier times, and he also satisfied his cravings as a historical realist. He set out to describe a society which he saw, and it would be a mistake to conclude, from the difficult mode of expression and the austere accumulation of facts, that the book is an essay in statistical interpretation.

The study of English history in the middle ages owes much to Vinogradoff. For ten years (1908–18) he was literary director to the Selden Society, and as chairman of a committee of the British Academy he planned a series of "Records of English Economic and Social History", of which the most impressive volume is Sir Frank Stenton's collection of Danelaw charters.

These ventures, however, were, for various reasons, not so happy as they might have been. They required a sustained effort of organization and co-operation which Vinogradoff seems to have found irksome. He was more successful in his "Oxford Studies in Social and Legal History", a series comprising several of the most helpful and illuminating books of recent times upon technical or obscure questions in medieval history. The editor's own share was confined to the duties of supervision, and many of the volumes bear witness to the wide range of his interest in and sympathy with the studies of others rather than to the course of his own labours, which became concentrated more and more upon the early history and the recent problems of jurisprudence. The first two—it is to be feared the only—volumes of his *Outlines of Historical Jurisprudence* appeared in 1920 and 1922, and were concerned, the one with introductory matter and tribal law, the other with the jurisprudence of the Greek city. The enterprise was an ambitious one, and all the more difficult because Vinogradoff could never be content with a philosophical exposition. He must follow the guidance of the thread of principle into the labyrinth of historical fact; he must take part with the family in the division of property or feel exactly what Demosthenes had at the back of his mind, while he is seeking to explain the general significance of their acts. Like Ihering, for whom he came to have a much greater admiration than casual references would suggest, he saw in the history of law the incessant working of strife and purpose. Law was not a force working without effort in history, a series of almost imperceptible adjustments; it was history itself.[1] How intensely Vinogradoff's mind was at work upon this aspect of history is best seen in the last few years. He wrote several essays upon the working of Roman maxims in medieval systems of law, and he was never willing to divorce the reception of these maxims from the particular circumstances of their application. Again, in his Leiden lectures, *Historical Types of International Law* (1923), and his lectures in American universities, he was concerned with the

[1] See the interesting contrast between Savigny and Ihering in J. Charmont's *La Renaissance du Droit Naturel* (Montpellier, 1910), ch. iii.

bearing of recent judicial decisions upon the problem of the state or upon the validity of recent speculation in the light of actual tendencies. "State and law are two aspects of the same thing", and, while we urge the necessity of the extra-legal sanctions, we must remember that they operate in an organized community bound together by law. In these lectures Vinogradoff constantly applied the views which he had expressed in some penetrating chapters, e.g., those on "Law and Psychology" and "Law and Political Science", in the introduction to his *Historical Jurisprudence*. Recent events, he evidently thought, gave fresh significance to a political philosophy which, in his later volumes, he would have expounded with an almost passionate earnestness.

Vinogradoff was an omnivorous reader. "In the Bodleian", we are told, "he read vastly." He read the whole of Troeltsch's works, for example, in preparation for the third volume of his *Outlines of Historical Jurisprudence*. There was a close relation at Oxford between his lectures and his books. Thus the volume on Greek jurisprudence was preceded by lectures, given during some years in the spring term, on Greek legal procedure. In these lectures he gave reality to the various γραφαί and δίκαι, and illuminated the public and private law of the Greeks. Some of the lectures were written, but he did not re-deliver them. The material was turned over again and re-planned. In their new form, Miss Moor tells me, and again in the next year, the lectures were taken down by his secretary when they were delivered, and the version which finally satisfied him became the basis of the book, "until some of the pages became a wonderful mass of almost illegible corrections and insertions. This—copied out—resulted in a typescript which was again subjected to a good deal of correction, but which with modifications finally went to the printer". Special lectures and articles were composed in much the same way, and were sometimes retyped as many as five times. He had an exceptional memory, rather like Acton's, and could carry in his head the references to volumes and pages, a faculty which, if applied to an elaborately annotated book like *English Society in the Eleventh Century*, could have its disadvantages.

His mind was always at work, and his knowledge always at the service of others. He was certainly formidable, but he was kindness itself to those who knew him, a big, lovable, generous man who was very different from the somewhat overwhelming person whom the less fortunate saw.

Vinogradoff belonged to a tradition and represented a type of scholar which is not common in England, where we are inclined to be sceptical and self-conscious in our attitude to learning. He knew how much men like Savigny and Ihering have done to form European civilization, and how much the learned world of Russia hoped to do. For him knowledge was a force in life, and a trust never to be depreciated. I shall never forget the occasion on which he took the chair at one of the general sessions of the International Historical Congress at Brussels in 1923, the grave courtesy with which, as one potentate addressing another, he acknowledged the presence of royalty, the emphasis with which he introduced Mr. Rostovtzeff as the "hope and the pride of Russia". He was at his best in an international gathering or committee, where his command of tongues gave him such an advantage, and the responsibility of sagacious counsel lay upon him. In our academic harbours—though he loved them and found a welcome in them—he lay like a great liner amidst all the bustle and hurry of the shipping. He will become a memory, and then a tradition; but the thought that he has gone on his last voyage leaves in those who knew and admired him a strange sense of desolation.

CHAPTER II

THE MANCHESTER HISTORY SCHOOL[1]

The late Professor Tout wrote about the Manchester History School in some racy and authoritative recollections which can be read in the first volume of his *Collected Papers,* published three years after his death in 1932. A chair of history was created in 1854. The trustees of the Owen College sought and took the advice of the historian Henry Hallam. They appointed to the new chair a stripling from Oxford, who had just graduated in the new Oxford school of history and jurisprudence, in which Hallam had acted as examiner. This young man was Richard Copley Christie, the friend and disciple of Mark Pattison. Shortly afterwards Christie was given two other chairs, one in political economy, the other in jurisprudence and law. He held all these chairs until 1866, when William Stanley Jevons, who, as a tutor in the college, had already published his books on pure logic and the coal supply, became professor of political economy and also of logic and philosophy, while a Cambridge man, A. W. Ward, was given the chair of history. Christie retained his chair of law until 1869. By this time he had become the leader of the Manchester equity bar and an influential public figure in the city. His successor as professor of law was James Bryce, fellow of Oriel College, Oxford, who in 1864 had won sudden fame by the publication of his *Holy Roman Empire.*

Adolphus William Ward was appointed professor of history and of English language and literature. In 1880 the appointment of a separate professor of English language relieved him of part of his duties, but until his election as principal of the college in 1889 he continued to be responsible for the whole of the historical teaching and for the teaching

[1] The introductory section of this chapter on the scholars Tout, Tait and Little consists of passages adapted from an article on the University of Manchester in *History Today,* May, 1951.

in English literature. It was he who organized an honours school of history in Manchester on the lines later developed by Thomas Frederick Tout, who succeeded him as professor of history in 1890, and by James Tait, one of Ward's former pupils, who had been appointed to a lectureship in 1887. Here are some impressions gathered by a student who first entered the college in 1896 at the age of seventeen, in Ward's last year as Principal. He was duly "entered" by the Principal, a remote, majestic figure, whose importance as a scholar only very gradually became a reality in his mind. He spent most of his time in the main block of the college buildings, where the lecture theatres, class rooms and library were adjacent to each other. The walls of one room, which was always locked after classes and lectures, were filled from floor to ceiling with the books of a man called Freeman. The student had read Macaulay's history and Carlyle's *French Revolution* and *The Letters and Speeches of Oliver Cromwell*, but he had never thought of history as a systematic study, and had never heard of Freeman or Stubbs or Gardiner or Acton or any other recent or living historian. He entered the history school, as it were, by accident, and was provisionally accepted by a professor called Tout. He attended lectures on history by Tout and another man, a lecturer called James Tait, and classes in Greek and Latin. He felt rather strange. Then in his second term, something happened. He was being taken in Tait's lectures, carefully and steadily, through ancient and medieval history, and was introduced by him to Tudor England. He was hearing Tout, in his exciting and discursive way, talking about modern history, and, four or five times in each term, he was learning how to write historical essays, and encouraged, actually encouraged, to browse in big books as he did so. This was history and these people were historians, and, as it and they became alive to him, the world about him began to seem more interesting and coherent. Then, in 1898 a new library, the Christie library, was opened and a room in it was set apart as a study and classroom, with Freeman's books all round it, accessible. There, in that room, the student, now in his third and last year, was guided into the mysteries of two special subjects, by Tout on Italy in the fifteenth century, by Tait on the Roman Republic in the time of Cicero. He read many books and realized what original authorities were and how they should be used. He discovered what it meant to handle the folios of Muratori, to study the Venetian ambassadors, and read Machiavelli and Guicciardini and Comines in the original. It was a bewildering, but also a wonderful experience.

After four years at Oxford, the student returned to the University of Manchester in the year of its charter, as a research fellow. By this time he was more familiar with history and historians, and also with libraries. He had worked in the Balliol College Library and read, rather timidly, in the Bodleian; and in Manchester he found a new library in the city, called the John Rylands Library, a noble place. A great scholar, A. G. Little, came regularly from Sevenoaks to give instruction to beginners in palaeography and kindred aids to study. There was also a University historical society; and there was a University Press. The first book published by the Press in its historical series, was James Tait's classical study of medieval Manchester and the beginnings of Lancashire. The student began to work on something himself and in due course began to teach. He learned all about the history of the history school in Manchester from Christie's time onwards and realized what Christie and Ward and Tout and Tait had done, and what had been done for himself. Later, after the First World War, he got to know Tout and Tait and Little as friends, and enjoyed also the friendship of the first professor of economic history, George Unwin. They were big men in a big place.

THOMAS FREDERICK TOUT[1]

Thomas Frederick Tout was born in London on 28 September, 1855. His father, Thomas Edward Tout, whose father, a Somerset man, had settled in London, did not enter much into his life and little is known of him. He would seem to have been a jovial, easy-going and generous man, popular among

---

[1] Taken from the memoir in *The Proceedings of the British Academy*, vol. xv, reprinted in *Collected Papers of T. F. Tout*, i (1932), 1-24.

his business associates, but not of the kind which makes a success of domestic life. Thomas Frederick's mother, Anne Charlotte Finch, who was born in January, 1821, and was married at Old Lambeth Church in March, 1845, is well remembered. Mother and son were devoted companions. One who used to visit Tout and his wife soon after their marriage remembers the old lady very vividly, how she used to sit by the fire with a long paper-knife, cutting the pages of some recent historical work and turning over in her mind recollections of her son's school and college days, and how the son was ever ready with thoughtful and tender attentions.

In 1869 Thomas Frederick entered St. Olave's Grammar School, Southwark, of which the Rev. Andrew Johnson was at that time the head master. Under Mr. Johnson's rule this Elizabethan foundation was brought into line with contemporary educational movements and began to send boys to the universities in greater numbers. It is pleasant to learn that at school Tout, in addition to becoming head boy and winning the Warden's Prize for an essay upon the British Constitution, received the long row of *Chambers's Encyclopaedia* as a prize, given on the vote of the boys to the one who had been most kind and helpful to other boys during the year, and that he took the part of Demea in the *Adelphi* of Terence. That he left a strong impression upon the mind of the head master may be inferred from a story told by another old boy who entered the school some years after Tout had left (1874). One day in 1892 when Mr. Johnson was taking the sixth form in the Greek Testament, the old man dozed, and waking up with a start, ejaculated "Go on, Tout".

In November, 1874, Tout won the Brakenbury History Scholarship at Balliol College. He came into residence in the following January. In 1877 he was placed alone—*unus, solus, totus*, as Stubbs remarked—in the First Class in the Honours School of Modern History. In the same year he was *proxime accessit* for the Lothian Prize with an essay on "The Place of Iceland in the History of European Institutions". In his time the men who read history at Balliol were sent to J. F. Bright, tutor and afterwards master of University College. With a few others, including R. L. Poole and J. H. Round, Tout had the privilege in 1876-7 of receiving tuition from Stubbs. When he became chaplain of Balliol in 1876, the professor agreed to take a limited number of pupils in the college. Tout always regarded Stubbs as his master. In later years he liked to describe the ritual observed at the professorial lectures in the Taylorian Institute, when those who attended were still required to deposit their fee in a bowl on the professor's desk. He generally walked home with Stubbs after the lecture. The younger man won the confidence and affection of the elder. Stubbs revealed his mind in a characteristic little note, written in 1889: "the older we grow the more difficult it becomes for me to write a testimonial for you. In fact I think our positions are reversed."

Although his influence is not so easy to trace, T. H. Green would seem to have cast his spell on Tout, who, after he had taken his Schools in History, read in the School of Literae Humaniores, and was placed in the second class in 1879. Tout was not a philosopher and was rather shy of showing his interest in philosophical speculations; but he was undoubtedly affected later by the *Principles of Political Obligation*, and was attached to Green's memory. It is not fanciful to see some connexion between Green's example and teaching and Tout's constant preoccupation, at Lampeter and during his earlier years in Manchester, with social interests and local affairs. Occasionally he would go further. I remember a remark of his to the effect that if he had to begin the study of medieval history over again he would start with the works of St. Thomas Aquinas. He always felt much more deeply about philosophical, as about religious, matters than he spoke. Indeed, he rarely allowed one to know what had moved him most. I was so unaccustomed to hearing him refer to influences of this kind that I was unreasonably surprised when he told me that Seeley's *Expansion of England* had been a revelation to him. The pupil is apt to forget that the master also has need of revelations.

At Balliol Tout was one of a remarkable group of future historians. Round was a commoner, already keen on genealogical problems, Charles Firth came up a year later, and other contemporaries were Richard Lodge, F. C. Montague, R. L. Poole, and Arnold Toynbee. Tout's friend William Ashley followed him from St. Olave's. If he made few friends at Balliol, they were very good ones and were lifelong. He was very shy, awkward, and though ambitious, still uncertain of himself. His powers of self-assertion grew very rapidly after he left Oxford, but in Balliol they do not seem to have been remarked, or if remarked were not yet linked with his still stronger genius for friendship. In addition to Firth, always his closest historical companion, his chief friend was C. E. Vaughan, afterwards Professor of English Literature at Leeds. One of the reasons why Vaughan chose to end his days in Manchester was his desire to be near Tout, with whom he consulted freely on all kinds of things. At Balliol Vaughan is said to have been "idolized", and his friendship with Tout was a matter of some surprise to his other friends; but all who knew Vaughan, however slightly, know that he always and instinctively saw beneath the surface.

At one time Tout had thoughts of the Civil Service, and he gained a place, but fortunately for the study of history he decided on a career as a teacher. The way was not open to him in Oxford, and after spending a year or two in private tutoring, he applied for and obtained the chair of history in St. David's College, Lampeter (1881). Two years later he won a prize fellowship at Pembroke College, Oxford; but henceforth his life as a teacher was passed in Wales and Lancashire.

During nine happy and intensely active years at Lampeter Tout found himself.[1] The man remembered with admiring affection by his friends and pupils at Lampeter is the man whom we knew in Manchester. He went exactly at the right time. St. David's College had been incorporated in 1828 for the purpose of training clergy for the ministry of the Church in Wales. In 1852 it was granted power to confer the degree of Bachelor of Divinity, and in 1865, by a third charter, to confer the degree of Bachelor of Arts. In 1880 it was affiliated

[1] I am indebted to a memorandum written by Tout's old friend and colleague, Professor Hugh Walker, and to conversations with Sir Charles Firth, for information about the years at Lampeter.

to Oxford, in 1882 to Cambridge; that is to say, its graduates, if they proceeded to Oxford or Cambridge, were permitted to sit for honours after two years' study. But, until the appointment of its second principal, F. J. Jayne, afterwards bishop of Chester, the college had not succeeded in maintaining the reputation expected of it. In 1880 a new period began, and it is interesting to reflect that the vigorous developments of the next few years were contemporary with the addition of the university colleges of Bangor and Cardiff as companion foundations to that of Aberystwyth, which had been founded in 1872. The success of St. David's was due in the main to three men, the principal, the late John Owen (a later principal, and afterwards bishop of St. David's), and Tout.

Mr. Walker gives an admirable summary of Tout's work at Lampeter:

> "He was making himself all the time." These words were spoken of Walter Scott, but they are no less true of Tout at Lampeter. In the College Library during term and in the British Museum in the vacation he laid broad and deep the foundations of his scholarship in history; in the Lampeter lecture-rooms he prepared himself for the wider stage of Manchester; and what better training in administration could be conceived than that which he found in facing the problems which arose in the process of reconstituting and reviving the almost moribund little College?

At Lampeter Tout, by unremitting and detailed labour, learned his craft as a historical scholar. Much of his work was of the popular kind; but much more was the result of original investigation. He could never live in a district without interesting himself in its history and antiquities, and at Lampeter he acquired a knowledge of medieval Welsh history which was maintained and extended in later years, and was even more important in guiding the studies of others than it was in his own work. His paper on "The Welsh Shires", published in 1888 in *Y Cymmrodor,* revealed his power of getting straight to the heart of a subject and treating it with force and lucidity. Many of the lives of Welshmen in the *Dictionary of National Biography* were written by him. As always, he desired to relate local or provincial or national history to contemporary history as a whole, and the great Dictionary edited by Leslie Stephen gave him his chance. Between 1885 and 1890 he wrote for the volumes iii–xxiv biographies sufficient to fill a whole volume; he used to say that he had written a volume of the Dictionary in the college library. It is hardly too much to say that some of our best scholars got their training as contributors to the Dictionary. The preparation of detailed articles inevitably brought with it a minute and critical acquaintance with the printed sources of British history. Tout continued to write for the Dictionary until 1910, when the last volume appeared.

Hence his pupils at Lampeter had a teacher who was working all the time himself. The result was remarkable. Needless to say it was not the professor's duty to give advanced instruction; it was his business to increase his knowledge of general history and to show his pupils what the study of history really involves; but Tout's pupils soon discovered that their master was no mere purveyor of information from text-books. He was both a kindly companion and a merciless critic, who made them, almost unconscious of what was happening to them, feel at home in the period of their study. The little school of history began to be talked about; several of its members won scholarships and exhibitions at Oxford; one of them succeeded Tout as professor. His experience at Lampeter was still more important for Tout himself. He became a vivid, confident teacher and talker, and acquired a knowledge of general history which was not only exceptional in its range but was also always at his command.

From the first Tout concerned himself with college business and local interests. It is significant that the first volume to bear his name was an edition of the college calendar (1882). He acted as librarian and was one of the leaders in the social life of the staff and in their academic deliberations. He had a large share in the foundation of the College School, which, first started to provide a matriculation class, rapidly became one of the chief schools for boys in South and Central Wales. Perhaps his most original role was played in municipal politics.

Before 1884 Lampeter, an ancient borough in name, was actually a village, ruled by a portreeve and a local board. The college was making it one of the most important places in Cardiganshire, and mainly through the energy of Jayne, the principal, it was at last raised to the status of a borough with mayor, aldermen, and councillors. As the ancient capital, to quote Mr. Walker, was situated in the extreme southern corner of the county and most inconvenient of access, Assizes, Quarter Sessions, and ultimately the County Council came to meet in Lampeter. Tout's knowledge of institutions had been of service during the time of transition from township to borough, and he was made one of Lampeter's first four aldermen. He frequently presided on the council in the absence of the mayor and tradition suggests that he took, as one would expect, a lively share in its proceedings. Once, when he protested that a councillor was wandering from the business and not speaking to a substantive motion, his angry colleague replied, "I maintain it is a very substantial motion, and I will not be insulted by Professor Tout or anybody else".

Although Tout's reputation grew during the Lampeter days, it naturally did not keep pace with the esteem of his colleagues and pupils. He never failed to arouse criticism, and doubtless had his critics in Wales, but his departure was generally deplored as a disaster. His forceful colleague, Canon John Owen, as he then was, expressed his confidence in Tout's future in vigorous terms. In letters written during the first years of Tout's career in Manchester, Owen frequently diverged from technical discussions upon the reorganization of the Welsh Church by Archbishop Pecham and from reflections upon the historical knowledge of that fiery young patriot, Mr. Lloyd George, to exhort Tout to make certain of the recognition which he deserved. He should write a big book and justify to all men the unshakeable belief in him of his friends. Owen regarded Manchester as a stepping-stone and no more. Happily for Manchester, Tout, after one or two unsuccessful applications for Scottish chairs, found satisfaction and full scope for his energy where he was. Manchester was fortunate in keeping him, and so was he in staying.

When Tout went to Manchester in 1890, the Owens College was already a centre of historical study. History had been taught by two great scholars, Copley Christie and A. W. Ward, the new principal, whom Tout succeeded. Many men who were to win distinction as historians or teachers had studied there.[1] One of these, James Tait, was already a member of the staff. This development was part of a movement which had made the college, always more concerned with men than with buildings, the home of a vigorous life, cheerful, optimistic, and earnest. There were some weak spots, but nobody who shared in this life could separate the interests of his own department from those of the college as a whole or fail to see that the success of the whole and of its parts were mutually dependent on each other. Tout was by nature aware of this, and, as a matter of course, he realized possibilities which, after his experience in Lampeter, were not strange to him. He was never concerned with elaborate plans. He was a man of vision and ideals, but he pursued the best as it was suggested to him by his daily experience.

A few clear principles of action, and a bundle of instinctive preferences and aversions, were sufficient for him. If he had to work in a university, he must try to make it a really efficient house of learning. If he were helping to manage a school, he must set his mind on seeing that the teachers were happy in their work, and not overdriven, regarded as friends, not as machines. He was a healthy opportunist, in the best sense of the term, with an uncanny ability to keep to the right path. In action he was always ready, giving the impression, as one of his friends puts it, of "a kettle bubbling over a brisk fire". He took his pupils as he found them, made friends with them, was solicitous about them, and would talk with them by the hour, but he never wasted their time and his by needless anxieties about them. He did not shut himself up to prepare

---

[1] Below p. 47. For Christie, Professor of History from 1853 to 1866, see *Selected Essays and Papers of R. C. Christie*, edited with a memoir by W. A. Shaw (1902). For Ward in Manchester, see Tout's memoir in the *Proceedings of the British Academy* for 1926, xi. 427-40, reprinted with additions and corrections in pp. ix-xxx of *Bibliography and Memoir of Sir A. W. Ward* (Cambridge University Press).

carefully wrought lectures, but, unless a detailed study of authorities was required, he made sure of just enough for his purpose and then let himself go. He seized the available hours for writing his text-books and reviews or an occasional learned article, but he was no recluse. Hence he was always fresh and ready for the transaction of college business and social intercourse and the multifarious duties which he undertook, whether as one of the founders and the first chairman of the University Settlement in Ancoats, or as an Extension Lecturer, or as chairman of the governing body of the High School for Girls. Perhaps his happiest trait was his firm belief, almost an instinctive belief, that what he did was worth doing. He believed in the place, in his work as a teacher, and in his students. Sometimes people speak of the Manchester history school as though it were a piece of deliberate invention, finished and shaped in all its parts, imposed from without by a powerful personality and achieving results which can only be regarded as surprising. Nothing could be farther from the truth. The department of history grew gradually; a conscious tradition was but slowly realized. The school was not an institution, but a little community, led by two fine teachers, and dominated by a strong, but very human, personality. Its success was the outcome of this companionship, in which every member had the opportunity of feeling that he had a share. The young people of the north who read history were taken seriously. Tout and his colleague assumed that they meant business. That they might not be worth guidance never occurred to them. If Manchester could produce physicians, chemists, and engineers, it could produce historians. Indeed, it had already done so. Lancashire people respond to this sort of treatment. I imagine that the irresponsive could be counted on the fingers of one hand. Nearly all in various ways gave the response expected of them and found something which they never forgot. In course of time the school became conscious of a living tradition. It had never been a mechanical society, but had grown and changed from decade to decade. It is still a living witness to Tout's administrative skill but yet more to his confidence in his work and his pupils.

During his first ten years the Owens College was a constituent part of the Victoria University. The association with Liverpool and Leeds had been fruitful; it had created common standards and helped to establish the work of each college on a broader foundation. But further development was felt to be impossible without independence. Tout joined wholeheartedly in the fight for independence. Opinion was divided, and some friendships were endangered for a time, for Tout was a hard fighter. The creation of the University of Manchester began a new period which lasted until the end of the war and Professor Tait's retirement. Freedom gave the opportunity for advance in all directions, and Tout was quick to seize every occasion. In University affairs he joined Sir Alfred Hopkinson and others in framing the new Faculty of Theology. He was primarily responsible for the establishment of the Manchester University Press, and acted as chairman of the Press committee until his retirement. He was one of the representatives of the University upon the board of governors of the new John Rylands Library, and helped to maintain its close association with the University, which has been of incalculable advantage to advanced students. The growth in the number of students had in the meanwhile justified expansion within the department. These years saw the successful culmination of the efforts to secure an increase in the staff, including the creation of a chair for Mr. Tait and the foundation of chairs in Economic and Modern History. The curriculum could now be dealt with. Although the main lines of the course —the insistence upon a broad general knowledge of ancient, medieval, and modern history, supplemented by a more detailed study of British history, especially of English institutions, and at the end by a careful study of selected special subjects—were never changed, important modifications were gradually introduced. The requirement of an essay or "thesis" in connexion with one of the special subjects had excellent results, and the reduction in 1919–20 of the special subjects from two to one was justified by the success of this exercise. The "thesis" has been criticized, and is certainly not suited to the systems of Oxford and Cambridge with their enormous schools, but at Manchester it gave genuine intellectual satisfaction to the students and prepared the way for those who wished to proceed to advanced study. The organization of advanced study indeed naturally followed. Much had already been done since the beginning of the century. The allocation in the new University Library of a special "Freeman Library" to hold the books of E. A. Freeman had provided a workshop which had hitherto been lacking.[1] The University Press and the Rylands Library had given facilities for the post-graduate work which, though always encouraged, had hitherto been rather casual. The appointment of Dr. A. G. Little as reader in palaeography had enabled advanced students to learn their way from the most delightful of teachers. In the years after the war still more provision was made for advanced instruction and for the recognition of advanced work as a natural and integral part of the history school. Moreover, the endowment of the Philip Haworth research library, founded by Mr. and Mrs. Haworth in memory of their son killed during the war, gave the advanced students a definite home inside the department. When Tout resigned, he had the satisfaction of feeling that, so far as external equipment and the influence of a strong personal tradition can give it, the history school at Manchester had an independent life of its own.

The Manchester history school is best known for its work in medieval history, yet it would be a mistake to conclude that Tout and his colleagues regarded it as exclusively a school of medieval studies. Such concentration as there was on medieval history came slowly and without premeditation. It naturally attracted the attention of Sir Paul Vinogradoff, one of the first to give public expression to the discovery that interesting things were going on in Manchester, and Tout's increasing absorption in his own field inevitably strengthened the impression. But Tout himself did not regard his academical work in this way. While he believed that a good grounding in

[1] Freeman's books were bought and presented to the Owens College after his death in 1892. A catalogue was compiled by Mr. Tait. At first they were housed in a lecture-room adjoining the old library; but after the new Christie Library was built, a large room suitable for purposes of study was provided for them.

medieval history was the best preliminary to historical investigations in later periods, he was far too well aware of the rich variety of interests which lay open to the student, and especially to a student bred in the industrial north of England, to drive his pupils into medieval history. Manchester owed an incalculable debt, during the years of Tout's greatest activity as a teacher of medieval history, to the work of George Unwin, one of the brightest spirits who ever cast his light on dark places and opened up new horizons to his pupils. Tout and Unwin were in many ways as unlike each other as two men can be, but they were alike in their belief in history, and in their capacity to inspire. The volumes of the University Press testify to Unwin's influence as they testify to that of Ramsay Muir and H. W. C. Davis, successive holders for brief periods of the chair of modern history. The possibilities of advance in all directions were, as they remain, very great, a fact which their past experience must have driven home to the two men, Tout and Tait, who for so long had borne nearly the whole burden of teaching and advice. It is worthy of record that two of the most distinguished medievalists in England spent the greater part of their teaching life in Manchester as lecturers on non-medieval subjects. Professor Tait was throughout responsible for most of the teaching in ancient history, and at times took a share in the lecturing on modern history. Tout, until the last nine or ten years, paid more attention as a teacher to modern than to medieval history. Indeed, it says much for the ardour and keenness of both men that they were able during this time, as an outcome of their own more private investigations, to direct the interest and the studies of so many young men and women in the investigation of problems of English history in the thirteenth and fourteenth centuries. It was done quietly, even casually, but it was done. Yet their general attitude was wider, and is perhaps best revealed in the volume of *Historical Essays* written by past and present members of the Owens College, which they edited in 1902.[1] This volume, gathering together the associations with the teachers

[1] Afterwards re-issued as the sixth volume of the Historical series of the Publications of the Manchester University Press (1907).

and students of the past, and prophetic of the development of the future, was issued on the eve of the emergence of the independent University of Manchester. In their preface the editors declared in general terms their hopes for the progress of the School of History in the years to come. The contributors ranged from Mr. Spenser Wilkinson, who had been a student in 1867, to graduates of two years' standing; the essays began with one on Caesar-worship and ended with one on Napoleon at St. Helena and with papers on the teaching of history in schools. The work as a whole was a most effective manifesto.

Tout's concentration upon the teaching of medieval history was made possible by the creation of the chair of modern history in 1912. But his impetus came earlier from the gradual discovery of the subject by which he will mainly be remembered as a scholar. He was always alert to the tendencies in continental scholarship in the history of institutions, and to the corresponding opportunities for advance in English history. His review of Viollet's *Histoire des institutions politiques* vols. ii, iii) in 1906 (I remember how at this time he carried this book about with him when he journeyed by train) shows him thinking about the comparative study which later gave us his Rennes lectures on *France and England* (1922). His edition, published in the same year, 1906, in collaboration with Miss Hilda Johnstone, of the State Trials of 1289 to 1293, illustrates his readiness, while he was at work on hand-books and text-books, to follow up and see the significance of new material. As Maitland wrote of this same work:

> One of the virtues which is placing Mr. Tout in the very front rank of our historians is his determination to leave no stone unturned, no thicket unbeaten. Out of the thicket may fly a bird worth powder and shot. Under the stone may lurk a toad with a jewel in its head.

This responsive activity found a direction two years later, in the course of investigations suggested by Monsieur Déprez's short study of the privy and secret seals. Tout realized as never before the connexion between diplomatic and administrative studies; still more, he realized that here lay an opportunity for using the calendared, printed, and unpublished treasures of the Public Record Office in a systematic way to bring together his own studies and his more advanced instruction. In their third year his students could study printed texts; those who were able to go further could proceed to the Record Office; and all the while he could, with nothing but happy results in his teaching, concentrate upon what might be his *magnum opus*. So it was that during the next twelve years, in spite of the reduction of numbers and all the pain and distraction caused by the war, he was able to inform the School of History as a centre of medieval study with a clearer purpose, to harmonize his activities as teacher and scholar, and to be ready for the changes which he supervised, as Director of Advanced Study, in the last five years of his professorship. His concentration steadied, but did not monopolize his activities. He did not force his interests upon others. He liked to see his colleagues doing their share in their own way, working with the victims, as he would put it, of their bow and spear. His own pupils by no means adopted his peculiar interests as a matter of course. He was far too good a teacher to insist upon that. But he now saw clearly how the department might be directed, and what a school of history might be; and his strength was increased by the growing appreciation of the world outside and by his intimate and far-reaching relations with scholars at home and abroad. Fellow historians looked to him for counsel, and younger men and women outside Manchester turned to him for advice and stimulus. He had come to his own.

Sir Charles Firth has observed that Tout possessed in an unusual degree the qualifications required for success in postgraduate teaching: wide knowledge, sound judgement, insight into character, and practical ability. A man who combines such qualities as these has no need to submit himself and his pupils to a rigid system; and indeed Tout was quite incapable of thinking of his work with his pupils in the academic terms of "graduate instruction" or "seminars". He was thoroughly English and realistic in his outlook on history, both in his more elementary teaching and in his supervision of advanced work.

From the moment of his entry into the school until the day when he could see his name on the title-page of a substantial book, the student who had run the whole course felt that he had been in a close personal relation with a teacher who had never confused the means with the end, or mechanism with stimulus. In the light of this experience it would be quite impossible for me to try to draw from his scattered addresses and papers upon the matter any systematic description of his views and "method". He would stress one theory at one time, another at another, as he saw occasion or as recent experience had prompted. He did not worry much about consistency. A man of strong common sense and very human affections, he knew how different people can be from each other. We had long desultory talk with him, quarrelled with him, were one day happy in the security of his warm encouragement, another day sore and bewildered after a touch of "the rough side of his tongue", or the uncomfortable experience of being "shaken over the pit". But all the time we knew that we were safe. Perhaps that intimate sense of safety, as one went away after a long evening by the fire, with the memory of a comfortable study filled with great books, of gossipy wandering talk in which one was made part of a wider world, was the greatest of his gifts to his pupils. He could be severe, even rather brutal, and his hot temper could make him unjust. At times he was even fussy and irritable, but he never made us forget that we were his fellow-workers. He never tried to impress or to envelop himself in a cloud of learned words. What mattered was, not what this or that learned person said, but what had happened and our own judgement about what had happened. And so we came quite naturally to feel about history as we felt about the interesting things and people of whom he talked. We learned to go our own way, and could safely be left to ourselves, for we knew that he was always there.

Needless to say, Tout felt very differently about different people, just as he aroused a strange variety of emotions about himself. The kind of man whom he admired and could like most was a man like Mark Hovell, who was killed in France in August, 1916: a man who had struggled against difficulties, had simple straightforward interests in life, was shrewd, clearheaded, humorous, and sharp-tongued, with no nonsense about him, and was blessed with the sort of self-confidence which rapidly sheds conceit. It is characteristic of Tout that he felt so strongly attracted to a Lancashire boy who had no desire to work at medieval history; it is a tribute to him that he retained as a matter of course the confidence as well as the affection of an able man who must very soon have outstripped his teacher in the particular study which he had made his own. After Hovell was killed, Tout laid aside his own work and spent many laborious months in finishing and preparing for the press his pupil's book on the Chartist Movement. The memoir which he wrote for this little volume is at the same time a memorial to his influence as a teacher. He lives in the memory of his other pupils, whether they only knew him casually through two or three years or were admitted to his more intimate friendship, by his kindness and geniality and eager interest in their welfare, by his continuous recollection of them, by his hatred of shams and pretentiousness, by his boundless energy, his uncertain moods and eccentricities, his vigorous, quaint, and absorbing lectures, his gift of racy narrative and anecdote, his alertness to everything that was going on both in the world of historical scholarship and in public affairs.

Tout's colleagues were all aware, although it was not easy for his pupils to realize the fact, that, while he gave to the work of his department time and energy enough to exhaust an ordinary man, he was one of the leading figures in the University and in the educational life of the city. Only when one sat with him in the Senate and committees did one begin to understand his influence. Some of his qualities had a double edge, and in a lesser man might well have obstructed his usefulness. In Tout they were, in a curious way, part of the physical basis of his strength. He was by nature a responsive man, and could be most tactful and sympathetic. His helpfulness in counsel, whether in private talk or in committee, struck all who had to do with him in normal and casual intercourse; and as the years passed he became an impressive as well as a vigorous "elder statesman". But in earlier years he was more formidable. When once roused he lost all sense of self-consciousness. He would show impatience without reserve at the dilatoriness or irrelevancies of others, while he exercised little restraint upon himself. If opposition was steady he was apt to lose his temper. Yet this masterful energy was combined with an unusual ability to disarm criticism. He had a very shrewd understanding of men and was anxious to make his position quite clear. He would begin with intimate, wandering conversations in the common room, and continue them as he walked home in the evening through the unlovely chain of villages in South Manchester, where talk was punctuated by the deafening clangour of the passing tram, and he would often end them over a pipe by his study fire. In debate he usually got his way, not by oratory, but by careful pungent exposition and good-humoured pertinacity. He learned to take his lapses of temper with equanimity and soon forgot all about them, so that others got into the way of doing the same. Whatever was said or thought about him, no one could doubt the largeness of his interest in the University nor fail to be influenced by his instinctive good sense and freedom from the meaner prejudices and passions of academic life. He was never deterred from a practicable reform by pedantry or vested interests. As he used to say of his politics, he was a conservative for radical reasons. His mind was very agile, and, however much he might wander, his thoughts were on the heart of things, on what really mattered. "Provoking little malice and bearing none, he preserved from first to last a direct and positive attitude to life which no difficulty could change into a defensive and which left no room for affectation or pettiness in any form." [1]

Tout felt the strain of the war intensely. He and his senior colleagues kept the school going—some of the best of his women students were trained during these years—but his interests were elsewhere, and he deplored what seemed to him to be inaction. In 1919 Mr. Tait retired and, with the close of this long and fruitful partnership, a new period began in

[1] From an anonymous appreciation which appeared in *The London Mercury*.

the history of the department. Tout became professor of history and director of advanced studies in a reconstituted school. In 1925 he retired, the date coinciding with his seventieth birthday. I doubt if anything in his academic life gave him more pleasure than the volume of essays in medieval history which was presented to him at this time, with its contributions from colleagues and pupils and from some of the foremost among his contemporaries, Liebermann, Bémont, Langlois, Pirenne, Poole, Haskins, and others.[1] The dutiful zest with which he read the essays was hardly less keen than his boyish delight in poring over the long list of subscribers.

The Owens College Essays of twenty-three years before had shown what Manchester had already done in the study of history. This new volume showed what Tout had done for Manchester. And it recognized his position as one of the leading scholars of Europe. The four years of his happy retirement in Hampstead were a time of still wider influence and recognition. They were not really years of retirement, but rather of activity in a wider field. For some time he had been a very prominent Fellow of the British Academy, which he served on the Council for more than one period of office, and as the second President of the Historical Association he had some years before enlarged his acquaintance with the teachers of history in English schools. In London he was free to extend these interests and to add to them. He was keenly interested in the Institute of Historical Research; indeed, two or three years before he left Manchester, he had instituted, on a plan more suitable to local conditions, a conference of teachers and research students suggested by Professor Pollard's Thursday evenings. He was now able to show a more continuous sympathy with the aims and work of the Institute. In 1926 he was elected President of the Royal Historical Society, and in his first address from the Chair, in February, explained very characteristically that he had made it his first duty to "look into the history" of the Society. "I should have been false to the principles of a lifetime", he said, "if I had not pursued

---

[1] This was the only occasion, I believe, on which Langlois could be persuaded to contribute to a volume of the kind.

these investigations in the original sources, and particularly in the record sources, the Minute Books and the Archives of the Society." This habit, so natural in him, of mastering all the bearings of any undertaking, gave him at once a position of influence rarely acquired by an elderly man who comes to London from active life in what, to use another phrase of his, are sometimes quaintly termed the provinces. When his last illness seized him, he was especially concerned with problems of organization, the future of the historical publications which he had directed, since the death of Sir Paul Vinogradoff, for the British Academy, and the work of the Union of Academies, and of the National Committee of the International Historical Congress. He was no novice in the direction of publications, and was familiar with the organization of conferences. He had presided over the medieval section of the Congress held at London in 1913, and was one of the leading figures at the Congress held at Brussels ten years later. He had also, with Vinogradoff, represented the British Academy at the meetings of the Union Académique. At first he had been disposed to be sceptical about the possibilities of this kind of development. When, however, he had once realized that, under the guidance of men like his friend Professor Pirenne, practical things could be done, he threw himself into the movement with his usual thoroughness. He made it the subject of one of his presidential addresses to the Royal Historical Society. He became president of the National Committee, and was ready to discuss with younger votaries of the cause all the difficulties and prospects of its schemes. "All were treated", says Professor Baxter, writing of one of his conversations with Tout, "with a kindly and understanding carefulness, a wide insight that at once grasped the essentials of each case and with no more than a gentle irony separated what was sound in it from what was merely sounding."

In the spring of 1928, after the third and fourth volumes of his big book on medieval administration had been seen through the press and were ready for publication, he went to the United States to deliver the Messenger Lectures at Cornell University. His friendship with many American and

Canadian historians, and his own love of travel and of new experiences, made it inevitable that this visit should develop into a prolonged tour. He gave lectures in more than thirty places and was fêted wherever he went. In addition he and his wife delayed their return so that he might spend a few quieter weeks in the inspection of the manuscripts in the Huntington Library in California.[1] Yet, although he may have over-exerted himself, he felt all the better for his arduous holiday. He returned in September, 1928, cheerful and rejoicing in what he had seen and done and in the honours which had been poured upon him. During the following months he worked closely at the fifth volume of his book, and completed the part which he had planned for himself. In May he had to undergo an operation which left him too weak to hope that his cure could be completed. His great desire was to see the book finished. After a gallant rally, he supervised the revision of his own work and made arrangements for the completion of the volume. He died on 23 October, 1929.

During his last years Tout gathered in the harvest of a long life of unremitting labour and of service to others. He was sure of the old friends; his genius for friendship brought him many more. Others who had known him imperfectly came with warm appreciation to know him better. He felt none of life's ennui or disillusionment and took a frank pleasure in recognition, especially in the doctorate conferred upon him by his own University of Oxford. The friends who worked with him in earlier days, while they shared his pleasure, felt, and still feel, that these distinctions have a somewhat fugitive interest, when set beside their jealously guarded recollection of the years spent in Manchester, where a more intimate and permanent memorial was slowly raised in the human companionship of the History School. And as I turn back for a moment to this, I cannot omit some reference to the home which was always generously open to his friends and pupils. Tout found great strength and happiness in his domestic life. Five years after he went to Manchester he married Miss Mary

[1] The Huntington Library has since bought Tout's own fine collection of books.

Johnstone, one of his pupils, daughter of Mr. Herbert Alison Johnstone, of Stockport. Both husband and wife were inspired by the same public spirit. She fully shared his academic and literary interests, and gave freely of her energy and enthusiasm, as he did, in the service of the social and educational life of the city. Tout had the satisfaction of having as fellow-workers in his own studies those who were nearest to him. His sister-in-law, Professor Hilda Johnstone, and his daughter, Dr. Margaret Sharp, were his pupils, both destined to win distinction as medievalists and to have a share in the last volume of the book which he had nearly finished.

Tout's historical work speaks for itself. The great book upon which his fame will mainly rest is a positive and unadorned contribution to knowledge, so massive that none can fail to realize it, so intelligently related to the facts of life that none can afford to neglect it. But whatever he wrote—lectures, articles, reviews, text-books, treatises—was concrete, vigorous, unaffected, and direct, even conversational, its merits obvious, its blemishes unconcealed. His master, Stubbs, was the outstanding constructive force in the historical scholarship of his time, and Tout, perhaps even more than the more brilliant and versatile Maitland, carried on this positive and energetic tradition. No critic, knowing what Tout did, need have the slightest hesitation in admitting his defects. He lived in a generation of very fine medievalists. He did not possess the finished scholarship of this scholar, nor the acute penetration of that, nor the fastidious, remorseless pertinacity of a third. He was an untidy builder; but he built, and his work stands, firm and four-square. He worked with a kind of deliberate fury, and very quickly, always going straight to the texts and manuscripts if he were engaged upon a piece of original work. He believed, and he insisted on this in advising his pupils, in mastering the published texts first and in reading them continuously as texts, not in consulting them as collections of raw material. He knew the pleasure of reading a chronicle in his easy chair. If he was not so thorough in his consideration of all the modern authorities, he knew where to look and rarely missed anything of significance. He wrote hard, not troubling much about form, but getting at the essentials with the pungent, vivid, direct, adjectival exuberance of his oral speech. His best writing, as in some of his published lectures (which remind one of Freeman), and in his survey of the character and policy of King Richard II, is very like his best speech.

Tout's work[1] illustrates a truth too often neglected, that good realistic history cannot be written unless the historian possesses a powerful and well-disciplined imagination. If we are conscious of seeing, as though for the first time, an old institution at work, or of understanding the significance of a group of apparently insignificant officials, it means that imaginative effort has given life to a mass of dreary details. This kind of imaginative faculty follows the facts; it is not the same as the artistic faculty—a much more dangerous thing in the historian—by which impressions are consciously re-created in the writer's mind. Each involves effort, and each is fed by the wide human interests of the writer. Neither is capable of "dry-as-dust" history, for neither is remote from life. Both make demands upon the reader, but the reader's attention may wander in the one case into misunderstanding, in the other into the realm of illusion. Tout, if he had ever cared to argue about it, would undoubtedly have agreed with a distinguished German contemporary that the science or learning of the romantic or of any other period of enlightenment was more important than its poetry. His work satisfied him in the way in which music or poetry satisfies other men. In this sense of satisfaction he was throughout consistent with himself. He could never quite understand the dissipation of interest which follows a divided allegiance. At Lampeter he was distressed when members of the staff absented themselves from a weekly social gathering started by themselves, and at Manchester I have seen him half-puzzled, half-indignant, if one of us deserted a historical conference for a concert. He had of course other strong interests of his own, especially in travel

---

[1] For details see Mrs. Tout's Bibliography of Tout's writings included in the volume of essays presented to him in 1925. This was brought up to date in a note appended to A. G. Little's memoir in *History* (Jan. 1930). A select and classified list is included in the *Collected Papers*, i, 207-213.

and archaeology and literature. He read his favourite authors, including Scott, Thackeray, and Stevenson, again and again. But he regarded these interests as relaxations which should never distract a man from the daily task. It was interesting to hear him talk about an old building, and he was at his happiest on a historical excursion, when he was describing to a group of students, in his racy and gesticulating fashion, an antiquity like Whalley Abbey or Conisbrough Castle. He always made them feel its interest as an expression of history, and I fancy that he could never quite enjoy a beautiful thing for its own sake unless he knew something about it and had set it in its various periods. Aesthetic pleasure without such knowledge would have seemed amateurish to him. On the other hand he could find real enjoyment in things which the more conventional historical student overlooks or rejects. He took a childlike pleasure in tracing, with his children, the courses of the wretched streams which trickle through the suburbs of Manchester to join the Mersey and the Irwell; and, with the imagination of the scholar, he saw in them the links with the past, when the marshy spaces were dotted with island hamlets, and Manchester was confined to the rocky triangle between the Irwell and the Irk. It was in this spirit of adventure, rejoicing in the details for the significance which could be found in them, that in later years he worked upon the problems of medieval administration. It is given to few men to feel, as the years close about them, the same zest in the bewildering contents of the Public Record Office as they felt in earlier days in exploring the antiquities of Gascony and Provence.

The *Chapters in the Administrative History of Medieval England* should be read in the spirit in which they were written. Tout was pursuing no learned by-paths. He was concerned to understand the methods of medieval government, and to adjust the generalizations of the constitutional historian to the salutary experience of men, great men and little men, ministers of state and clerks living their lives of routine among associations now long forgotten. He went back and appropriated the traditions of the great scholars of the seventeenth century, in whose time the medieval institutions of England were still at work, and in whose eyes the methods of chancery and exchequer practice, and the co-operation of the royal household with the state which it supervised, were still of obvious significance. And with opportunities for investigation greater than those open to Spelman and Prynne and Madox, he tried to work out in detail the interplay, from year to year, of administration and policy. The outcome is not all of equal value. It lacks proportion and some of it is not inspired; but it is undoubtedly one of the outstanding achievements of English historical learning.

JAMES TAIT[1]

My first mental picture of James Tait belongs to October, 1896, when he was thirty-three years old. It was the custom in those days in the Owens College in Manchester to open a new session with a formal lecture. Tait had just been promoted from his assistant-lectureship to a lectureship in ancient history, and the principal, A. W. Ward, paid him a compliment by inviting him to give the lecture. Ward opened the proceedings and then introduced Tait as "one of the most distinguished of our sons". I do not now remember what the lecture was about, but I can still see the lecturer. I was much interested, for I had just entered the College and I knew that this man would be one of my teachers. I saw a serious, reticent young man, determined to go through with his task, a man of firm, well-defined features, sturdy in build, rather tall, shy but composed.

Reticence, composure, self-reliance, were throughout qualities of James Tait; but he was not imperturbable. Underneath he was sensitive, anxious and, until success and a competence were assured, easily worried. Like scores of other boys who have entered the new colleges and universities he had to make his own way in the face of a hazardous future. He had also, like many others, to stand up against the solicitude of relatives who had little knowledge of the academic world and wished to see him settled in a way which they could under-

[1] From the memoir in The Proceedings of the British Academy, vol. xxx.

stand. He was born in Manchester on 19 June, 1863. His father, Robert Tait, was a seed merchant and James was his second son. James described himself as privately educated, but he cannot have been badly educated. His sufficient acquaintance with Latin and his love of English literature show that he had not lacked the stimulus at home and school of books and ideas; but it is clear from letters which A. W. Ward wrote to him that his college career was beset with perplexities. He entered the College when he was sixteen (1879), just before the Victoria University, with the right to confer degrees, came into existence. For two years he attended classes in various subjects. He must have made a favourable impression upon Ward, the professor of history, who had a large class of a hundred or so; for on 31 July, 1881, the professor wrote to him a wise, balanced, and on the whole encouraging letter in reply to a request for advice:

> I have no doubt but that your abilities are sufficient, with continuous application and systematic study, to qualify you for success as a teacher of literature or history. And I should say that under the circumstances you could not do better than work for one of the Honours Schools of the Victoria University. ... *Possibly* you might go in for History first and the other [English] afterwards. Possibly you might prefer to pass on from us to Oxford or Cambridge or to a foreign university.
> And this brings me to another aspect of the question. It is never desirable, I think, to look too far ahead—and in education especially, so long as one is working hard and with a real love of one's subject. The question of what is likely to pay need not always be before one's eyes. Still, it is well to form some general idea of the future and its possibilities.

After discussing alternative plans which might be adopted after the boy had taken Honours, his mentor proceeds:

> Do not commit the very natural error of supposing that literature is to be relied upon as a supplementary resource. Only one kind of literary employment can be made to answer in that way, viz. journalism; and to be a journalist is in nine cases out of ten to relinquish being a man of letters. To succeed in the time of which you are thinking, you will either

have to serve an apprenticeship as an assistant which may be long and which may not be all delight—*or* you will have to give up some time to hard work which may enable you by rapid distinction as a writer to obtain a fairly independent position more speedily.

Lastly, remember that though we look forward to great progress in the next few years, yet at present there are not many Professorships or Lectureships, assisting or otherwise, in History and Literature open to competition, and it is just possible that the progress may not be immediate or that it may be interfered with.

In case you should think me inclined to pessimism, I will add that if a man can (in more senses than one) afford to wait, and if he is willing to be passed in the race at first by many of his contemporaries in so far as position and money and even reputation are concerned, he cannot do better than choose the line of life of which you are thinking. If you decide on trying with that end in view you may trust to me for giving you what help I can towards it.

Tait kept this letter, as well he might. I have quoted from it freely for several reasons. Tait had not yet made up his mind whether to specialize in history or in English, but he already wished to devote his life to one or other of these subjects. He laid his hopes and fears before Ward. Ward's reply shows the regard in which he held his pupil, and also the purpose which had directed the University from stage to stage and established the firm tradition into which Tait and his contemporaries entered, and which he, more than most, was to do so much to maintain. But the most impressive thing about this letter is the grave and patient courtesy with which an eminent Victorian, conscious of important movements in a great age, wrote to a promising lad of eighteen. His prudent counsel is shot through and through by the encouragement of a priest who admits a neophyte to a temple. He takes the boy's capacity and desire to rise to his opportunities for granted. He treats him almost as an equal. "There are not many professorships." At the age of seventeen I saw Ward for three minutes, when he admitted me to the College. I never saw him again except at a distance, but in that short interview he gave me exactly the same impression as his letter to Tait conveys. He made me feel that I was entering a new world. The new universities were created in this spirit of high endeavour and companionship. Practice kept pace with precept. Ward, we must suppose, lectured about history with the same dignity with which he wrote. If history was to be taught, this was the only way to teach it, for this was what it meant. There could be no condescension. And the seriousness was so much a matter of course that it had its effect. Spenser Wilkinson, John Holland Rose, J. P. Whitney had felt it a few years before Tait went to the Owens College. The names of Thomas Alfred Walker, the historian of the law of nations, and Robert Dunlop, the historian of Ireland, appear on the first honours list in 1882, the year after Tait joined the History School. William Arthur Shaw was Tait's contemporary, George Arnold Wood, later the honoured and beloved professor of history in the University of Sydney, and one of Tait's closest friends, was a year or so his junior. So the work of Copley Christie and A. W. Ward came to fruition. The way was prepared for the notable partnership of Tout and Tait.

Tait entered the History School in 1881 and graduated with first class honours two years later. He then sat for a scholarship at Balliol and was elected to an exhibition. He was matriculated on 15 October, 1884, the day on which Freeman gave his inaugural lecture as Regius Professor. In 1887 he was again placed in the first class in history. His examiners were York Powell, A. L. Smith, Richard Lodge, and S. R. Gardiner. The signatures on his certificate—for in those days the examiners testified to the achievement of each candidate separately—give it palaeographical interest. Other firsts in this year included two Balliol friends, Owen Edwards and J. W. Allen.

At this time Tait's habitual reserve was growing upon him. It disturbed his father and was noticed by Ward. The two men had exchanged letters about James's future. He wrote a good deal of poetry and would seem to have been especially drawn to the English poets of the early seventeenth century. There may have been a religious crisis before he gradually settled down into a quiet agnosticism. He was always scrupulously careful to respect religious beliefs and practices in others. As often happens he was probably more free and easy with his companions in college than, in spite of his steady domestic affections, he could feel at home. Certainly the few letters which he kept from his Balliol friends, J. W. Allen, Raymond Beazley, George Gregory Smith, and especially Thomas Seccombe, do not suggest reserve, though they reveal deep respect. Unhappily no letters from George Arnold Wood, who followed him to Balliol as a scholar in 1885, seem to survive, for he was, I think, Tait's closest friend until the oceans separated them and Seccombe took his place. Wood was the subject of a story which the group of friends long remembered. One day, A. L. Smith started an inquiry into their ideas about the greatest book ever written. Some said the *Iliad*, some the *Divine Comedy*, and so on; but Wood, "fearing nought", exclaimed with a firm voice "John Morley on Compromise."

The earliest of the little diaries or rather note-books of miscellaneous jottings which survive from Balliol and later Manchester days tells us something about Tait at Oxford. A reference to "Freeman's pedantry" in calling Rochester "Hrofesceaster" suggests that he attended the professor's lectures. Then come a note on the genealogy of his cousins, the Cases of Liverpool, a description of the Tait family arms with the motto "pro Rege et Patria", a quotation from Pope, and the characteristic entry heavily underlined "May 6, 1886. Lent Crum my note-book on Ed. ii—Hy. vii. See it is returned." These entries are followed by memoranda of a week-end in London with an uncle and a quotation from Machiavelli, "you must either crush or you must conciliate". After term began he attended meetings of the Society for the Promotion of Religious Unity including one in the Lincoln Common Room where Dr. Fairbairn discoursed on "Theology as an Academic Science". Tait notes the speaker's contention "that every theological student should take the arts course before going on to theology". On 31 May Tait was elected a member of the Seminar "of which I am one sixteenth". This was a small group of dons and undergraduates who met to discuss historical subjects. W. H. Hutton read a paper on the *Utopia* with York Powell in the chair. "Carlyle, Wells, C. H. Firth, Y. P. spoke", and Tait notes the main points of the discussion. These are followed by a well-known story of Jowett, told apparently by H. Stuart Jones:

> Jones loquitur: Tatham said logic was a science, Nettleship maintained it was an art. I asked the Master which was right and he said "It's neither, it's a dodge".

A list of books shows that Tait, as early as 1886, was taking a special interest in the occupation of northern France by the English in the fifteenth century, but he was still more interested for the moment by a lecture given by Herkomer in the Sheldonian on "Notoriety in Art" (17 June) and three days later by the speeches given in Wadham Hall at a meeting of the Layman's League for the Defence of the National Church:

> Sir W. Anson, T. H. Warren (Magd.), R. E. Prothero (All Souls), Henson. Anson clear and fairly good, W. confused, involved and Latinistic, P. vigorous and stumpy, Henson very fiery and incisive. The makings of an orator in him. "The besetting sin of Oxford men is—*slackness*, the slackness of too many interests, that of dilettantism, the slackness of no interests at all—that of the cynic and the simpleton".

A jumble of quotations, references to books, stories, a journal of a holiday in north Wales, a list of Anglo-Saxon kings and bishoprics, follow. Then comes on 20 January, 1887, a passionate little outburst on his longing for spring, stirred by a day as balmy as May. Only then and in summer "do I live in any true sense, it is only then that I lay in the poor little stock of health and strength which scarcely suffices to carry me through the damp chills and blood-curdling frosts of the other half of the year". (As a matter of fact, Tait was never ill in his life.) The rest of the note-book contains memoranda of his first holiday in Germany, with sketches, lists of German books that he needed, and so on. Some of the sketches of mountain scenery and of churches show power and feeling.

A letter from one of his friends, written in the Michaelmas Term of 1887, after Tait had gone down, links Tait's Oxford friendships with his new life in Manchester. Wood had shown the writer a letter from Tait, "and I was so pleased with it", says the latter, "that I was seized with an irresistible desire to get one from you for myself. The very house where I am now installed (16 St. John Street) is haunted by memories of you.... I have not yet ventured upstairs into your old room, but on leaving my own to go out I often catch a glimpse of your figure vanishing round the staircase corner and the other night, coming back from college in the dark, I had a most distinct vision of you in [St.] John Street, walking along in front of me". The letter continues:

> I must insist upon congratulating you on the place you have got more recently—though indeed Wood tells me that you wrote to him some time back about it in a discontented state of mind! This I don't understand at all and it seems to me you have got a pretty good start. Doubtless eleven lectures (is it?) a week must be trying—especially as I am told that you have to lecture on Greek history! I was aware that your knowledge of modern history was unfathomable, but I did not know you embraced the ancients also.

This sprightly passage takes us back to Manchester, where in July, 1887—a month after his success in the Schools at Oxford—he was recommended by a committee of Senate to fill a vacant assistant-lectureship in history and English. Firth, writing as president of the Oxford Historical Seminar, testified to his merits: "He read us a most excellent and careful paper and frequently took part in our discussions." The reference to the paper read to the Seminar helps to explain a passage in a later testimonial (1891) from Gregory Smith. Were it necessary to emphasize his high literary qualifications, "I should point to some of his Oxford essays, but especially to the admirable paper on 'The Spasmodic School of Poetry' which he published at Manchester."

The letter in which Ward told Tait of his appointment was kind, but rather alarming. The professor sketched a programme of lectures under headings of day and evening classes and the "Women's Department". The work was not so formidable in fact as it seemed to be on paper, but the prospect of his duties may well have reminded him of Ward's words six years before about the apprenticeship "which may be long and may not be all delight". His quality was revealed to his colleagues a year after his appointment. Ward was away ill during the greater part of the session 1888–9, and Tait was made responsible for the historical side of the department. This experience, and the strain which it must have involved, doubtless decided him to apply in 1889 for the chair of history and English language and literature in University College, Cardiff. He had as yet nothing or little to show and was unsuccessful. Then came Ward's appointment as Principal and the election of a new professor of history. Tait was one of the three selected candidates, but again was unsuccessful. The new professor was T. F. Tout, who was Tait's senior by ten years and already a scholar of repute with professional experience. Tait, as we learn from one of Seccombe's letters, talked at this time (1890) of going to Sydney, by which is probably meant making an application for the chair which Wood got. Encouragement came from an unexpected quarter. Tout's prize fellowship at Pembroke College, Oxford, fell vacant in this very year. Tait sat for it and was elected.[1] In the following year he made a more determined effort to get a chair. He applied for the chair of history and English at the Queen's College, Belfast, with strong support from Ward, Sidney Lee, Gregory Smith, and R. L. Poole, who had been greatly impressed by him while he acted as external examiner in Manchester and placed "entire confidence in his knowledge and judgement". Again he was unsuccessful. The only thing left was to work hard and to see others pass him in the race, as

[1] Tait was not required to reside. In 1898, after his fellowship had expired, he was invited to accept nomination by the college as proctor. Since his election as proctor would, of course, have involved residence, he had to refuse the suggestion.

Ward, in that wise letter of his, had said. His time would come. He settled down with his new chief, began to write regularly, and at last, in February, 1896, he got his promotion. "I enclose you", wrote the Principal in his grand manner, "certain resolutions of the Council which affect your position here, I hope in a way that will not be unacceptable to you. . . . Let me express a hope that you will accept the appointment and my pleasure in having been able to be instrumental in obtaining whatever recognition it involves of your services to the College and the History Department. The arrangement is one of which Tout and I most cordially approve". This appointment, a lectureship in ancient history, to be held concurrently with his assistant-lectureship, really meant that the long partnership with Tout in a reorganized history school had begun. Six years later, in the year of the college jubilee (1902) he was made professor with the title "professor of ancient and medieval history".

Tait had worked very hard during his apprenticeship. A link between his duties as a teacher and his aspirations as a scholar was Freeman's library which Christie and his colegatees presented to the Owens College in 1892. They were anxious that a special catalogue of the collection should be compiled and published; and Ward invited Tait to undertake this task. "As you are so thoroughly conversant with the kind of literature of which Freeman's library in the main consists, I can hardly think that the task will be an over-laborious one to you." Tait immediately complied and had finished the catalogue by October in the following year. It was published in 1894. From one of Ward's letters it would seem that the plan had been to distribute the books in the College library, each in its appropriate class and section, but this idea—obviously inconsistent with the preparation of a separate catalogue—fortunately came to nothing, though later developments have recently made it advisable to act upon it. For a few years the Freeman collection was kept in a lecture room, but when the new university or Christie Library had been completed, it was given a special room there. The "Freeman

Library" was an inestimable boon. It was the centre of the History School, a study and lecture room for undergraduates in their last year, and a home of graduate research. Tait's catalogue lay on the table. Generations of students became familiar, or had the chance to become familiar, with the working library of a famous historian. And it is easy to imagine how much Tait must have learned from his work on the catalogue, and from his later access, as in a private study, to the books which a young scholar might require. As the years passed, additions were made to the library, and all of us who were medievalists began our investigations there and had constant recourse to it later.

In 1891, the year in which Seccombe was made an assistant-editor, Tait began his connexion with the *Dictionary of National Biography*. His first articles had at once satisfied Sidney Lee who, as early as May, suggested that he might consider appointment to an additional assistant-editorship, and later testified to his "very thorough research and clear literary style". In the next year he began his lifelong connexion with the *English Historical Review*. He wrote long notices of the first volume of Karl Lamprecht's *Deutsche Geschichte* and of Sir Charles Oman's *Warwick the Kingmaker*. His sound and independent judgement is apparent in his scepticism about Lamprecht's theory of tribal origins and of early kingship. And his quality as a critic shines out in a later review (January, 1895), of Mrs. Green's *Town Life in the Fifteenth Century*. This is the work of a mature scholar. It anticipates much that he had to say in his erudite study of the English borough forty-one years later, and it has all the freedom and verve of his best days. Tait's early training is a very important clue to the significance of his historical work. He was anything but a narrow specialist who gradually emerged as the author of a treatise. He began his work as a historian with an unusually wide range of knowledge and a keen appreciation of literature. He had traversed the whole range of history, ancient and modern, had taught himself to read German as well as French, and was already a traveller of some experience. On the other hand, he had little time to spare for independent work. Apart from a short note in the *English Historical Review*[1] his literary activity was confined to reviews and to articles for the *Dictionary of National Biography*; but this was precisely the opening which he needed. In the *Review* he was encouraged to apply his mind, with its stores of well-ordered knowledge, on new books about a variety of subjects and to make sure where his true interests lay. There also he could, as occasion served, practise his gift for clear, vigorous and sometimes very neat terse prose. In the *Dictionary* he could prove his power to handle original material, in all its complexity, in articles which, as more important subjects were entrusted to him, offered ever-increasing opportunities. His activity in these years 1891–1901 is astonishing, especially when we remember that he was lecturing on ancient and medieval and Tudor history and taking a responsible part in the life of the History School and of the College. Yet it was, in a sense, a cover, behind which he could probe into Domesday Book and chronicles and local records. It strengthened his grip on history and satisfied his desire to express himself, and at the same time it gave him a greater sense of freedom for quiet investigation on matters to which he was not yet ready to commit himself. In fact, a rare opportunity to show what was in him came in 1897. This was the publication of Maitland's *Domesday Book and Beyond*, which R. L. Poole, with his usual insight, offered him for review. The editor's praise was characteristic:

> I admire the review very much and am sure Maitland will be all the more pleased because you are critical. He has suffered from too much adulation. This is the first serious review the book has received.

The review[2] established Tait's position as one of the best historical scholars in England. It does not, if carefully read,

---

[1] "On the date and authorship of the Speculum Regis Edwardi", *E.H.R.* xvi (1901), 110-15. This work, usually ascribed to Archbishop Islip, Tait tentatively ascribed to an earlier archbishop, Simon Meopham.

[2] *E.H.R.*, xii (1897), 768-77.

reveal him as a past master of Domesday problems. This, as the previous pages should have shown, was physically impossible. It revealed something much more important, a scholar so sure of his ground as a student of history that he could submit a fine and carefully wrought book by the most brilliant man in the historical world to independent scrutiny, and shake its two main contentions. With the courtesy of a just and modest mind, Tait used his own criticism to confirm the author's point of view:

> We cannot now enter into a discussion of the remoter and wider question, or analyse as we should have liked to do the remarkable chapters in which Professor Maitland subtly unfolds the complicated and obscure processes which may be supposed to have gradually dimmed the lustre and impaired the fulness of early English freedom even before the Normans came to complete the degradation of the free villager. Suffice it to say that, so far as we are capable of forming a judgment, he seems to have made out a case which the supporters of the "manor theory" will find it hard indeed to meet. It may be thought that if, as we think, his explanation of the Domesday manor as a unit of assessment will not hold good, the strength is taken out of his case. On the contrary, for he has certainly proved that "manerium" in Domesday often means something which cannot be the "manor" in the sense in which it is used in the controversy [between the Romanists and Germanists]. Our own view is that the term was far less precise than even he supposes.

Maitland's letter of thanks must be set out in full:

Downing College
Cambridge
20 Oct. 1897

Dear Sir,

Will you allow me to take an unusual step and to offer you my warm thanks for the review of a book of mine which you have contributed to the *English Historical Review*. If the step is unusual (and I have never done anything of the kind before) the occasion also is unusual and in my experience unprecedented, for I have never seen a review of anything that I have written which has taught me so much or gone so straight to the points that are worth discussing. I cannot refrain from telling you of my gratitude. If ever I have to make a second edition of that book I shall have to alter many things in it in the light of your criticisms. Certainly this would be the case in the matter of the boroughs, and I must confess that you have somewhat shaken one [of] my few beliefs in the matter of the *manerium*, namely that this term had *some* technical meaning. I can't give up that belief all at once, but may have to do so by and by.

                        So repeating my thanks
                        I remain
                              Yours very truly
                                  F. W. Maitland.

Tait enlarged his acquaintance as his work was more widely known. His contributions to the *Dictionary* brought him in touch with other scholars, for he took trouble to submit his articles, if he were in any doubt, to those who might be able to help him. Also, he began to receive invitations to write books and articles. Early in 1897 York Powell asked him to contribute to an Oxford school-book, and Lord Acton offered him a choice of chapters for the Cambridge Modern History. Would the siege of Vienna appeal to him? "Besides Klopp's great volume, a series of works and documents came out for the centenary, and are chronicled in the Jahresberichte for 1883, 1884. Through the immense addition of knowledge it has become a new topic." In the course of the next ten or twelve years he was frequently approached by editors. Tait resisted these temptations. He had had enough of this kind of work and in any case was now co-operating with Round and Farrer in the Victoria County Histories, a much more congenial and original field. One invitation, however, he did accept. Sir Paul Vinogradoff enlisted him as a supporter of the international "Zeitschrift für Sozial- und Wirtschafsgeschichte" and followed this up by a suggestion that he should write a critical survey of the work so far done in the Victoria County Histories on Domesday Book (22 February,

1903). This paper was written during the next six months and appeared in the form of a review of the volumes published between 1900 and 1903. As Tait pointed out, "the comparative study of the various sections in detail"—he was referring especially to Round's "admirable introductions" to the shire surveys—"brings out features which elude a partial or superficial examination". And he proceeded to criticize Round's interpretation of "inland".

For some years (1903-8) Tait spent a good deal of time on Domesday Book. He was responsible for the introduction to the survey of Shropshire (1908). This interest is reflected in some of his reviews and articles and, less directly, in the increasing attention which he was giving to the history of the English boroughs. It also brought him into closer relations with Round. Tait took a detached view of Round and his controversies.[1] His obituary notice of him in the *English Historical Review* shows this; and, long before, in 1897, he had gone out of his way to call Hubert Hall's attention to some doubtful points in Round's first broadside against Hall's edition of the *Red Book of the Exchequer*. Hall was very grateful for this unexpected support from a stranger. As he wrote, "When one is isolated it is cheering to have an ally." But, while his keen sense of justice forbade him to approve Round's extravagances, and his sound learning enabled him to express his own views without any undue deference, he corresponded with him at intervals for a quarter of a century, and kept several of his letters. Round, as one would expect, had a high regard for Tait. He had greatly admired his map of northern France in 1066, the earliest of four maps of great value contributed to Poole's *Historical Atlas of Modern Europe*. In a letter to Poole, dated 19 January, 1898, he says, "I was greatly pleased with the way of shewing the places where English families came from, which seems to me both clear and remarkably accurate. He was wrong in the *E.H.R.* in questioning Bémont's derivation of the Balliols from Picardy. Some

---

[1] Cf. a sentence in Tait's obituary notice of Round in the *E.H.R.* xliii (1928), 576: "He accused Green of misstating the extent of the Norse settlement in the Wirral peninsula, when Green was perfectly right."

may have come from a Norman Bailleul, but *the* Balliols (yours and mine) came from Picardy. I have an important charter proving both this and their early pedigree." Poole passed the letter to Tait, who kept it with the letters which he later received from Round. I quote a few passages from these:

> I write to thank you for your review of my book [*Peerage and Pedigree*] in the *E.H.R.*, which is peculiarly welcome. Knowing the value of your criticism, I am not surprised that this review is worth more than any other I have had. The reviewers have been more than kind but me[re] uncritical praise is not what one wants. I was particularly anxious for a critical estimate, whether favourable or not, of the *legal* portion of the book, but . . . I failed to get this. So you have supplied precisely what I wanted to have. [1910.]

Again, in a long letter of 2 June, 1919, he wrote:

> I wish to thank you for your review in the *E.H.R.*, of my *Magna Carta* paper last year, which was really too favourable.[1] I had selected the subject as being to my thinking one of the most difficult still to be solved in the Charter, but I could not satisfy myself about it, partly because I had to write the paper before and after a serious operation.
>
> I believe you would be greatly interested in my Borough paper, if I have the health and strength to finish it, because it is based on special knowledge and information, not on mere hypothesis.
>
> Please excuse an invalid's scrawl.

The last letter to Tait, dated 19 May, 1925, was written from bed, when he was "absurdly weak". It is a reply to a friendly letter about the article "Liber burgus" which Tait had prepared for the volume of essays presented to Tout, and about William Farrer's work "left unfinished. It is a warning", adds Round, "to those of us who are getting old." He quotes an

---

[1] "Barons and Knights in the Great Charter", in *Magna Carta Commemoration Essays*, ed. H. E. Malden (1917), pp. 46-77; see Tait in *E.H.R.* xxxiii (1918), 263.

entry about the liberties of Colchester from the proofs of the Pipe Roll of 2 Richard I, and refers to letters which Farrer had written to him about his difficulties in selecting the method to be used in his work *Honors and Knights' Fees*. The letter ends "I cannot write more".

Round wrote to Tait as to a scholar whose interests in Domesday problems, feudal institutions, borough origins, royal and private charters, and local history coincided with his own. The elder man was more nimble and discursive, as he pounced with furious intensity on every significant detail; the younger was cooler, took a wider view and, without the genius of the other, had surer ground beneath his feet; but both were concerned to explain the nature of medieval society, not merely to add to knowledge here and there. The field of their operations was one. It is a mistake to say that Tait was first a Domesday, then a local, then a borough specialist. All these interests were expressions of a single desire, the elucidation of English society. They gradually transcended the more political interest which had first attracted him and had been fostered by his work for the *Dictionary of National Biography*. At one time, like Sir Charles Firth before him, he had thought of working on the English occupation of northern France during the later stages of the Hundred Years War. Firth, indeed, handed the subject over to him and gave him some of his books. Tait soon deserted this plan and became absorbed in the history of England in the later fourteenth and in the fifteenth century, especially during the reign of Richard II, which he chose as a special subject for his honours students. He maintained this interest to the end of his life, but it became a secondary interest. After he had closed his long list of articles in the *Dictionary* with the life of William of Wykeham (1900) and printed in 1902 his well-known essay[1] "Did Richard II

---

[1] *Historical Essays by members of the Owens College, Manchester* (1902), pp. 193-216. Twenty-one years later the late A. E. Stamp, Deputy Keeper of the Public Records, produced evidence which cast doubt on Tait's conclusions: *E.H.R.* xxxviii (1923), 249-52; cf. R. L. Atkinson, pp. 563-4; but in 1932 Mr. H. G. Wright, in an able paper, showed that other evidence confirmed them; *E.H.R.* xlvii, 276-80; cf. Tait's review of A. Steel's *Richard II*, ibid, lvii (1942), 382.

murder the Duke of Gloucester?"—known to his pupils as "Prof. Tait's detective story"—he published apart from reviews only one work in the period. This was his edition of the *Chronica Johannis de Reading et Anonymi Cantuariensis, 1346–1367* (1914) a good, solid, definitive book, profusely annotated, but not a work of outstanding importance. Everything that Tait wrote has lasting value, but his finest contributions to learning must be sought elsewhere.

To return to the interests which he shared with Round, then with William Farrer, and rather later with Professor Stenton, Tait found a congenial field for their exercise in the history of Lancashire and Cheshire. Although no hard and sharp lines can be drawn, his life as a scholar, after what I may call the *D.N.B.* period, falls roughly into two halves, a middle period, lasting from about 1900 to 1924, and a later and overlapping period which began soon after he resigned his professorship in 1919 and culminated with the publication in 1936 of his book on the medieval English borough. In the middle period the emphasis lies on his work for the *Victoria County History of Lancashire* and the Chetham Society. Throughout this time he enjoyed the literary companionship of his friend William Farrer. Tait's fine obituary notice of this remarkable man[1] is his best bit of writing. It betrays the warmth of feeling which made him such a firm and loyal friend. And, with unusual care and freedom, it brings out the significance in Farrer's work of those qualities which he himself possessed in a still higher degree. Except in his indifference to municipal history—for Farrer, a country gentleman and sportsman, avoided cities and everything to do with them as much as he could—Tait found in him a kindred spirit. Farrer was not a local historian of this place or that, but studied local history as a key to the history of England. "Like Robert Eyton, the historian of Shropshire, whom he took for his model, his historical curiosity carried him far beyond the bounds of merely local antiquities. As Eyton became the

---

[1] Printed in the *E.H.R.* for January, 1925, xl, 67-70. Another brief memoir of Farrer, based in part upon this, appeared later in the year as the preface to the third volume of *Honors and Knights' Fees*.

pioneer of Domesday study, Farrer's real distinction lies in his detailed researches in the lower ranges of the Anglo-Norman feudal hierarchy. His *Honors and Knights' Fees*, so far as it goes, supplies the under side of Dugdale's great work on the *Baronage of England.*" Tait pointed out how the arrangement of Yorkshire charters (in his *Early Yorkshire Charters*) under the Domesday fiefs "gradually shifted his main interest from the documents to the general Norman distribution of baronial estates upon which they cast only a broken and local light".

Some years before he transferred his attention to this wider subject Farrer had secured Tait's co-operation in the *Victoria County History of Lancashire*, in which he had merged his earlier plan to prepare a history of the county to the death of Queen Elizabeth. In 1895 he had bought the collections of J. P. Earwaker and "he spent large sums in completing them". A man of means, he was able, after he had "taught himself the technique of research" to work from transcripts of public and other records, and his great collections were at the disposal of his colleagues, in so far as they were not already printed in his numerous books.[1] Tait's interest in the history of Lancashire and Manchester was finding expression at the same time. He gave two public lectures on "Manchester under lords of the manor" on the Warburton foundation, and a few years later his first book, *Mediaeval Manchester and the beginnings of Lancashire*, which had grown out of these lectures, was published by the new Manchester University Press as the first volume of its historical series (1904). In the interval Farrer's publications, especially his *Lancashire Pipe Rolls*, had appeared. They had, in Tait's words, "put the study of Lancashire history in the middle ages on an entirely different footing", and the necessity to take full account of them was one of the reasons for Tait's

[1] Most of Farrer's transcripts are now in the City Library or in the John Rylands Library in Manchester. His Yorkshire material was secured by the Yorkshire Archaeological Society, which has sponsored the continuation of his *Early Yorkshire Charters* by Mr. Charles Clay. His library, which, in Tait's words, "may well have been the finest private library in the country of books on local and feudal history", was unfortunately sold and scattered.

delay in publication. "My debt", he wrote in the preface, "to Professor Maitland, Miss Bateson and Mr. Farrer is apparent on almost every page." This book is both a piece of baronial history and a study in borough origins. The growth of a town as distinct from the manor of Manchester raises many problems, and, assisted by Miss Bateson's recent investigations, Tait sought to "reconcile Manchester's possession of burgesses, a borough court and a borough reeve with the formal decision of 1359 that she was no borough but only a market town". The gradual process by which the county of Lancaster came into existence, by the amalgamation of districts within the wider honour of Lancaster created by William Rufus, was traced through a careful analysis of baronial charters. How tricky inquiries of this kind can be is illustrated by an attempt made by a competent young scholar over thirty years later to question Tait's crucial distinction between the district "between Ribble and Mersey" and the honour as it was in Stephen's reign. The critic overlooked the fact that the place which is the subject of two precepts of King David of Scotland and the place from which he dispatched them were not, as one might well think, in the district south of the Ribble, but places of the same or similar names in North Lancashire and Cumberland.[1] It was always dangerous to challenge Tait on a point of this kind.

The book has been rightly regarded as a model. Mary Bateson spoke of it with enthusiasm. Its influence has been far-reaching, though not far-reaching enough. Tait, for example, in his discussion of the barons of Manchester, called attention to the fact that "barons who held of mesne lords and not directly of the crown were commoner in the first age after the Norman conquest than is usually supposed". But the subject was still generally ignored until Professor Stenton explored it in his masterly way in the third chapter of his *First Century of English Feudalism* (1932). More important at the time, however, was Farrer's desire, which the book must have intensified in his mind, to have Tait's co-operation in the preparation of the *Victoria County History of Lancashire*. The

[1] *E.H.R.* l (1935), 670-80, with Tait's correction in li (1936), 192.

great book in eight volumes, "as near to the ideal county history as can be expected in a world of compromises", appeared at the average rate of a volume a year between 1906 and 1914. Farrer himself, of course, wrote or directed the sections whose subjects he had made his own. Tait wrote in the second volume (1908) the important sections on the political history to the reign of Henry VIII, the ecclesiastical history to the Reformation, and the detailed histories of every monastic house, priory, and cell except the account of Furness abbey, which he asked me to undertake. It was a privilege to be introduced to the study of local history under such auspices, to have the run of Farrer's transcripts, and to see something of the two men at work.

Tait was as interested in Cheshire as he was in Lancashire. He busied himself with plans for a Victoria County History of Cheshire, and made friends with the two men, Fergusson Irvine and R. Stewart-Brown, who were almost as capable as Farrer himself to direct the enterprise. This plan came to nothing, but it encouraged Tait to turn his attention to the county and to use the Chetham Society, just as Stewart-Brown and Irvine used the Record Society for Lancashire and Cheshire, as a medium. The Chetham Society was founded in 1843 for the publication of "remains historical and literary connected with the palatine counties of Lancaster and Chester". In forty years, under the guidance of its main founder and president, James Crossley, it issued more than a hundred volumes. In 1883 a new series began after the Society had surmounted a crisis and with it began also a very much closer connexion than had existed hitherto between the Society and the Owens College. The new president and "second founder" was R. C. Christie, then professor of history and other subjects in the College. In 1901 he was succeeded by Ward, and in 1915 Ward was succeeded by Tait, who held office for ten years.[1] Tait took this

[1] Tait was invited to contribute an account of the Society to the hundredth volume in the new series *Chetham Miscellanies,* vol. vii, shortly after the election of Professor Jacob as president and Dr. Tupling, lecturer in local history, as vice-president, the first time that both offices had been held by members of the University staff. This retrospect gives a full account of the work of the Society and of the share in it of members of the University.

pleasant duty very seriously. Having got the chronicle of John of Reading off his hands, he had already set to work on the *Domesday Survey of Cheshire*, published by the Society in 1916. Other contributions which he made to its publications were the first (and only) volume of *Lancashire Quarter Sessions Records*, an edition of the Quarter Sessions Rolls, 1590-1606 (1917), *The Chartulary or Register of the abbey of St. Werburgh, Chester*, in two volumes (1920–3) and *Taxation in Salford Hundred, 1524–1802*, an edition of the records of four lay subsidies, 1524, 1543, 1563, 1600, of the hearth tax of 1666, and of the land tax, 1780–1802 (1924). This last volume owed its being to a suggestion by Farrer.

In his edition of the Cheshire survey, originally intended for the abortive Victoria County History, Tait was following up his work on the survey of Shropshire (1908). In his introduction he emphasized exceptional points, rather disappointing, as he says, to the student of the status and organization of a palatine earldom, but important to the student of borough customs and of the salt industry. In his edition of the *Chartulary of St. Werburgh's*, one of the most valuable of his books, he broke new ground, for which his comprehensive history of the Lancashire monastic houses had prepared him. He spent much time and trouble in tracking down the copies in royal *inspeximus* or made by seventeenth-century antiquaries, of the original charters, "of which summaries only, with the witnesses omitted, are usually given in the register of the abbey" (Harley MS. 1965) and he met with a good deal of success. He examined the life of St. Werburgh and the history of the foundation to distinguish fact from legend. And he attempted to sketch from the charters the administrative system of the palatine earldom in the twelfth century. His elaborate discussion of the charters of earls, including the "great charter" issued by Ranulf III to his barons, is perhaps the most valuable part of the book. He put the early history of the shire and earldom on as firm a foundation as the evidence admits and brought to bear upon his task, at the height of his powers, his unrivalled knowledge of feudal institutions, social conditions, and local topography.

In 1919 Tait resigned his chair and, subject to the need to avoid strain on his eyesight, was free to devote his working time to historical work. Two other interests, in place-names and in medieval boroughs, took a more purposeful place in his mind than they had had before. In 1923 he accepted an invitation to become the first President of the English Place-name Society, founded by the late Sir Allen Mawer and Sir Frank Stenton. Professor Stenton, in the annual report of the British Academy for 1944-5, has paid an authoritative tribute to Tait's work for the Society:

> He took an active part in the discussions which preceded its establishment, made suggestions of the highest value towards the determination of its plan of work, and contributed to our Introductory Volume an article on the feudal element in place-names, of which the importance becomes steadily more apparent with the passage of time. In those early days he brought to our help the support of an historian, eminent among English medievalists, who was one of the first modern scholars to appreciate the significance of place-name studies as an aid towards the solution of historical problems.

Tait's interest in boroughs, like the strong attraction which place-names had for him, began early, and, as we have seen, sprang naturally enough from his study of Domesday Book and feudal institutions. The stead impetus which it received about 1921 was due to a casual suggestion. The Syndics of the Cambridge University Press were looking for an editor to prepare the second volume of Adolphus Ballard's *British Borough Charters* for publication. They approached Tait, who came to an arrangement with them in the spring of 1921. He had the book ready by the summer of 1923. Although Ballard had left the text nearly complete, Tait put much work into the volume. In a long introduction, he anticipated in tentative outline the problems and developments with which he was to cope during the next twelve years; also, his work on the book suggested to him the theme of his lecture to the British Academy in May, 1922, on the study of early municipal history in England.[1] As he wrote later, the invitation to complete Ballard's book "induced me to lay aside other plans of work and confine myself to municipal history". The Academy lecture, the best introduction in our historical literature to a difficult subject, was followed in 1925 by his paper *Liber Burgus* in the essays presented to Tout, and by four other papers contributed to the *English Historical Review* between 1927 and 1931. As he approached his seventieth year he worked more slowly and wrote less than in earlier years. His book on *The Medieval English Borough* appeared in 1936.

In each of his books Tait made it his practice to explain exactly, in a lengthy preface, how and why he had come to compose it. He regarded himself, not as an isolated worker who had staked out a claim to a subject, but as the modest continuator of a noble succession of scholars whose traditions it was his duty and privilege to maintain. His preface to *The Medieval English Borough* is especially instructive. During the greater part of the century which followed the Municipal Corporation Act a true understanding of the medieval borough had been prevented, as he points out, by the influence of Merewether and Stephens, whose big book had appeared in the same year (1835). The false trail which they set had been deserted by Charles Gross, F. W. Maitland, Mary Bateson, and others, but hopes of an adequate history were deferred "by the early death of nearly all the leaders in these investigations". Tait, after his decision to finish Ballard's book on the municipal charters of the thirteenth century, had decided to resume, at any rate for the later twelfth and the thirteenth centuries, the work which these distinguished scholars had left unfinished. He worked for a decade upon half a dozen papers. He would probably in any case have collected them in a volume; but whatever his plans may have been, they were revised by the appearance in 1930 of a revolutionary article by an American scholar, Carl Stephenson, upon the Anglo-Saxon borough. Professor Stephenson already had behind him a fine record of stimulating and forceful work, part of the

[1] Reprinted, after some revision, from the Proceedings of the Academy in *The Medieval English Borough*, pp. 339-58.

abundant harvest of the seed sown by his master, Henri Pirenne. He writes with energy and clarity. He looks at his subject all round, with a wide comprehension of the medieval history of Europe. When he turned his attention to England he approached the history of the Anglo-Saxon and Norman boroughs with the outlook of a continental scholar. He saw in our island an outlying product of western civilization, subject to the same influences which had shaped the municipal destinies of the Low Countries. In Tait's view he both exaggerated the bearings of Pirenne's views and misunderstood the structure of Anglo-Saxon England. He suffered from a "tendency to interpret ambiguous evidence in the light of a theory".[1] He virtually made the Norman Conquest, with the mercantile elements alleged to have come for the first time in its train, the starting-point of English urban development. He was a victim of the garrison theory and misunderstood Domesday Book. "Hence", says Tait, "my attention was diverted to the pre-Conquest period."

The *Medieval English Borough*, therefore, consists of two parts, the first on the Anglo-Saxon period, largely concerned with a detailed examination of Stephenson's theories, the second a revised version of the papers written between 1922 and 1931. Although Tait had not been able to write his projected chapters on borough jurisdiction and the history of formal incorporation, the book is the most comprehensive study in existence on the origin, history, and developments of the English borough in the middle ages. It puts the whole subject on new and firm foundations. Perhaps its most important contribution is the study of the town councils, which finally dissipated the democratic *aura* with which former historians, before the days of Gross and Miss Bateson, had mystified the story. Tait will be mainly known, to many only known, by this book, the only book which he ever wrote on a large scale about a great subject. This outcome will not altogether do justice to him either as a scholar or as a writer, for the book is not easy, is written in his more austere manner,

[1] From Tait's review of Stephenson's *Study of Urban Origins in England*, in *E.H.R.* xxvii (1912), 720-8.

abounds in detailed disquisition of a learned and critical kind, and lacks those lighter touches which make some at least of his earlier work so readable and attractive. It is a pity that he never tried his hand at sustained biography or narrative. There is nothing elsewhere in his writings so intimate as his little sketch of James Crossley, the first President of the Chetham Society:

> Crossley presided at his last Council meeting on 20 April 1883 and signed the minutes of the previous meeting in his large, firm handwriting. He died on 1 August partly as the result of an accident in London a few months earlier. . . . He was the very reverse, Raines said, of the general editor who is reported to have said: "I'd sooner drive a team of tigers than a team of editors." His Johnsonian figure and fresh complexion even in his last years were familiar to me in my youth when living in Cheetham Hill and passing his book-crammed dwelling, Stocks House, Cheetham, on my way to Owens College and, if my memory does not deceive me, I once came upon him seated in the small shop of a second-hand bookseller in Oxford Street, which he seemed nearly to fill, turning over books which the proprietor was submitting to him.[1]

Before I leave this survey of Tait's historical work, I must refer to the loss to English learning due to his failure to continue his studies in Magna Carta. Tait, being but mortal, had his heavy days and even his bad days, but his note on *"waynagium and contenementum"* (1912),[2] was written on his very best days. Poole wrote, "I rejoice to have the Wainage and Contenement which will be very much in place in this Review. Wainage had long troubled me, and your explanation seems for the first time to account for the facts. Contenement I had blinked at, feeling certain that I did not really understand it and silently suppressing the *con*." Tait intended this masterly piece of exposition to be the first of a series of studies, but it had no successors. Nothing that he wrote gives a better

---

[1] "The Chetham Society: a retrospect", in *Chetham Miscellanies*, vii, 10, 11.
[2] *E.H.R.* xxvii (1912), 720-8.

idea of his range and insight. His vindication of Spelman's gloss on contenement, "aestimatio et conditionis forma" (1626), and his exposition of the underlying idea common to it and to the word "wainage", as used in the Great Charter, brings us to the heart of thirteenth-century thought about the social order. A series of studies of this quality would have been a boon indeed. But first the Chetham Society and then the boroughs stood in the way.[1]

Tait's life was given to Manchester and the University. His partnership with Tout made the Manchester School of History. The epigram that they were "dual manifestations of a single personality" is at any rate a tribute to a common devotion to a single purpose. It is unnecessary here to repeat a story which has already been told, and rightly told, in the memoir of the senior man.[2] While Tout took the lead, Tait kept the balance. His sagacity was never at fault, his reliability was taken for granted, his loyalty was unfailing. And, if Tout made himself a Manchester man, Tait was a Manchester man already, deeply rooted in the life and traditions of the city and university. After his appointment as a lecturer in 1896 he settled down. None of us knew anything about his earlier restlessness. He was a part of the place. His lectures, as Professor Galbraith has remarked, were dry but not dull; yet I doubt if his pupils minded very much whether they were dull or not, for he was Tait, the man with whom they felt safe, the constant sharer in their activities, their companion on walks and excursions, their minstrel. If he lived remote, he was always accessible. If he expected too much, he at least "delivered the goods". His retirement from his chair in 1919 seemed for a time to be a disaster, but did not in fact make so much difference as was feared, for his colleagues, the conference of teachers and research students, and for some years the undergraduates, saw almost as much of him as before.

Tait had become professor two years before the Owens

---

[1] For a wider appreciation of Tait's work than I have attempted here, the reader should turn to the admirable memoir by Professor V. H. Galbraith in the *E.H.R.* lx (1945), 129-35.

[2] See above, pp. 30-38.

College ceased to be combined with the colleges at Liverpool and Leeds and was merged in the Victoria University as an independent University of Manchester. He took his part in the discussions which preceded the change, and was always a force behind the scenes in academic life; but his most important contribution to University administration was made in the day-to-day work of faculty, senate, and council, on the committee of the University Press, of which he was chairman from 1925 to 1935, and in more incidental ways, especially as the chairman of the committee which was concerned with the erection and internal arrangements of the fine arts building, the home of the Faculty of Arts (opened in 1919).

In 1920 Tait was made an honorary professor and Litt.D. of the University. In 1921 he was elected a Fellow of the British Academy. In 1933 he was elected an honorary fellow of Pembroke, and was given an honorary D.Litt. by the University of Oxford. This was the year of his seventieth birthday. The event was commemorated by the preparation of a splendid volume, *Historical Essays in Honour of James Tait*, edited, with a drawing by Ronald Allan and a bibliography, by J. G. Edwards, V. H. Galbraith, and E. F. Jacob. The book was given to Tait after a dinner on 19 December. Lord Crawford, the Chancellor of the University, presided. It was a happy occasion.

During the greater part of his life as a teacher and for about six years after his retirement Tait lived in Fallowfield. Many of us could not pass 9 Beaconsfield without recalling, as some of the most satisfying of our lives, the hours we spent in his sitting-room, among his books. In 1925 he bought a house at Wilmslow, where he lived with one or more of his sisters for twenty years. He continued to spend every Thursday afternoon in Manchester and to take tea in the Senior Common Room at the University. He served on committees, was for three years a Governor of the John Rylands Library, and for a longer period a member of the Art Gallery Committee in the city. He had his garden and fruit-trees, his favourite cat, his regular clock-like walks, his carefully arranged holidays in Langdale and Eskdale, and above all his study. "He was", writes Miss

Beatrice Tait, "as methodical in the home as in his work. He rarely gave advice unless sought for and it was always worth having. He considered the matter from every angle, then gave his opinion. He was very rarely angry and I always admired him for apologizing when on consideration he felt he was in the wrong; not an easy thing to do, but it proved the kind of man he was."

Tait had travelled much in his early and middle life. After 1887 there was hardly a year in which he did not roam, generally with one or two friends, in Germany or France, or, if this were not practicable, in England and Wales. He kept note-books in which he described and sketched, in the manner of Freeman and quite as well, towns and buildings, with plans and architectural details. Few historical scholars have known England so well as he knew it. He liked to wander about London—where he always found time, if he could, for the Zoo—and to identify places of literary or historical interest, not antiquities only, but streets and houses associated with famous men or with the characters of Dickens and other novelists. His reading was very wide, especially in biography. In his youth he was attracted by Walt Whitman, as passages copied into his note-books show; they come between his careful little accounts of expenses. In later life he read less poetry. He preferred the company of poets as revealed in their lives. Scott's life and letters were often read, and the lives of historians, especially of Freeman, whose realism and range appealed to him. His letters, if they could be put together, would be found to be full of raw material. He must have given of his best in them, for so many people used to consult him, as he liked to consult others, about historical and topographical details. When he ceased to wander far afield and settled down to regular holidays in the Lake country, especially in Eskdale, he gradually mastered the history of the district. With the aid of the very full verdict of an Elizabethan jury of twenty-four, known in local usage as the Twenty-Four book, he traced the site of every vanished farm in Eskdale, and followed up every sheep-walk, which, so far as they remain, are still the same.

Indeed, Tait's constancy to all his historical interests was very impressive. A list of his writings after he reached the age of seventy shows every one of them. And there was still more to come. Stirred by recent Domesday discussions and instigated by Galbraith, he returned to an old battle-ground, and plunged into the minutiae of the Herefordshire Domesday. The outcome, published in 1950, six years after his death, as a volume of the Pipe Roll Society, was the *Herefordshire Domesday*, edited by Galbraith, the text of a twelfth-century revision of the earlier survey, from Balliol College MS. 350. This book incorporates Tait's careful and voluminous notes.

"Iuvat eum, ut fertur, per montes vagari; eundem iure dixeris per ardua investigationis culmina prospere tulisse vestigia."[1] Tait was a historian who took broad views. He was much more than a delver. He raised up his eyes to the hills in more senses than one. In the summer of 1943 he made his last ascent of Scafell. He kept a record of all the hills, of 2,500 and more feet above sea-level, which he had ascended in Great Britain. He wished to add one more, to reach, I think, the total of thirty-five, so we went up Grey Friar together. For his Easter holiday in 1944 he went as usual to Langdale with his friend Joseland. Tait clung to his routine. One day, although Joseland was compelled to pause and return, he insisted on pushing on alone to the top of Pike o' Blisco. On his way down by a different route, he had a bad fall and lost his eye-glasses. Unable to see clearly, bruised and shaken, he took some hours, in the increasing darkness, to grope his way down to the dale, where he was found by a search-party. For a time he seemed to to be little the worse for his experience, but it had been too severe. He died suddenly at Wilmslow in the early hours of 4 July, 1944, a fortnight after his eighty-first birthday.

I have written about Tait as I think he would have preferred, step by step, under the guidance of documentary evidence as well as of personal recollections, and in more detail than is usually required. His life and work added distinction to the university in which he found his first opportunities and to the historical movements in which he took so large a

---

[1] From the oration delivered by Dr. Cyril Bailey, the Public Orator, when Tait received his honorary degree at Oxford on 9 May, 1933.

share. He is part of their history, and they in their turn add significance to him.

ANDREW GEORGE LITTLE[1]

Andrew George Little was born on 28 September, 1863. He was the second of the three sons of Thomas Little, the rector of Princes Risborough. His mother was Ann Wright, a woman of great charm, whose home had been at Chalfont St. Giles. Thomas Little was the very best kind of parish priest. The eldest of eleven children, he was born and brought up at Corrie, six miles from Lockerbie in Dumfriesshire, and had the good fortune to be taught at the village school by a Mr. Monsey, one of those inspiring dominies who have shaped Scottish boys and sent them on to the universities. The stories told about Thomas as a boy and man are singularly consistent. He had a remarkable influence upon others, whether he knew them well or made friends with them in a casual meeting. His memory was long cherished with gratitude and affection in Princes Risborough.

Andrew lost both his father and mother when he was about thirteen years old. On medical advice the rector went with his wife to Italy—the boys were at school—but had to leave owing to an illness contracted by Mrs. Little. She died suddenly at Paris on the way home, and her husband, a sick man, never recovered from the shock. He died a few months later, in November, 1876. The three boys were given a home by their uncle, Dr. David Little, of Manchester, one of the leading ophthalmic surgeons of his day. Many years later, in November, 1902, two days before the doctor died, Andrew wrote to his aunt: "I have felt for many years very deeply and the present circumstances bring it home to me still more nearly what an enormous lot we three owe to Uncle David, ever since the day of my Father's funeral when he took charge of us and rescued us from the danger of slack surroundings and brought

---

[1] From the memoir in *The Proceedings of the British Academy*, vol. xxxi. It is based mainly on Little's correspondence which Mrs. Little placed at my disposal, with other information, and on the recollections of Little's cousin, Miss Dora Little.

us back into the bracing atmosphere of work and duty." All the same, life in Manchester was dull for Andrew and his brothers until Dr. Little married a lady nearer their own age than he was. Then, in a house with a good garden in Victoria Park, they were very happy with the doctor and his wife, whom they called by her Christian name and regarded as an elder sister, and, as the years passed by, with the children. One of these cousins, Miss Dora Little, writes:

> I always loved Andrew from a small child upwards, but, alas! never saw enough of him. His wit and tremendously hearty laughter will always remain vividly in my mind. Our old nurse had the greatest admiration for "Mr. Andrew"... He was always so delightful with children and my mother remembers him saying that the greatest hell on earth would be never to see a child....

And, referring to later years, Miss Little speaks of his instinct for doing "charming little things". In 1887 the three nephews had Mrs. Little's portrait painted "as a token of gratitude for the happy home my father, as their guardian, had given them, and for all he and my mother had been to them. It was Andrew's idea and he who chose the artist, Sir William Richmond." [1]

Andrew was sent by his parents to a preparatory school, Durham House (better known later as The Grange) at Folkestone. His brother Frank recalls that the headmaster, the Rev. A. L. Hussey, had no great opinion of Andrew's abilities. He thought that he was very slow and that he did not make much effort to learn. If this were so Andrew certainly woke up at Clifton, where he went in 1878, two years after his father's death. In May of this year Dr. Percival, then headmaster of Clifton, had offered the post of master of the upper fifth to Charles Edwyn Vaughan, a young man of twenty-four, afterwards well known as a writer on English literature and political thought and as professor of English language and literature in Cardiff, Newcastle, and Leeds. Andrew Little owed more to Vaughan than to any other man. His influence upon

[1] Mrs. David Little survived Andrew, and died in November, 1946.

him during his Clifton days and afterwards was profound. He gave him both the stimulus and the wider outlook which he needed and made him aware of the mental and spiritual values which came to mean most to him. Among other things he taught him that writing is the surest refuge from boredom and that something of philosophy is indispensable for a fruitful knowledge of history.[1] In 1882 Andrew went up to Balliol, just bereft of the presence but not of the influence of Vaughan's cousin, T. H. Green. And his first teaching post was at Cardiff, close to Llandaff, where Vaughan's uncle, the famous dean, was still at work with his pupils in the companionship which Dr. Coulton has described so well in his autobiography.

At Oxford Andrew read for honour moderations in classics and then turned to history, in which he took a first class in 1886. He had adequate means, made friends easily, and worked steadily. Riding, until he gave up his horse in 1918, was his only recreation. From his undergraduate days until he left Cardiff he hunted, generally riding to hounds once a week during the hunting season. His interest in politics was strong. A letter written on 8 February, 1885, just after the news of the fall of Khartoum had reached England, shows deep feeling controlled by the good sense always so characteristic of him. After he had taken his degree he decided to study in Germany. He told Bishop Stubbs that he "intended to go into *Domesday Book*. Stubbs chortled and said it was much more important to get out of it", and foretold that nothing would come of it. The prophecy was justified, for Andrew, in his own words, found himself in a Serbonian bog. He attacked a difficult subject in the wrong way and in the wrong place; but he learned a great deal from his experience.

He went first to Dresden where he studied German with Fräulein Gottschalk, well known to Oxford scholars as a teacher. He then went to Göttingen where he worked for about a year, from the spring of 1887 to the spring of 1888, under

---

[1] After Vaughan's death in 1922, Little prepared for the press his *Studies in the History of Political Philosophy before and after Rousseau* in two volumes (Manchester University Press, 1925). He prefixed to this work a fine memoir of his friend.

Ludwig Weiland, the disciple of Waitz, and one of the editors of the volumes of "constitutiones et acta publica imperatorum et regum" published in the *Monumenta Germaniae Historica*. Weiland was a good scholar and a stimulating teacher. In one of his letters to Mrs. David Little (28 April, 1887) Andrew writes:

> This evening at 6 o'clock took place something which I have looked forward to as a vague possibility for two years now, it ought to be something great, oughtn't it? It was a discussion between students and professor on the principles and practices of the critical examination of original historical documents— a pretty heavy and dull affair to have on one's mind 2 years! Weiland was the professor; he is quite splendid—only spoke today generally—of methods etc., and quoted a few screamingly funny examples of documentary falsifications. I did not know the subject was capable of such a treatment. Next Friday we begin real work on original documents. I am afraid my pleasure will be a little spoiled when I have to make a speech in German—but never say die! He is going to examine some of the English documents this term and I shall try to show then that even an Oxford historical student doesn't get all his knowledge at secondhand.

Andrew obviously got what he felt that he needed in Göttingen. He enjoyed the discipline in historical method. He talked German with an old lady, Frau Dr. Hummel, who was exceedingly kind to him and, when the tête-à-têtes in German became wearisome, proceeded to teach him Italian. As he acquired proficiency in the language he entered more easily into the interests of his companions. One day he read a paper to the historical society, and won much approval, though the paper was "somewhat too highpitched for the rather beery atmosphere that pervades a *Kneipe*". He found good friends. He wrote: "It made me really very dismal to leave Göttingen: people were very good to me and seemed very sorry that I was going. One gets up a lot of affection for a place where one has been for a year. I felt too that my time there was very well spent and that an era of my life had come to an end." At times he had not been happy. The subject which Weiland had suggested to him was not congenial and, as the professor ruefully admitted, he had led him on a wild-goose chase. It made him feel that he was stupid and dispirited him. And he was depressed by the news of his greatest friend, Charles Warrack, who was seeking health in vain in Italy and Algeria. His happiest time was when Vaughan came to stay with him. Vaughan helped him to carry the four big folios of *Domesday Book* from the University library to his room, and read to him bits of his history of political philosophy.

Weiland was impressed by Little and testified to his capacity to treat historical problems "even of a difficult sort, thoroughly and according to the scientific methods". The outcome of his researches was a note in the *English Historical Review* for 1889 on "Gesiths and Thanes".

On his way home Little went to Berlin to see the body of the Emperor William lying in state before his funeral. He wrote a detailed and vivid description of the scenes in the city and of the crowds, and added an appreciation of the new Emperor, Frederick (13 March, 1888):

> The funeral takes place on Friday and ought to be very imposing. I shall try to get a decent place somewhere. The new Emperor will probably not take part in it—the weather is too unfavourable. There is a report that he was in Berlin today; but I don't believe it. The more one hears of him the more one hopes he may live. There is an old prophecy said to date from the 16th century to which the old Emperor is said to have attached importance (as he certainly did to others of the like kind) that an Emperor would arise who would restore the Empire to its old might and conquer all its foes, and would live longer than any of his predecessors; he would survive his son and hand on the Empire to a weak grandson, under whom, however, the Empire would rise still higher. Who knows whether this may not have depressed the Crown Prince? A new spirit is visible already in the Emperor's decrees—in the mourning-decree that he would leave the time to the people themselves in their various localities; and in the Manifesto to the People that appeared yesterday—also in [a] letter to Bismark. One sees a reverence for the Constitution worthy of an Englishman, which Emp. Wilhelm and Bismark have not

shown. Everything is not, it would seem, to be ordered from the head-centre, not to depend on a few men, but Government is to become the business of the people; they are not to have everything done for them, but are to do things themselves, and feel their own responsibility. The mention of Arts and Sciences in the Manifesto is very remarkable, and I should think quite original in a document of this kind. I don't know whether the Germans will in their hearts agree with the very peaceful character of the policy sketched out—with the truth, which every paragraph of the Manifesto would seem to bring out—that "Peace hath her victories no less renowned than war". The German youth of the present day seems to me to be distinctly war-loving.

After his return to England Little spent four fruitful years in research in Oxford and London. He deserted Domesday Book and the Anglo-Saxon laws for the friars. A casual remark made by his tutor, A. L. Smith, had already aroused his interest: "Read Brewer's introduction to *Monumenta Franciscana*; you would like it." He *had* read it, and now he determined to devote himself to ecclesiastical and academic history, and especially to the history of the Grey Friars or Franciscans or Friars Minor.[1] He lived mainly in London, but spent a good deal of time in Oxford. One letter, written from Oxford to Mrs. David Little, describes "a great thing" which had happened to him on 12 November [1890], the day on which the letter was written.

> Just as I was starting for a ride, a youth came up to me and said, "The G.O.M. is coming to tea with me to-day: do you care to come?" It is needless to say that I did care to come. There were only four of us—the other three being undergrads. and younger than myself. We waited, not expecting that the old man would turn up as it was raining hard. Presently Mrs. G. turned up and we hailed her joyfully as an earnest of better things to come. Soon after the well-known

---

[1] "Fratres Minores is the best Latin translation of Grey Friars. Fratres grisei is occasionally found as a popular and non-official translation, e.g., *Political Poems and Songs*, ed. Wright (R. S.), i. 256: 'Inter fratres griseos sic est ordinatum'." (MS. note by A. G. L.)

head appeared in the doorway. He looked beaming but very muddy and said he had a tragedy to tell. Coming along the High [to Magdalen] with his umbrella in front against wind and rain, he had fallen over some sacks of coal on the pavement (that is rather characteristic of Oxford streets by the way, in the dark). He was none the worse and seemed to regard it as a huge joke, but it might have been very serious. He is extraordinarily young—really blessed with eternal youth— the youthfulness of the soul. He merely frivolled, humbugged his wife, and talked about the historic significance of pork, which he had discovered was of great ethnological importance, especially in relation to Homer and the Phoenicians. He had just met Burdon Sanderson for the first time and was tremendously impressed by his appearance; it was evidently a problem to him how a vivisectionist could look so magnificent. I did so want to talk politics but thought it better not to begin; they were not mentioned.

Little had his share of interruptions and domestic anxiety, but his life was uneventful, placid, and happy, and its story is soon told. In the autumn of 1892 he became the first independent lecturer in history in University College of South Wales at Cardiff. In July, 1898, he was made professor. In 1901 he resigned his chair on account of the bad health of his wife, whom he had married in 1893. In 1902 he settled in Sevenoaks in a house called "Risborough" in recollection of his father's and his own early home, and there, on 22 October, 1945, he died. His wife was Alice, the daughter of William Hart of Fingrith Hall, Blackmore, Essex. He had first met her in 1882 at her aunt's home, Waltons Park, a beautiful place on the borders of Essex and Cambridgeshire, where Andrew and his brothers and the Hart family were wont to spend some of their holidays. "We had a married life", writes Mrs. Little, "of great happiness, in spite of my frequent indifferent health, which Andrew bore with unfailing and amazing, kindest patience." How much he, in his turn, owed to the companionship and to Mrs. Little's encouragement is known to all their friends. They had a full life. Little was a good citizen, deep in many academic activities, in frequent touch with scholars at home and abroad. The envelope of a foreign letter which he once sent to me was addressed, I noticed, to "The University, Risborough"; and in a sense Little did build up a "school" of his own in his Kentish retreat.

He had been a good professor. As a teacher at Cardiff he set a high standard and enlarged the scope of his subject. This involved him in controversy with the "patriots", which seems to have come to a head in the senate in 1900. His refusal, which caused some debate, to draw rigid distinctions and to provide independent instruction in the history of Wales at the expense of other subjects, was probably wise at the time and certainly did not imply indifference to Welsh history. He wrote a capital little book on *Medieval Wales* (1902) which, though it appeared after his retirement, was the outcome of a course of popular lectures given in 1901, and found an immediate welcome in the other colleges of the University of Wales. He brought to Cardiff, young though he was, a mature judgement and the influence of wide historical movements in scholarship. The memory of his work still lives in Wales. He was always so much more than a learned man. After the establishment of the University of Wales in 1893, and especially after his promotion in 1898, his quiet influence was felt throughout the academic life of the country. He inspired trust and affection. I cannot do better than quote the testimony of Vaughan, who had been made professor of English and History in 1889 and had surrendered the teaching of history to his new colleague, but old pupil and friend, three years later. Vaughan left Cardiff in 1898, but after Little's retirement he wrote an appreciation of him for the college magazine. Here are a few excerpts:

> For the last nine years he has been inseparably bound up with all that is best in the life of the College; with its social intercourse, with the working of its various Societies, with the transaction of its business; and, above all, with its intellectual energy. And it is no small thing for the College to have had, during that time, a man of such wide sympathies and so sound a judgement, as well as of such deep learning and scholarly training, on its Staff. . . . Though he had started life with no intention of becoming a teacher, he soon took to the work like

a duck to the water.... His distinction as student and teacher is but a small part of what he has contributed to the life of the College. Where, for the last nine years, would the College have been without his disinterestedness, his energy in extending its influence, his sound judgement, his keen interest in individual students, his self-sacrificing devotion?

Except for an application at Edinburgh in 1899, Little made no attempt to get another chair; but he was not a recluse. In 1901 he accepted an invitation from Professor Tout to teach palaeography to graduate students who were engaged in research work in Manchester, and, after the necessary arrangements had been made, he began in 1902 those weekly or fortnightly visits to the northern University which continued with few breaks during the greater part of each academic year until 1928. He was not the first to lecture or give instruction in palaeography in a British university, but I think that he was the first to gather about him, in a systematic though informal way, groups of students who, as members of a school of history, were trying to learn how to write history. Neither Tout nor his colleague Tait believed in "spoon-feeding", but they did believe that graduate studies are as important as undergraduate studies in any academic society which professes to advance learning; and Little, with his vivid recollections of all he had looked forward to as an undergraduate and all he had learned in Göttingen, was just the man to supplement the guidance given by the professors to their pupils. He took much care. He prepared collections of facsimiles of manuscripts ranging from Carolingian minuscule to Tudor script and distributed them, at a ridiculously low charge, to the members of his class. He was patient and precise in the exposition of technicalities, but he also made his pupils realize the significance of the texts as historical documents, and encouraged them to write papers on the manuscript sources upon which each of them might have to rely. Above all, he made them feel that they were his fellow workers, whatever their particular interests might be. The hours which some of us spent in Little's class were some of the happiest and most stimulating in our lives as students of history. His accuracy and learning won our immediate respect; his gentleness and humour and personal interest made him our friend.

His public spirit made him a familiar figure in much wider circles. His high sense of duty was combined with wide human sympathies; and he was a source of strength to learned bodies, the Royal Historical Society, the Canterbury and York Society, the Historical Association, and, after his election as a Fellow in 1922, the British Academy. On the whole he was able to relate his special interests in Franciscan history to his furtherance of educational and learned enterprises. His frequent contributions to the *English Historical Review*, the sixteen biographies which he wrote between 1890 and 1895 for the *Dictionary of National Biography*, his accounts of the friaries of various orders in Lincolnshire, Worcestershire, Oxfordshire, Dorsetshire, Yorkshire, and Kent which, between 1906 and 1927, filled more than 150 closely packed pages of the *Victoria County Histories*, and a score or more casual essays and papers, in books, magazines, and local periodicals, all either extended or popularized knowledge of the history of the friars, and of the English Grey Friars in particular. They were to a large extent preparations for what was to have been his greatest work, a history of the Franciscans in England. On the other hand, his sense of duty was responsible for his failure to fulfil this purpose. The secretaryship of the ecclesiastical section of the International Congress of Historical Studies held in London in 1913 or the co-editorship of the volume of essays presented to Professor Tout in 1925 might be taken in his stride, though they involved much correspondence and other labour; but his work in the War Trade Intelligence Department (1916–18) during the First World War,[1] his preparation for the press of Professor Vaughan's big book on

[1] H. W. C. Davis, the vice-chairman of the department, admitted him with reluctance. He observed, "it is like cutting wood with a razor". A report on the iron and steel resources of Austria and Germany is said to have won warm praise from Earl Balfour; but most of his work was done as one of the editors of "Daily Notes". He left the department in November, 1918, and received a grateful letter from Davis for his care and thoroughness in this uncongenial task.

political philosophy (1922–5), and his devoted service as President of the Historical Association (1926–9) made serious inroads on his time and energy. He undertook the last responsibility only after much hesitation, but as a former chairman of the publications committee and as a warm advocate of the aims of the Association he felt that he must accept the nomination. It meant that he would have to attend many meetings and travel among the local branches, and it came just when he was ready to settle down to his comprehensive history. Then, in 1928, his friend Paul Sabatier died, and he found himself committed to the preparation for the press of the famous scholar's new edition of the *Speculum Perfectionis* (2 vols., 1928, 1931), a labour of love, no doubt, but also a most tiresome and perplexing task. After this the state of his health enabled him to do little more than finish various pieces of work which he had in hand and to put together some of his earlier papers. He had already had one operation in April, 1916. In 1937 he had to undergo a much more serious one. Throughout the Second World War he lived in a dangerous area in a time of incessant anxiety, and without the domestic help upon which his wife and he had always been able to rely. He worked hopefully in his house and garden, kept in touch with local life and his old friends, made new friends of those who were given a place in his home, and published a collection of papers. His last work, a revision in an English form of his edition of Eccleston, was published after his death.

He had been a Fellow of the British Academy since 1922. He received the honorary degree of Doctor of Letters from the University of Oxford in 1928 and from the University of Manchester in 1935.

At first sight Little's historical work may seem narrow and to lie outside the main field. He was not so widely known as some of his contemporaries were, either at home or abroad. He received no foreign distinctions, although he devoted his life as a scholar to the poor man of Assisi. Yet this way of looking at him is most misleading. His first book, *The Grey Friars in Oxford* (1892), has the same sort of importance in English historical literature as had those other Oxford books, R. L.

Poole's *Illustrations of the History of Medieval Thought* (1884), and Rashdall's *Universities of Europe in the Middle Ages* (1895), and it probably had a more immediate and continuous effect than they produced. It gave fresh and wider significance to medieval history, submitted a neglected subject to the standards of exact scholarship, greatly broadened our knowledge of unpublished material, and linked with learning, some of which was his own, but more of which lay hidden in the treasure-house of western thought and endeavour, a theme of perpetual charm and interest to the spirit of man. As his powers grew and his range broadened, Little's work became in itself a source of inspiration, not alone for students of his subject but for all who wished to see the barriers between this and that field of learning broken down. Never forgetful of the early influences under which he had learned history and always ready to advance them, he was one of those who can explain the unity of life in the past, and in doing this make a great library a less mysterious place. The man was not lost in the scholar. Those who knew him well would be inclined to agree with his oldest contemporary, who wrote after his death that Little, since Maitland, came nearest to the idea of what an historical scholar can be.

Most of Little's work consists of studies in critical scholarship. Its range and intensity can best be realized by an examination of the bibliography printed with the address presented to him in 1938. Its value as a contribution to medieval history can only be estimated by specialists. A mere detailed summary of it would be tedious and unsatisfactory. Some general observations, however, should be made before I refer to Little's outstanding books and papers. From the first he saw the Franciscan movement as part of a wider development in religious, ecclesiastical, and educational life. He was no naïve enthusiast devoted to the *Poverello*. Indeed, I fancy that his concern with the lives of St. Francis and his disciples was mainly due to the efflorescence of Franciscan studies which followed the publication of Paul Sabatier's famous book shortly after his own *Grey Friars in Oxford*. Inevitably and eagerly he took his share in a movement of which he can hardly have been aware when he began; yet he regarded the history of the mendicant orders as a whole, and of their academic activities in particular, as his subject. From one point of view his work was an expression, suggested by his special interests, of his belief in the value of local history and of his desire to make more accessible to the general student and to specialists the technicalities of his craft. It was connected with the influence which he exerted, as a leader in the Historical Association, in the promotion of the study of local history and in the preparation of annual bibliographies of current historical literature, and with his wise and skilful direction of the committee which prepared, for the Institute of Historical Research, a report on the way to edit documents. The publication, early in his career, of his *Initia operum latinorum*, to which I shall return, was the finest example of a natural quality which, throughout the history of learning, has blessed scholars of generous and gracious minds—the wish to share with others the profits of their labours. Little, like the late P. S. Allen, regarded our academic society as an unselfish brotherhood with no frontiers except the frontier imposed by the duty to maintain a high standard.

His Franciscan studies widened Little's circle of friends both at home and abroad. He did not labour, like P. S. Allen, under the pleasant compulsion to make a systematic survey of manuscript sources in foreign libraries, but he was familiar with the chief collections and made some important discoveries, and, like Allen, he had ties, sometimes very close ties, with fellow scholars in the west of Europe and Italy. Numerous letters to him from Sabatier and the Franciscan brothers in Quaracchi, notably Father Livarius Oliger, show how the discussion of minute points of scholarship was enlivened by warm personal regard and the memories of happy visits. He spent a summer in Paris during his Cardiff period, was in Florence in 1895, in Rome, Assisi, and Florence in 1909, in Florence, Assisi, Siena, Ravenna, and Venice in 1922. Co-operation with continental scholars became a matter of course after the publication in the *English Historical Review* in 1902 of a long review of recent researches into the sources of the history of St. Francis, a paper which was translated into Italian by Professor R. Casali for the *Miscellanea Francescana*. The French and Italian periodicals devoted to Franciscan studies sought contributions from him. As his correspondence reveals, he was regarded by scholars in related fields of study as a source of information about manuscripts. His work on Roger Bacon provides a good example of this and of his ability to bring scholars together. His account of Bacon in the *Grey Friars in Oxford* was the first expression of an interest to which he returned throughout his later life. He gave vigorous encouragement to, and for many years prevailed upon the British Academy to support, Mr. R. R. Steele's *Opera hactenus inedita Rogeri Baconi,* the first fascicle of which appeared in 1905. He organized the commemoration in 1914 of the seventh centenary anniversary of the traditional date of Bacon's birth (1214). A volume of essays was compiled and a memorial stone was erected on an old wall which is regarded as a remnant of the medieval friary in Oxford. While he was preparing the volume of essays, Little approached the distinguished scholar, Pierre Duhem of Bordeaux, who, in the course of his labours on his great cosmological work, *Le Système du monde,* had already published an unedited fragment of the *Opus Tertium*. Duhem ultimately sent to Little his essay on "Roger Bacon et l'Horreur du vide" (*Commemoration Essays,* pp. 241–84), but at first had thought of writing on Bacon's early *questiones* on the *Physics* of Aristotle. Little lent him a rotograph of the important manuscript at Amiens (Amiens no. 406) containing most of Bacon's earliest work, which had not been thoroughly examined since Victor Cousin had described it in 1848 in the pages of the *Journal des Savants*. After Duhem's death in 1917 another Baconian scholar, the Franciscan Ferdinand M. Delorme, used the rotograph, in co-operation with Mr. Steele, in his edition of the *questiones* published in the *Opera hactenus inedita* (1928).[1] During these years Little did much

---

[1] Letters from Duhem and Delorme, and information from Mrs. Little. Little had first examined the Amiens MS. about 1907 and in 1928 seems to have had it sent for his use or for Mr. Steele's to the British Museum. The rotograph was later given, with other rotographs, to the British Museum.

work on Bacon. In 1928 he delivered to the British Academy the masterly lecture in which he summed up the results of all recent work on this "master mind".

At this point we naturally come to his best-known enterprise, the formation of the British Society of Franciscan Studies, for three of the twenty-two volumes issued by the Society between its reconstitution in 1907 and its dissolution in 1936–7 contain editions of works by Roger Bacon. The Society was originally founded in September, 1902, as a British Branch of the International Society established by Paul Sabatier in the previous July. Sabatier was its honorary president until his death in March, 1928. The desire to give more emphasis to the publication of texts and studies and to provide money for the same led in 1907 to the reconstruction of the Branch as a British Society. The story of its activities has been told by Little himself.[1] It is a part of the history of Franciscan studies and only concerns us here in so far as it throws light on Little as organizer, editor, and scholar. Throughout his was the leading spirit. From 1905 he was chairman of the committee as well as honorary general editor and, after Sabatier's death, honorary president. He arranged the preparation of all the twenty-two volumes published for the Society, was the author of two, one of the authors of three, and contributed papers or bibliographies to seven of them. Then there was his revision in two volumes of Sabatier's edition of the *Speculum Perfectionis*. Moreover, with the enthusiastic support of his friend Dr. Walter Seton, who was secretary of the Society from 1923 until his early death in January, 1927, he was actively concerned in two commemorations, one the celebration at Canterbury on 10 September, 1924, of the seventh centenary of the coming of the Franciscans to England, the other the arrangement of a course of lectures in University College, London, in October, 1926, to mark the seventh centenary of the death of St. Francis. The lectures with other papers, edited by Dr. Seton, were published by the London University Press under the title *St. Francis, Essays in Com-*

---

[1] *Franciscan Essays* II (1932), pp. vii-xii. This volume is the third in the Extra Series of the Society

memoration, 1226–1926. They comprise, in addition to F. C. Burkitt's study of the sources and other remarkable works, a survey by Little of the first hundred years of the Franciscan school at Oxford, always the theme closest to his mind and heart. The Society came to an end, in accordance with a resolution passed at a general meeting on 31 October, 1936, with the publication of two fine volumes on *Franciscan Architecture in England* (1936) and *Franciscan History and Legend in English Mediaeval Art* (1937), due respectively to suggestions made by Sir Charles Peers and Mrs. Bardswell. The decision was taken with reluctance, but lack of funds and support, the consciousness that, though much more remained to be done, most of the sources of primary interest in Franciscan history had been published, and the difficulty of finding a successor to Little as editor made it inevitable. As Little says, in the preface to the concluding volume, "there are fashions in historical as in other movements". From 1918 the volumes of the Society were published through the agency of the Manchester University Press. Little's friendly relations with the publications committee in Manchester must have spared him much anxiety. It had already undertaken his *Initia Operum* and his Ford lectures, and was to publish his last collection of essays (1943) and his new edition of Eccleston (1951).

Little was always at work, quietly, steadily, placidly, but with unfailing thoroughness. And it should not be forgotten that he inspired or improved as much work by others as he wrote himself, not only books prepared under his direction while he was engaged in advanced teaching in Manchester, like Miss Margaret Toynbee's *S. Louis of Toulouse,* and Miss Decima Douie's *Nature and Effect of the Heresy of the Fraticelli,* but the work of fellow scholars who relied on him for advice, for assistance in the search for and handling of manuscripts, and in countless other ways. Whether they knew him personally or not there can be few of his contemporaries and none of his juniors interested in the history of medieval thought or education or ecclesiastical institutions who have not learned of him. Everything that he wrote is straightforward and to the point, and so wisely related to the criticism of texts. It would be hard to distinguish between his learned and his popular essays or lectures as sources on influence for the learned work is so easy to follow and the popular work is so free from padding, reflecting the best of his thinking and expressing with more freedom his disciplined feelings. As I have said, he returned again and again to the subject of his first book, both in learned and popular studies. One of his most important pieces of work is the long paper on "the Franciscan School at Oxford in the thirteenth century", which Father Oliger induced him to write for a special number of the periodical of the Quaracchi fathers, *Archivum Franciscanum Historicum* (1926). This includes a revision of the lives of the earlier Oxford scholars dealt with in the *Grey Friars in Oxford* (the articles on Pecham and Duns Scotus are notable), with a masterly account of the academic exercises in early Oxford. It leads naturally to the book which Little prepared, in collaboration with his friend, Father F. Pelster, S.J., for the Oxford Historical Society in 1934, *Oxford Theology and Theologians c. A.D. 1282–1302*. Four years before, the two scholars had discovered that both were working on the same manuscripts, and in particular on Assisi 158 (*quaestiones* at Oxford and Cambridge 1282–90) and Worcester Cathedral Library Q 99 (*quaestiones* at Oxford, 1300–2). They joined to describe these *quaestiones* and to add a precious section on the university sermons preached at Oxford in 1290–3. The outcome is a strong and practical study, enriched by texts, notes, and biographies, of academic life in the last years of the thirteenth century. I do not know a better introduction to life in a medieval university. An outcome of Little's work on the Grey Friars at Oxford was his edition of Eccleston's *Tractatus de adventu fratrum minorum in Angliam* published in Sabatier's *Collection d'études et de documents* (Paris, 1909) and his edition of the *Liber Exemplorum* or practical manual of illustrations for the use of preachers, contained in a Durham Cathedral manuscript (British Society of Franciscan Studies, i, 1908). In the former he established and annotated a well-known text, first edited by J. S. Brewer in 1858; in the latter he broke new ground,[1] and notably promoted the literature, now greatly extended, about medieval preaching. These books, with his various studies in local Franciscan history and his numerous papers, prepared him for his more comprehensive and best-known book, the Ford lectures, *Studies in English Franciscan History*, delivered in 1916. During the years which have since gone by, many readers and university students, in their successive generations, must have learned from Little's lectures what the coming of the Friars Minor meant to England and how a fine and sympathetic scholar can throw fresh light on the society of the past by the skilful arrangement of scattered evidence. Dr. Coulton, who had made Little's acquaintance some years before, read the proofs with warm appreciation. The lectures have won and will long retain a place in our historical literature undisturbed by changing fashions and enthusiasms, for they are firmly rooted in knowledge and humanity. How far removed is the spirit of the following passage from the fleeting vogue of the *Fioretti*:

> It would ill become a Balliol man lecturing in the Hall of Balliol College to maintain that the Franciscans were exclusively devoted to schemes for the maintenance of their own Order. It is well known that Franciscans took an honourable part in the foundation of Balliol, and for more than two centuries were associated in the government of the College. And there are other instances of Franciscan confessors directing their penitents to apply their property to the advancement of learning—notably in the case of Pembroke College, Cambridge. But these instances, so far as I know, are too few and too exceptional to allow us to alter our general conclusion that the necessity of maintaining themselves on alms impaired the social usefulness of the friars, and their spiritual force. The pressure of material needs was too insistent. The cares of poverty proved as exacting and distracting as the cares of property.

Two other books call for attention, the *Initia Operum* and

[1] At first Little thought he was the first to discover this manuscript. He wrote ruefully to his wife in 1904, while he was examining in Oxford, that W. P. Ker had called his attention to a study of it by a French scholar. This scholar was Paul Meyer.

Sabatier's new edition of the *Speculum Perfectionis*. One of the projects of the original or branch Society of Franciscan Studies was the compilation of a catalogue of Franciscan manuscripts. Though Sabatier warmly encouraged this proposal, it fell to the ground, but Little had begun to compile a catalogue of Franciscan manuscripts in Great Britain. His preliminary studies grew into the more general *Initia Operum Latinorum quae saeculis xiii., xiv., xv. attribuuntur* (Manchester University Press, 1904). The interleaved volume of 275 pages, containing close on 6,000 *incipits*, is now very rare and costly. Little made extensive additions in his own copy, now in the possession of the Institute of Historical Research, but no second edition has ever appeared. The list is obviously provisional; it was primarily intended to help Franciscan students; but Little cast his net wide and produced a book which is still the only attempt of a general kind to cope with a crying need. Since 1904 much other work has been done, notably in Vatasso's *incipits* of writings printed in Migne's *Patrologia Latina*, in the *Catalogue of the Royal Manuscripts in the British Museum*, in the catalogue of *incipits* of medical manuscripts, and in other more limited ways. An exhaustive work, to comprehend every kind of medieval Latin literature, would be quite impracticable; but a catalogue of the *incipits* of theological and philosophical texts, which would take account of all discussion and identifications during the last fifty years, might well be undertaken by an international group of scholars. Nothing could be a better memorial to A. G. Little.

The *Initia*, of course, was of inestimable service to Little himself. He could proceed more surely with his investigation of manuscripts. In 1910 he had the pleasure of discovering among the Phillipps manuscripts (no. 12290) one precious text, which he was able to purchase. It is now known as the Little MS.[1] He later discussed its relation and the relations of other recently discovered Franciscan documents to the *Second*

---

[1] Little gave this and other manuscripts and his working copy of *The Grey Friars in Oxford* to the Bodleian Library. It is now MS. Lat. th. d. 23 The latest study of the place of the text among the sources will be found in J. R. H. Moorman's *The Sources for the Life of S. Francis of Assisi* (1940), pp. 90 ff. and 134-5.

Life by Celano and the *Speculum Perfectionis*, in the *Proceedings of the British Academy* for 1926. By this time the problem of the sources was known to be more complicated than Sabatier had thought in 1898 when he issued his edition of the *Speculum* or was yet disposed to think, and the drift of opinion among Franciscan scholars was opposed to his conviction that the *Speculum* was written *d'un trait,* less than a year after the death of the saint. Hence when, after his friend's death in 1928, Little undertook to arrange Sabatier's materials and bring out the second edition of the *Speculum,* he was faced by a delicate and difficult task. Only a careful student can appreciate the amount of labour which the preparation of all this material had involved, and the punctilious loyalty with which Little discharged his obligation. The critical study in the second volume gives the considerations which had led Sabatier to the view that, even if the date 1228 in the Mazarin MS. was a scribe's error, the early date of the *Speculum* and the close intimacy of its author with St. Francis was proved by internal evidence. Little himself was convinced. "I think", he wrote, "that Sabatier's penetrating criticism proves that a great part of the *Spec. Perf.* was written by Brother Leo soon after the death of St. Francis. . . . In one of his sketches for the unwritten Introduction to this volume Sabatier has the heading, 'La victoire de frère Léon'. When the long struggle over the historical value of the *Spec. Perf.* is ended, I have no doubt that the result in essentials will be 'la victoire de Paul Sabatier'." If we stress the words "in essentials" this judgement has on the whole been vindicated. Sabatier's book was criticized, even violently criticized; yet scholars now seem to agree that, although the *Speculum Perfectionis* as a separate work was compiled in 1318, and is not an original work at all, but incorporates material collected a few years earlier, the greater part of this material is derived from the *Scripta Leonis,* the lost rolls and schedules submitted by Leo and his companions in 1245–6 as contributions to the *Vita Secunda* of St. Francis by Thomas of Celano. So, in Dr. Moorman's words, "Sabatier was perfectly right to see in the *Speculum* a work which clearly emanated from the circle of the Saint's intimate friends."

In a fine survey of Little's work[1] Dr. Moorman has included him among the "excavators" who make possible the work of others, and whose work remains a storehouse when the work of perhaps more famous men is forgotten. Little was certainly an excavator, but, as we have seen, he was also an incessant interpreter. For my part I could not draw a hard-and-fast line between his writings. His reviews, for example, especially in his later years, are full of learning, sympathy, and wit. Little was always himself. In him, more than in any scholar I have met, the man was inseparable from what he did. And the consciousness of this fact can be felt in all the letters written about him after his death by all sorts of people. I shall not try to illustrate this single-mindedness. I prefer to close this memoir with the words which he spoke on 14 June, 1938, when his friends gathered about him in the rooms of the Royal Historical Society to present the slender volume which had been prepared in his honour during his seventy-fifth year. The address, with more than two hundred signatures, and the bibliography of his writings were given to him. Then came Little's reply:

> I thank you all very much for the honour you have done me in presenting me with the bibliography and for coming here. Historians are a generously appreciative body. I am deeply impressed with this large and distinguished gathering and by the long list of distinguished names in the book; each one will recall memories. I should like to say how very greatly I appreciate the presence here of representatives of the Franciscan Order and would especially thank my old friend Father Gregory Clery who has come all the way from Dublin. I would add that in the course of my researches I have invariably met with the utmost courtesy and help from the sons of Francis in all countries and in all Orders—Friars Minor, Conventuals and Capuchins. I have been treated as a brother, not as an interloper. . . .
>
> You all know and will remember with relief that I am not an orator and do not "yoke the Hours like young Aurora to my car". But when I was young I heard somebody, who wasn't

[1] *Church Quarterly Review*, cxliv, 17-27.

accustomed to public speaking and had to make a speech, say: "When in doubt talk about yourself." This seems an appropriate opportunity of trying that recipe—with this book as the text.

The first entry is 1889: *E.H.R.* 1889–1938. I have been contributing to *E.H.R.* for 50 years. I am reminded of the Scottish minister's comment on the passage about there being no marriage or giving in marriage in heaven—"chilling thought, my brethren". The whole book illustrates a kind of rake's progress—the specialist's progress—learning more and more about less and less till he ends—The end is not quite yet. But I seem to see the lines converging to a point—and one used to learn in Euclid that a point is that which has no parts and no magnitude—is nothing. I see there is a blank page at the end of the book.

I sometimes think that the best excuse for printing anything is that it forms a nucleus for additions and corrections. The most useful book I ever had printed was printed on one side of the page only in order to catch additions and corrections; *Initia Operum Latinorum* in the later Middle Ages. It made no attempt at being complete. My copy has some thousands of entries added, and is intended for the Institute of Historical Research when I have ceased to enter fresh *incipits*. The late Father Lacombe once talked to me about it, and wanted a complete list. I told him that if he waited for that he would never do anything—and probably quoted to him the saying: "The best is the enemy of the good." (It is a dangerous doctrine and only suitable for really conscientious people—such as we all are here.) Vattasso's *Initia*—containing all *incipits* of the *Patrologia Latina*—is much more systematic than mine (they don't cover the same period). I was in Rome soon after they both came out, and I remember Vattasso and I were introduced to each other (I think by [Cardinal] Ehrle) as *Initiatores patrum*. Both Vattasso and I made our compilations during a period of enforced leisure (he was on sick leave from the Vatican)—not a bad way of using temporary unemployment, but it implies holidays with pay or its equivalent.

Turning over the leaves of the bibliography I note "Authorship of the Lanercost Chronicle" (1916) which also gives me satisfaction—partly because it was written in much pain (and so is a triumph of mind over matter) but chiefly because there is nothing new in it—no new material. All the sources had been printed for many years and were open to everybody: the only thing was to see what the sources meant and put 2 and 2 together: I put 2 and 2 together and made 22—a very good score on a medieval wicket.

Almost all my printed works relate to the Middle Ages—Croce has a dictum that all history is contemporary history. I am not quite clear what it means but am pretty sure it isn't true—like most clever sayings. I will give you another: the only ancient history is medieval history. I do not think that the most valuable function of the historian is to trace back the institutions and ways of thought which have survived, as though we were at the end and climax of history. It is at least as important to retrieve the treasures that have been dropped on the way and lost, which, if restored, would enrich our civilization. There are many of these in the Middle Ages. Even a difference of emphasis may have profound importance. Thus in the Middle Ages most good and serious-minded people worked for the glory of God: now they work for the good of man—or rather of some men—not very successfully, owing to mistaken ideas of what is good. There are two Great Commandments: and unless and until both are kept the world will be a lop-sided place.

I have wandered off the autobiographical track. I will only thank you once more and express a hope that more of my colleagues may have their bibliographies printed; they would be useful and save time and mistakes. This bibliography of mine is due to my wife who has kept from year to year a record of my writings, following the excellent example set by Mrs. Tout. May I commend this example to others? There are marriages made in heaven.

CHAPTER III

HENRI PIRENNE[1]

The death of Professor Henri Pirenne, in October, 1935, brought to an end a career which can have few parallels in the history of learning. In this country a career of the same kind is almost inconceivable. We have had great British scholars and scientists who have been distinguished in our public life and two or three, like Lord Macaulay, who have been among our foremost citizens, but their careers were quite different from that of Pirenne. His nearest counterpart in England is, perhaps, his friend the late Sir Paul Vinogradoff, but Vinogradoff was a voluntary exile who was rather an international figure than a leader of British opinion. Pirenne, a man of immense force of character, was a leader in the historical world, but he was especially, as a historian and teacher, a great Belgian citizen whose influence and importance were generally recognized. Indeed, the position which he won for himself is only possible to a man in a small country, and only then if his country makes the organization and advancement of science one of the objects of its being. His dominating personality was fortunate in its environment; he became, so to speak, an embodiment of learning in his own land and, in the learned movements of his time, was accepted as the living expression of Belgian scholarship. Nobody who ever met him could regard him as a symbol—he was much too human and forceful—yet he seemed to catch up and represent the current movements in thought about the study and teaching of history, the organization of learned enterprise, the policy of learned academies, and the combination of patriotic endeavour with international co-operation. Honours and distinctions were showered upon him almost as a matter of course, tributes to his massive scholar-

[1] From *The English Historical Review,* li (1936), 78-89, with a few excisions and additions.

ship and personal achievement, but also to the value of the things for which he stood.

He was born at Verviers on 23 December, 1862. He studied for his doctorate at the University of Liége, where he had the good fortune to be taught by Godefroid Kurth, the historian of the Franks, and Paul Frédéricq, the historian of the inquisition in the Low Countries. It is easy to trace the influence of these masters upon Pirenne. Kurth, whose life of Clovis and studies in Frankish sources and hagiography are classics, revealed to his pupil the significance—and the delights—of exact scholarship, and aroused in him the zest for early medieval history.[1] Pirenne never lost this interest; he inspired his best pupils with it, and he returned to it at the end of his life. Frédéricq, a master of Belgian history in the splendid Burgundian period and in the period of transition to Spanish rule, was a scholar of wide outlook as well as an indefatigable editor of texts. Perhaps the most readable and stirring volume of his former pupil's *Histoire de Belgique* is the third, devoted to this exciting time, and written when Pirenne was at the height of his powers (1903-7). Moreover, Frédéricq was keenly interested in the historiography and study of history in other countries,[2] and it is not fanciful to suggest that he helped to open Pirenne's mind to the importance of encouraging international relations among teachers and scholars. But Pirenne's fame rests on his work in social history. His history of Belgium was deliberately conceived as a study in the development of a people, and the foundations of this study had to be found in the great Flemish towns. Hence, in considering the growth of his interests, we must remember, in addition to Kurth and Frédéricq, Schmoller, with whom he worked in Berlin, and Giry, with whom he worked in Paris. Schmoller's two studies on Strasbourg (1875) had prepared the way for the deeper consideration of economic factors in medieval municipal

---

[1] Cf. Pirenne's "Discours prononcé à la manifestation en l'honneur de G. Kurth", in the volume *À Godefroid Kurth* (Liége, 1899), and his obituary notice of Kurth in the *Annuaire* of the Belgian Academy for 1924.

[2] The Johns Hopkins University published authorized translations of Frédéricq's essays on the study of history in England and Scotland (1887), Germany, France, Holland and Belgium (1890).

history and, while his influence lacked precision, it was provocative and far-reaching. He helped to free historical investigation from the preconceptions of contemporary liberalism.[1] Arthur Giry's history of Saint-Omer (1877) and his two volumes on *Les Établissements de Rouen* (1883-5) are still more in line with Pirenne's work. Other well-known scholars with whom Pirenne came in close contact at Berlin, Leipzig, and Paris were Bresslau, Gabriel Monod, and Thévenin. When he became "chargé de cours" at Liége in 1885 at the age of twenty-two, the young scholar was singularly well equipped.

Pirenne taught for only a year in his old university. In 1886 he was appointed to the chair at Ghent, which he was to occupy for over forty years. He made his name as a professor at Ghent. From 1919 till 1921 he was rector of the university. He retired, and became professor-emeritus, in 1930. He died at Uccle, near Brussels, on 24 October, 1935, in his seventy-third year.

The impressive volumes of *Mélanges d'histoire* presented to Pirenne in 1926 on the completion of his fortieth year as professor at Ghent is a testimony to his world-wide reputation, while the bibliography of his writings, included in the first volume, reveals the wide range of his interests. The record was not complete in 1926, for the two last volumes of the *Histoire de Belgique,* the revised edition, in French, of his American lectures on medieval cities, and a number of subsidiary papers, in which he expounded more minutely his view on the unbroken continuity between the late Roman and the Merovingian world, were yet to appear.[2] A detailed survey of Pirenne's writings would be wearisome, and is not necessary, for most of his papers were prepared with a view to his great *Histoire de Belgique,* and their conclusions are summarized in that work. Yet it is worth while to point out that a study of his publications prior to 1890 would show that Pirenne by that year had revealed his quality as a critic of

[1] Cf. G. von Below, *Der deutsche Staat des Mittelalters* (1914), pp. 61-2, 83.
[2] For Pirenne's later work see *Études d'histoire dediées à la memoire de Henri Pirenne* (Brussels, 1937).

sources, an editor of texts, a student of medieval municipal history and of Belgian history in the sixteenth century, and a guide in the organization of historical and subsidiary studies.

The first volume of the *Histoire de Belgique* appeared in 1900. It traces the history of the Low Countries, in so far as they bear upon the political, social, and economic development of the county of Flanders, from the earliest times to the war with France in the first quarter of the fourteenth century. The foundations on which this volume was raised were broad and deep. Indeed, a study of Pirenne's publications during the preceding decade gives an exceptionally clear idea of the way in which a great historical work should be written. In 1893 we have the first edition of the *Bibliographie de l'Histoire de Belgique*, a systematic and chronological list of the sources and main works relating to the history of the Low Countries prior to 1598 and of Belgium prior to 1830. In 1894 we have, in the third volume of the *Histoire Générale*, edited by Lavisse and Rambaud, a chapter on the Low Countries from 1280 to 1477. In 1895 Pirenne contributed to the *Mélanges Julien Havet* (1895) a paper on the chancery and notaries of the county of Flanders before the thirteenth century. In 1891 he had published, in the *Collection de textes* issued by Picard in Paris, an edition of Galbert of Bruges's history of the murder of Count Charles the Good in 1127. He followed this up in 1896 with an edition of the polyptyque of William I (1249–72), abbot of St. Trond, to which he had called attention five years before; and in 1900 he produced a volume of unedited documents, entitled *Le Soulèvement de la Flandre maritime de 1323–1328* (Publications de la Commission royale d'histoire). Throughout these years, 1890–1900, a continuous stream of papers on the criticism of sources and on early local history, appeared in the *Bulletin* of the royal commission. But the most important contribution made by Pirenne to historical learning at this time was the essays in which he worked out his views on the origin of medieval towns. Most historical students are now familiar with these views through Pirenne's little book, *Les anciennes démocraties des Pays-Bas* (Paris,

1910), issued ten years after the first volume of the History[1]; but they were the outcome of his work on the History, are expounded in it, and can be studied in detail in a series of papers and reviews which appeared in learned periodicals between 1889, when they were foreshadowed in his history of Dinant, and the end of the century. The well-known articles in the *Revue historique* for 1893 and 1895 are a masterly critical survey, culminating in a new solution, of a great historical problem and of the abundant literature which it had produced. Whatever fate may be in store for Pirenne's own theory, these articles will endure as a model of historical criticism.

Many attempts had been made to explain the origin of municipal institutions, and most of them had been influenced by some prevalent school of thought about medieval German history. W. Arnold saw in the municipal constitution a product of public law (1854). K. W. Nitzsch, from a more social and less juristic point of view, saw a differentiation of classes under the protection of the lord's administration. The later burghers were patrician descendants or successors of the episcopal *ministeriales* (1859). "Germanists", like W. E. Wilde (1881), and the more powerful Gierke, insisted that the town-organization was the outcome of free association; their influence was marked in France and England, and strengthened, if it did not inspire, the "gild" theory. R. Sohm identified urban law with market law (1890). G. von Below, in the tradition of Maurer, brushed aside all theories of *Hofrecht*, gild, and *Marktrecht*, and saw the burgesses, not as merchants, but as men in possession of land; the condition of land and people was the same in the village and in the town, and the town grew out of the village community (1893). Pirenne, while he insisted that each town must be studied separately, and recognized much that was suggestive in these various theories, perhaps especially in that of Sohm, took as his guiding clue the establishment of a merchant community in a trading centre or *port*, alongside the earlier and non-mercantile *burg*. The first urban

---

[1] Translated into English by J. V. Saunders with the title, *Belgian Democracy, its Early History* (Manchester, 1915).

groups were "colonies" of merchants and artisans, and these groups gradually fused with the earlier inhabitants of the fortified castle or episcopal residence by which they had settled. Fusion was not complete until the thirteenth century.

Pirenne's view was expounded with a precision and qualifications which cannot be analysed here. One of his later pupils, the late Carl Stephenson, discussed it in detail and adopted it as a guide to English municipal history.[1] It is appropriate, at this point, however, to say something about its stimulating influence in Belgium. Unlike so many attempts at simplification, it did not commit its supporters to a formula or a juristic principle. It was based upon the fact of early social life in the Low Countries and there, for most of the Flemish towns, it holds good; it directed attention to the general structure of feudalism in the Frankish counties to the west of the lower Rhine and provoked further investigation into administration, land tenure, trade, and foreign relations. Pirenne belonged to no definite school, although he had studied in many and was glad to learn from all. His experience in Germany had strengthened his conviction that the true way to write the history of a community is to trace its social developments and to regard it from an economic rather than a political point of view; but he was at heart a realist, not a theorist.[2] Hence his vigorous and stimulating influence as a teacher encouraged his pupils to think for themselves, and to work out the problems which he set them without preconceptions. The work which can be traced to his seminar at Ghent is exceptional both in quality and quantity. Before the first volume of his History appeared, his pupil, the late Professor G. des Marez, had published the first of his remarkable books, his *Étude sur la propriété foncière dans les villes du moyen âge et spécialement en Flandre* (1898). In 1915 W. Blommaerts produced his study, *Les châtelains de Flandre,* which, like the later work of H. Nowé, *Les baillis contaux de Flandre* (1929), is of funda-

[1] Above, pp. 66, 67.
[2] Pirenne has sometimes been described as a pupil of Lamprecht. Professor Ganshof, who has kindly given me information about Pirenne's early life, writes that Pirenne was a close friend of Lamprecht until 1914, but had never worked with him. His great friend in England was Vinogradoff.

mental importance for the history of the *burg* and of administration in Flanders. Since at least 1920 onwards, F. L. Ganshof has thrown light on the growth of social classes and of judicial administration, notably in his *Étude sur les ministeriales en Flandre et en Lotharingie* (1926) and his *Recherches sur les tribunaux de châtellenie en Flandre* (1932). In the same year (1932) Paul Rolland's *Les origines de la commune de Tournai* was published with the assistance of the "Fondation H. Pirenne", which is administered by the Royal Academy of Belgium; and it is worth while to notice that this book illustrates the necessity for serious modifications, in the history of particular cities, of the master's generalizations. Other pupils, like H. Nélis, have distinguished themselves as archivists, or, like G. G. Dept, by their investigations into the history of foreign trade and foreign relations. These scholars, and others might be mentioned, have, in the main, devoted their attention to problems suggested by Pirenne's work for the first volume of his History.

From 1900 to the outbreak of the First World War, Pirenne was at work on the next four volumes of his History. The second volume (1902) ends with the death of Charles the Bold, the third (1907) with the arrival in the Low Countries of the Duke of Alba, the fourth (1911) with the treaty of Munster, the fifth, not published until 1921, with the revolutions, the restoration of Austrian rule in 1790, and the outbreak of the continental war against France in 1792. These four volumes cover a period of nearly four hundred years, from the Flemish victory over Philip the Fair to the eve of the invasion of the Austrian Netherlands by the French Republican army. Like the first volume, they were preceded by numerous articles and editions of texts, of which the *Collection de documents relatifs à l'histoire de l'industrie drapière en Flandre* (2 vols. 1906–9), prepared in collaboration with Georges Espinas, the historian of Douai, calls for special mention. In the developments and events and historical persons described in the second, third, and fourth volumes of his History, stretching from the preliminaries of the Hundred Years' war to the end of the Thirty Years' war in 1648, Pirenne had a very great theme. He rose to the occasion; and it is by these volumes, written with such verve, penetration, and mastery of detail, that he will probably be best remembered. He never swerved throughout the exercise of his great task from the path which he had decided to follow: the study and the explanation of the national life. "Changes of parties, political theories, religious ideas, institutions, economic phenomena, and social conditions have absorbed my attention rather than wars and diplomacy."[1] Hence, just as he had realized the necessity to understand the origin and rise of the Flemish towns, so, in his later work, he realized the far-reaching significance of the industrial development known as the "new drapery", in the course of which capitalism captured the countryside,[2] the big towns lost their leadership, and the system of estates took their place as the expression of a national consciousness. Writing in November, 1920, two years after the armistice, he explains how, in his view, this national consciousness had been aroused under the discipline of Spanish and Austrian rule, and in the later times when Belgium had continued to be the "cockpit of Europe". National feeling is the guarantee of the unity of Belgium:

> La communauté de ses souvenirs, de ses besoins et de ses libertés a fait naître chez elle cette conscience collective dont la guerre a révélé toute la profondeur. Et cette conscience ne doit rien qu'au peuple même en qui elle réside. Elle ne découle ni de l'unité géographique, ni de l'unité linguistique. La Belgique—c'est l'originalité et la beauté de son histoire— est le produit de la volonté de ses habitants." In a common experience they have found "une dignité qui les relève à leurs propres yeux et qui les distingue des peuples qui se sont docilement laissés former par l'État ... Nous avons une patrie, non point parce que la nature nous l'a assignée, mais parce que nous l'avons voulue.[3]

The *Histoire de Belgique* was completed by the publication of the seventh volume (1830–1914) in 1932. The last two volumes are a worthy continuation of their predecessors; they

---

[1] Preface to vol. iv (1911).
[2] *Histoire de Belgique*, iii (1907), 258.
[3] Vol. v (1920), pp. xi, xii.

involved immense labour, and demanded all Pirenne's powers of presentation and control; but, although these never failed him, he was obviously working under a sense of greater strain. He felt that it had been a rare privilege to have been able to write his History; a work which had filled the greater part of his life and had brought him much joy. His health had not failed him, and his companionships, especially those of his home, had never ceased to sustain him. Looking back over his work, he uttered a word of salutary warning to those who think that they can attain a complete mastery of their subject or who refuse a big task because they cannot attain it. Historical science, like all other science, is never final. "Il n'y a de science que du général." The materials can never all be collected, for they can never be known. Problems cannot all be solved, for, as they are solved, new aspects are perpetually revealed. The historian opens the way; he does not close it.

It is from this point of view that a generalization which occupied Pirenne's mind in his later years must be approached. While he was working on the last two volumes of the History, his thoughts went back to his earliest studies, which still engaged the attention of his best pupils. The very old problem of the continuity between the Roman and the medieval world was attracting scholars in new ways. For example, the writings of Professor Dopsch of Vienna had aroused the learned world to controversy. To Pirenne the problem naturally presented itself as a challenge to the investigation of the earlier history of those economic movements which he had analysed in his studies of municipal origins. When and how did the medieval revival of trade, commerce, communications begin? His view was that it was late rather than early. He agreed that there was no serious lapse of continuity between late Roman and Merovingian times. The Mediterranean was still open. But there was a break, and this came with the closing of the Mediterranean by the Arabian conquests.[1] Medieval trade and

[1] In some respects, e.g., in the survival of domanial organization, Pirenne thought that there may have been much uninterrupted continuity. See his paper, "Le fisc royal de Tournai", in the *Mélanges d'histoire du moyen âge, offerts à M. Ferdinand Lot* (1925).

communications developed slowly and painfully, making a fresh start in the Carolingian age. This view was expounded by Pirenne with all his usual energy in a series of papers and lectures, in which, whether they confirmed his theory or not, many new and interesting points were raised, and many neglected facts were subjected to penetrating analysis. The clearest exposition will be found in the first two lectures of a course delivered by Pirenne in the United States during the autumn of 1922, and printed in 1925 by the Princeton University Press under the title *Medieval Cities, their Origins and the Revival of Trade*.[1] Although Pirenne's argument has received powerful support, for example from Professor Ferdinand Lot, it is generally regarded as a stimulating incentive to thought rather than as a definitive contribution to knowledge.[2]

The completion of the History and the investigation of early medieval economic problems by no means exhausted Pirenne's energy in the years after the war. During the fifteen years 1920–35, he won recognition as a foremost citizen of Belgium and as one of the leaders in every international historical enterprise. From the beginning of his career as a teacher he had taken his full share in discussions on the organization of historical study and the teaching of history, but after the war his interest in these and similar matters was intense, and doubtless was encouraged by his public activities. As a historical writer, he expressed it in a series of more popular writings, such as the chapters which he contributed to the two volumes, *La fin du moyen âge*, in the series "Peuples et civilisations", edited by Halphen and Sagnac, and his last important work, a survey of economic and social history in the volume, *La civilisation occidentale de xiie siècle à la fin du xve*, part of the "Histoire générale" planned by Gustave Glotz. As a leader of academic thought, he did more than any man to revive the International

---

[1] The French version, *Les villes du moyen âge: essai d'histoire économique et sociale* (1927), is more satisfactory.

[2] See especially the criticism of Professor Norman Baynes in the *Journal of Roman Studies*, xix, part 2 (1929), 230-3.

Historical Congress, which met in Brussels in 1923 under his presidency. The congress decided to institute an International Historical Committee which should make arrangements for the next congress on the widest possible basis. The committee, with its *Bulletin* and its numerous commissions, was organized at Geneva in May, 1926. Proposals adopted at Brussels for a new annual bibliography of historical literature, for an international review of economic history and other activities, were thus given form. Most important of all, Austrian and German scholars sat from the first on the governing body of the Committee, and came in large numbers to the Congress held at Oslo in 1928.[1] Pirenne's statesmanship was largely responsible for the successful creation of this elaborate piece of academic machinery. He had suffered more than most civilians of his age during the war. On 3 November, 1914, his son Pierre, born in 1895, was killed in action on the banks of the Yser. In March, 1916, he was taken from Ghent, which, "collective prison" though it was, was also his home, and deported to Germany.[2] He had lost his German friends and seen the book which had won such high praise in Germany reviled as a tendentious piece of "Belgian imperialism".

His courage and resource did not fail during this desperate time. He required to be left "alone with his thoughts". In the camp at Holzminden and later (August, 1916, to January, 1917) at Jena, he studied Russian and lectured. When, at the end of January, 1917, he was sent, as a dangerous person, to live alone in a Thuringian village, he at once determined to steady his mind by daily work on a history of Europe. A note of his intention, dated 31 January, is now the preface to this unfinished work. Every afternoon until the armistice he wrote in small exercise books, aided only by a little historical manual

---

[1] G. des Marez and F.-L. Ganshof, *Compte rendu du ve congrès international des sciences historiques*, Brussels, 1923; *Bulletin of the International Committee of Historical Sciences*, no. 6, May 1929; H. W. V. Temperley in *The Times*, 29 October, 1935.

[2] See preface to *Histoire de Belgique*, vol. v. (1920). This volume was finished at Ghent on November, 1915, during the German occupation. Pirenne wrote his recollections of his captivity in Germany for the *Revue des deux Mondes*, 1920.

used in the local schools. He wrote down the outcome of his daily thoughts to occupy his mind. After his return to Belgium he did not continue his history; he did not even read it through. It was published after his death by his son, Jacques (1936). *The History of Europe to the XVI Century* was, and probably still is, the most popular of his works: and some would describe it as his masterpiece.[1]

When he returned to his work in Belgium he put aside bitter memories and worked for international understanding where it seemed to be most practicable—and where national animosities are least respectable—in the world of science. But the company in which he expatiated still more happily was that smaller gathering, the Union Académique, which, until 1935,[2] met annually at Brussels in the Palais des Académies. Here, on his own ground, he renewed, year by year, his friendship with members of the learned academies of Europe and America.

A foreigner who was not an intimate friend of Pirenne cannot write with any authority about him as a man and a citizen. But his pre-eminence was obvious to anyone who attended the meetings of the Union Académique, or worked with him while he was still a member of the International Historical Committee. When the electors—an international body—met to award the Prix Franqui, their choice fell inevitably upon Pirenne. He added it without affectation to his decorations, his membership of the Institute of France and thirteen foreign academies, and his sixteen honorary degrees. His outstanding position was not altogether due to his learning, for Belgium possesses many scholars of distinction whose critical insight is as fine as his was; it was due even more to his abounding personality. The historian of Belgium had become part of his own subject. And in Belgium he had become the living embodiment of work upon his subject. When he died he was president of the council of the royal library, of the commission for the publication of the dictionary of

---

[1] An English translation appeared in 1939.

[2] The Union Académique met at Copenhagen in May, 1935. At this meeting the Austrian and German academies were elected members of the Union.

national biography, and of the committee which controls the Belgian historical institute at Rome; and, as secretary of the royal historical commission, he had behind him many years of service which had virtually given him the control of the publication of Belgian historical texts and monographs.

Once seen, Pirenne could not be forgotten. He looked like, and indeed was, one of those big, vivacious burghers whom the Flemish artists of the seventeenth century liked to paint. His face in repose was somewhat heavy; the features did not quite fit their setting of trim beard and hair brushed smoothly back from his forehead. But when his interest was aroused and he began to talk, any impressions of this kind were forgotten. He was a most exuberant man and seemed to put all his strength into whatever he said or did. He could be overwhelming, though without intention; he was never overbearing, and one never felt the least frightened of him. It would not be surprising to learn that he had enemies or ruffled the feelings of the susceptible, but he was essentially kind-hearted, friendly, generous. His strength and vitality, not design, made him redoubtable; but he was single-minded, and never tried to be impressive. His services to Belgium and his unpleasant experiences during the war had made him, so to speak, a chartered freeman of his country. Walking with a friend one day by the high railings in front of the palace, he is said to have embarrassed both his companion and the illustrious objects of his attentions by his boisterous salutation of some members of the royal family whom he descried within the enclosure. The story may be true; it is certainly characteristic. He ate, smoked, wrote, and planned with a sort of vehemence, and was very hospitable. He was a rapid and vivacious talker, gesticulating wildly. His life was spontaneous, useful, and happy, rooted in the social realities. His last days were clouded by sorrow and ill-health—he had lost a second son in 1931, and a third, Henri, died in the summer of 1935—but he worked to the end, sustained, as always, by his able and devoted wife, his family, and his friends.

CHAPTER IV

CHARLES HOMER HASKINS[1]

Charles Homer Haskins was born at Meadville, Pennsylvania, on 21 December, 1870. He passed through the earlier stages of a successful academic career with unusual rapidity. At the age of sixteen he graduated at Johns Hopkins University. He studied in Paris and Berlin while still a boy, earned his doctorate, and became an instructor in Johns Hopkins before he was twenty years old. In 1890 he went to the University of Wisconsin, where from 1892 to 1902 he held the chair of European history. His connexion with Harvard began in 1900, and in 1902 he went there as professor. Only thirty-one years of age, he had already made his mark as a scholar, teacher, and academic administrator. He had been one of a committee of seven appointed by the American Historical Association to report on the study of history in schools. He had collaborated with William I. Hull in a *History of Higher Education in Pennsylvania*. As a pupil of Ch.-V. Langlois, he had begun at Paris his investigations in the history of medieval thought and institutions,[2] and he had found his way about the Vatican Archives. From the outset of his life as a teacher, he made it his business to relate, as closely as he could, his work as a scholar to the guidance of his pupils and the furtherance of historical study. It was characteristic of him that (apart from an early paper in quite a different field of study)[3] his first published essay was an article on the Vatican Archives, in the *American Historical Review* (1896). When he went to Harvard, he was

[1] From *The English Historical Review*, lii (1937), 649-656.

[2] See "Opportunities for American students of History at Paris", in *American Hist. Rev.* iii (1898). 418-30. Haskins's first historical article, on the life of medieval students as illustrated by their letters, appeared in the same Review in the same year (iii. 203-29).

[3] "The Yazoo Land Companies", in American Hist. Assoc., *Papers*, v. 4, pp. 59-103.

prepared for the work which was to continue, without haste and without rest, for thirty years.

At Harvard Haskins had various chairs in succession (the last being the Henry Charles Lea chair in medieval history) before he was compelled to retire by illness and became Professor Emeritus in 1931. His most important work was done as Dean of the Graduate School in the Arts and Sciences (1908 to 1924) and as the teacher of graduate students. Few teachers of history can ever have had so many pupils who were later to win distinction as scholars and who bore so clearly the stamp of their master. The *Anniversary Essays in Medieval History by students of Charles Homer Haskins, presented on the completion of forty years of teaching* (Boston and New York, 1929) contains papers by eighteen men and women, several of whom are known by their own works throughout the historical world. These are his greatest, possibly his most lasting memorial, for through them Haskins spread an influence which has profoundly affected for good the study and teaching of history in the United States of America.

The guidance of advanced pupils was, however, but one source of the impression which Haskins made upon the academic life of his time. He was a leading figure in the American Historical Association, or corporation of university teachers of history. From 1901 to 1907 he was responsible for the Reports of Proceedings in the annual meetings of the Association; in 1922 he was its President, choosing as the subject of his presidential address "European History and American Scholarship". He helped to found the American Council of Learned Societies which has done such important service in assisting scholars to continue their investigations, and he was its chairman from 1920 to 1926. He was concerned also in the formation of the Medieval Academy of America and was its president in the year 1926–7. Throughout his active life at Harvard he was ready to speak or write on matters relating to the study and teaching of history and the organization of historical work. As he was never one of those people, not unknown in educational circles, who talk for the sake of talking, his words carried weight. They were the expression of firmly co-ordinated experience, and were never vague or sentimental or aspiring. Haskins regarded them as part of the business of his life. And all the time he was a great man at Harvard. His position there was consolidated by gradual but incessant effort, like one of his own books, and was as firm as a rock until the end came. He refused to go back to Johns Hopkins as its president. He would not leave Harvard and was regarded as a future president of Harvard. Then the end came, when he was about sixty years old. Whether the strain of his work, which he seemed to do with such remorseless ease, broke him down, I do not know. The anxious and responsible work which he had done in Paris during the Peace Conference as one of President Wilson's lieutenants, had certainly told upon him. During the last years of his life he was an invalid. He died on 14 May, 1937, of a sudden attack of bronchial pneumonia.

Haskins's historical work falls into no periods of development. He never sat down to write a treatise. He wrote learned papers and special series of lectures, which were later published or re-published in book form. His two main subjects, the history of medieval science and the development of Norman institutions (science and institutions interpreted in the broadest sense), were studied together and, although he concentrated more intensely on Norman history before 1915, the year of his first book, *The Normans in European History*, his articles on both subjects appeared contemporaneously in various periodicals. After the First World War Norman history was discontinued, and from 1920 to 1931 we have a stream of articles of a special and technical kind on the history of the transmission of learning and, later, on formulary books. The papers appeared or reappeared as *Norman Institutions* (1918), *Studies in the History of Medieval Science* (1924; 2nd edn. 1927), and *Studies in Medieval Culture* (1929). Two more popular books, the Colver lectures on *The Rise of Universities* (1923) and *The Renaissance of the Twelfth Century* (1927), brought the results of some of his research to the notice of a larger circle of readers.

This body of various and detailed material has a unity

which says much for Haskins's singleness of aim. A man whose grip was less firm, or whose judgement was less well-balanced than his, might easily have scattered his energy to little purpose; but Haskins chose a theme; he was not merely concerned to follow this or that interesting line of investigation. He saw the big important things, the interplay of the intellectual and the administrative life, the most likely centres of influence or ways of communication, the most significant developments, and, having these always in mind, he turned to the texts and followed the lead of the evidence without any bias or preconceptions. He made few if any startling discoveries, and he rarely indulged in a bold generalization. His suggestion, for example, that Adelard of Bath introduced the use of the abacus to the English treasury, and his conjecture that the Conqueror got the idea of the Domesday survey from some specimens of Roman cadastres, preserved in South Italy and Sicily by Byzantine or Saracen mediation,[1] were, as he was aware, no more than interesting hypotheses; he would never have tried to base an elaborate theory upon such foundations. For he was emphatically a builder, and the foundations of a building must, in his view, be sure and enduring. His greatest works, *Norman Institutions* and *Studies in the History of Medieval Science*, are the outcome of intense investigation among manuscripts, traced in Norman archives, Paris and South Italy, and, for the study of the transmission and translation of Greek and Arabic learning, in collections all over Europe. He had no difficulties with languages, and his genial, impressive personality opened the doors to him, wherever he went. In France he could rely on the friendship of such men as Léopold Delisle, Ch.-V. Langlois, and Charles Bémont. In Spain he made the guardians of local treasures realize that he knew his way about better than they did themselves. On one occasion he asked for a catalogue of the manuscripts in a Spanish cathedral. After some delay a document was triumphantly produced, which he saw at once to be a list, not of the manuscripts which he had come to examine, but of those which had been

---

[1] See "Quelques problèmes de l'histoire des institutions anglo-normandes", in *Congrès du millenaire normand* (Rouen, 1911); tirage à part, p. 9.

transferred to Madrid, and which he had already seen, The canon, who was in residence at the time in Rochester, still relates a lively memory of an invasion during the long vacation by Haskins, who had recently discovered, in a Rochester lectionary in the library of the Vatican, the account of a visit to Jerusalem and Constantinople by Joseph, a monk of Canterbury. Haskins wanted to trace some evidence that Joseph had brought relics of St. Andrew from Constantinople to Rochester.[1] No clue was too insignificant to be disregarded, and few men have been as quick as Haskins was to notice clues. So in his patient orderly way an article was written, in which the new material was firmly placed in a lavish setting of erudition. Some of these articles are classics, others are brief and technical contributions; but very few of them are casual, or unrelated to his main purpose. The only exception of importance is the fine paper on "Robert le Bougre, and the beginnings of the inquisition in Northern France". This was first printed in 1902, early in his career, and was doubtless suggested by his preliminary studies in Paris.[2]

His more popular books revealed the qualities which distinguish Haskins's specialized papers. They grew out of his other work and are as uncompromising in their form and their avoidance of rhetorical devices. Haskins preferred to be his own "popularizer". He knew that his theme had significance and he believed in sharing his knowledge. Moreover, in general lectures and essays he could take a wider view and call attention to the work of others. But the method is the same. A good example is the address on the spread of ideas in the middle ages, which I was privileged to hear during the meeting of the American Historical Association at Richmond in December, 1924.[3] As I listened, the simile of the builder came into my mind. Each sentence was like a block of hewn stone, laid in

---

[1] See "A Canterbury Monk at Constantinople, c. 1090", in Eng. Hist. Rev. xxv (1910), reprinted in Studies in Medieval Culture, pp. 160-3.

[2] American Hist. Rev., vii (1902), reprinted in Studies, pp. 193-244. The next paper, "The Heresy of Echard the Baker of Rheims", ibid. pp. 245-55, was suggested by Haskins's work on Parisian university sermons.

[3] Speculum i (1926). 19-30, reprinted in Studies, pp. 92-104.

its place by a skilful mason. The operation was directed by a clear and powerful mind, but every stone, so to speak, was left to make its own impression, without the aid of external graces. Anything wild and extravagant was unthinkable, yet as the lecture went on, I found myself hoping, and knew that I hoped in vain, for a touch of mischief or something just a trifle hazardous. Not that Haskins was a solemn person or did not admire the bold, constructive work of other men. In this same lecture he paid a generous tribute to Monsieur Bédier and to Professor Kingsley Porter. But his own mind, though searching and positive, did not lead him into their kind of adventure.

The comparison which I have made may give an impression of heaviness; but a finely proportioned building, honestly built, is massive rather than heavy in appearance. It speaks of purpose and achievement; its austere lines reveal unexpected lights and shadows. It excites interest and holds the attention, and is neither dull nor wearisome. Haskins's work always seems to me to be like this.

The peace negotiations of 1919 made the first and only break in Haskins's academic career. In December, 1917, he wrote the preface to his book, *Norman Institutions*.[1] He was then caught up in war work and was selected by President Wilson to accompany him to Paris as chief of the division of Western Europe in the American delegation. He acted as American member on the Commission on Belgian and Danish affairs, and on the committee which dealt with Alsace-Lorraine. His most important task, however, was the arrangement made for the Saar Valley; this was the joint work of Monsieur Tardieu, the late Sir James Headlam-Morley, and Haskins. Haskins gave his thought and energy to his responsible duties with his whole heart, yet I doubt if they were as congenial to him as they seemed. I remember the relief he felt one afternoon when he took a holiday; we walked together, talking about history, and ended up with a visit to Charles Bémont in the Rue Monsieur le Prince. After his return to

---

[1] The book is dedicated "to the spirit of France, humane, unflinching, clear, and free". Cf. his paper, "L'histoire de France aux États-Unis", in the *Revue de Paris*, xxvii (1920). 654-72.

America, he joined with Professor Robert Howard Lord, who had had charge in the American delegation of the affairs of Eastern Europe, in a course of lectures in which the two scholars tried to explain to a Boston audience and to a wider American public the meaning and responsibilities of the peace settlement. The lectures, under the title, *Some Problems of the Peace Conference*, were published in 1920. Haskins wrote the first four lectures, on the tasks and methods of the conference, Belgium and Denmark, Alsace-Lorraine, and the Rhine and the Saar. He did not feel any doubts about the justice of the arrangements with which he had been concerned, nor about the general nature of the attempted settlement; but insisted from the first that success depended on the ratification of the peace by the United States. Speed in continuous co-operation was essential. The League of Nations was an experiment, whose smooth working was largely contingent on the activities of the commissions which some idealists regarded as foreign to its purpose.[1]

Both his academic and his political labours brought Haskins numerous distinctions. He was made officer of the Légion d'Honneur, commander of the order of the Crown of Belgium, member of the Académie des Inscriptions et Belles Lettres and corresponding fellow of the British Academy, and received many honorary degrees. But he valued most the confidence of his colleagues and pupils, and his friendship with other scholars in all parts of the world. As a scholar, he takes his place beside Lea and Gross; as a teacher and man of affairs he set an example. He did more than anyone in recent years to give a much-needed sense of the value of discipline and direction to the study of history in America.

Haskins was a well-built man, with broad shoulders on which his massive head was planted rather low down. He had a very straight look. He talked freely, with a touch of formality, in short incisive sentences. He listened as easily and naturally as he spoke, but conversation with him tended to take the form of question and answer and the interchange of opinions rather than of rapid give and take. I have heard him described

[1] *Some Problems of the Peace Conference*, pp. 32, 149, 150.

as an ambitious man. If this means that he strove for dignity and power for their own sake, the judgement is beside the mark; if it means that he was aware of his ability and was ready to shoulder responsibility, it is true. He disliked pretentious and slovenly-minded people just as he disliked pretentious and slovenly work, but his criticism was generally conveyed by inference rather than by definite words. He never indulged in historical controversy, but let his views speak for themselves, after he had given the evidence. He welcomed good work and did not harp on trifles. It would be very hard to deduce his private opinions on political or spiritual matters from anything that he wrote. Perhaps he expressed himself most freely in his ungrudging tribute to Henry Charles Lea, whose view of history was "that the study of the past in the scientific spirit would render us not only more tolerant of outgrown ethical standards, but also 'more impatient of the present and yet more hopeful of the future' ".[1] Haskins was very generous to young men, had a kind, somewhat whimsical, manner, and was blessed with a large capacity for affection. He endeared men to him. I have reason to remember how, when a young man, of whom he had never heard, began to wander into his chosen field of study, he asked Charles Gross to make inquiries in England, welcomed the beginner as a fellow-worker, and made him a friend for life.

Until his health gave way, Haskins had a full, strenuous and happy life. The memory of it must have helped him to keep his courage undaunted. The spirit in which he had worked is reflected in the preface to *Norman Institutions*, the book in which I feel he must have found most pleasure:

> He has made the personal acquaintance of a number of workers in the field of Norman history, and has enjoyed several summers of study and research in some of the pleasant places of the earth. And as the work comes to a close, the memories which it recalls are not so much of dusty *fonds d'archives* or weary journeys on the Ouest-Etat, as of quiet days of study in provincial collections, long evenings of reflection by the Orne or the Vire or in the garden of some cathedral

[1] *Studies in Medieval Culture*, p. 262.

city, and rare afternoons at Chantilly with Léopold Delisle, now gone the way of the Norman historians and chancellors on whom he lavished so much labour and learning. *Requiescant a laboribus suis, opera enim illorum sequuntur illos.*

Of the last years, a friend and colleague, Professor E. K. Rand, has written:

> This lamentable breakdown of a great career was mastered by Haskins with the strength with which he mastered everything. Even in the latter years, in the latter months, of his life, his friends who were permitted brief visits saw within the prison of the body the will of iron, the keen mind, the gay humour, the loyal friendship that they had known of yore. Those who were his constant attendants, his devoted wife and children, his faithful nurses, heard no syllable of discontent, no sound of pain escape his lips. It was the triumph, not the defeat of Charles Haskins, and the best of his legacies to our age. For more notable even than his works in the world of scholars and of nations was the moulding of a noble soul through joys and pain. *Requiescas in pace, anima candida.*

CHAPTER V

H. W. C DAVIS[1]

Henry William Carless Davis had what is called an uneventful life. A scholar of Balliol at the age of seventeen (1891), a fellow of All Souls at the age of twenty-one, then for a generation a teacher and writer of history, he followed a quiet, successful course. There was nothing unconventional or startling in his life and conversation. Yet Davis, simply because he was Davis, could always give distinction to the commonplace and exert influence through the ordinary opportunities of life. He was one of the outstanding men of his time. Both as teacher and as writer few men have been so effective. He was shy and reticent, and most of those who are grateful to him would not claim to have known him. They saw in him a very fine, perhaps the best, type of Englishman, but a man with whom it was not easy to be intimate. Those who did know him can hardly speak about him so soon after his death. They can only remember his generosity, his loyalty, his devotion to duty; and leave time to reveal the measure of the influence which, in his quietness and strength, he had upon Oxford, and through Oxford, upon the world outside.

His life, in all that he did, was the expression of mental and moral integrity. The adjectives brilliant, clever, penetrating, sound unreal and banal when applied to him. He would set himself a task and do it, with all his strength yet with a deft economy of energy and phrase. He was lacking in imagination perhaps, but he was very clear-sighted and also very simple and massive. He was, in a word, absolutely honest and always self-controlled. He had his prejudices, both personal and historical,

[1] From *The English Historical Review*, xliii (1928), 578-584. For a more detailed appreciation of Davis's life and work, I refer my readers to *Henry William Carless Davis* (1874-1928), a memoir by J. R. H. Weaver and a selection of his historical papers, edited by J. R. H. Weaver and Austin Lane Poole (London, 1933).

but they were his own, never gathered elsewhere, and he never hesitated to drop them, silently letting them go, if he saw that he had been wrong. This integrity, in social intercourse and in writing, made an impression, especially upon the young, which those who did not know him well did not always understand. One of his pupils writes:

> "No man stood more consistently for loftiness of mind, for calm and unprejudiced judgement, for absolute purity of motive in his every thought and decision."

The judgement expresses the impression of bigness which no stiffness could hide, and it expresses, moreover, the affectionate awe with which his friends and pupils responded to his lofty standards. The effect produced by his book on the Normans and Angevins was, in its own way, very similar. Here was a man who could take a difficult theme, which much teaching and writing had reduced to unmerited dullness and conventionality, and make it really interesting and important, not by any display of literary brilliance, but by virtue of honest living into the period. Here was a man who could write, had taken immense pains, and had insisted on looking at his facts and authorities entirely afresh, for himself. A scholar who afterwards became one of Davis's most valued colleagues once told me that the reading of this book, when he was a young undergraduate, made him realize what history was.

The industry of Davis and the wide sweep of his interests were almost proverbial among his friends and colleagues. His industry was untiring and seemed, though it was not, effortless, a form of self-expression. It was always directed, and was not the same quality as the thoroughness or the patient waiting for results which have been characteristics of some great scholars. Mentally he was like the mountaineer who cannot rest until he has climbed one peak after another, and who is never daunted by the knowledge that he cannot hope to climb them all. He disliked the discipline of minute investigation, and he was, I think, impatient if he could not come to a conclusion. He was not like those who are never satisfied, 'though winning near the goal', because Clio always vanishes round the next corner. He was satisfied to find a message waiting for him on the hill-top. Hence the 'deftness' of his work, and hence too the sense of something lacking in it felt by those who do not quite like the process of 'ticking off' historical truths. Yet no one who regarded these things as defects in his work would deny that they were the defects of exceedingly fine qualities. All that he did was so safe and imperturbable, like himself, so neatly grouped, yet so strong in its solidity. It was his habit to arrange his reading and reviewing around the bit of work which he had in hand. Thus his first contributions as a reviewer were notices of books on the eighth and ninth centuries, written while he was writing his *Charlemagne* in the "Heroes of the Nation" series, a series which he was later to edit. Many of his best short contributions to medieval English history were suggested while he was reading for his *England under the Normans and Angevins*. His note-books were filled by neatly written extracts from chronicles, and he characteristically worked through the great uncharted volumes of the earliest Close Rolls. His plan for a collection of royal charters, which resulted in the first volume of his *Regesta Regum Anglo-Normannorum* in 1913, led to deeper researches, carrying on his earlier work. Hence we have the series of papers in *The English Historical Review*, beginning in 1903 with an article on *The Anarchy of Stephen's Reign* and ending in 1914 with the fine little paper on *The Chronicle of Battle Abbey*. And during the last years of his life he was amassing an extraordinary knowledge of the sources for the political history of England in the middle of the nineteenth century and finding work for his pupils in Manchester and Oxford. This economy of energy, in the best sense of the term, was thoroughly characteristic. It enabled him to do the work of three or four men at once, to edit series, revise other people's books, advise the Clarendon Press, direct the last supplement of the *Dictionary of National Biography*, and quietly prepare for the terrifying task of revising the whole of that great work. He was never daunted. Experience would seem to have taught him that if he worked steadily and methodically, difficulties would vanish away. And he had the rare ability to take up a piece or several pieces of work without waste of energy and temper, just where he had left off. I shall never forget the impression which he made upon me when I went to see him at Manchester a day or two after his arrival in the university. A large section of his library was already neatly arranged upon the whole available wall-space of the little room allotted to him; his papers were spread out before him; and when I entered he raised his head from his work as many a time I had seen him raise it in Balliol and in the War Trade Intelligence Department. He might have been in Manchester a couple of years instead of a couple of days.

Davis began to lecture in Balliol College in 1899. In 1902 he became fellow and tutor, and so remained until 1921. During these years his chief work was done and his unique position among the teachers of history in Oxford was established. From the first he was singularly mature, just as, until the last, he showed little, if any, sign of advancing age. The young fellow of All Souls whose lectures on Thucydides some of us still remember was very like the regius professor nearly thirty years later. But his range widened, and his methods of study were deepened. As an historical writer he concentrated more and more upon the Norman period, and if the war had not broken into his life, as it broke into everything, he would doubtless have gone on steadily with his *Regesta* and cognate investigations. The papers which he contributed later to the volumes of essays presented to Professor Tout and Dr. R. L. Poole reveal in some measure the extent of his inquiries into the charter evidence for the reigns of Henry I and Stephen. The *Regesta* is not a perfect work of its kind. It was planned as a co-operative enterprise and was carried through with the aid of only one helper, Mr. Whitwell. If it is compared with the great French series of royal *Chartes et Diplômes* it is seen to be both too ambitious in range and too modest in plan. In any case it was a work which demanded a scholar's undivided attention during a long spell of years, not the limited energies of a busy college tutor and administrator. The pitfalls which beset the worker in this field can be seen by any one who cares to turn to J. H. Round's examination of the first volume, one of his most searching, and also, it should be added, his more sympathetic, reviews.[1] Yet the *Regesta* is of great value and should be completed. Only Davis could have achieved it in the face of such difficulties, and it is more than adequate to justify his high place as a scholar.

The war, with the costly experience gained in a government department, hastened, if it did not actually occasion, a change in his outlook as a teacher and writer. As a tutor, Davis had never confined his attention to one branch of history. He was a classical scholar and had all the interest of a good Greats man in political theory. He was an omnivorous student of history who had never drawn a sharp distinction between ancient, medieval, and modern. He felt no hesitation about the justice of his country's cause, and when war came he took his share in the ways in which he was most likely to be helpful. He edited the Oxford pamphlets and wrote a book about Treitschke with the quiet intensity and objectivity which he had displayed in his work on Anglo-Norman charters. He was asked to join a few others, under the chairmanship of the late Sir T. H. Penson, in the organization of an intelligence department connected with the Admiralty and the Board of Trade. This, the Trade Clearing House, afterwards became the War Trade Intelligence Department, and was definitely connected with the Foreign Office as part of the Ministry of Blockade. During four long weary years Davis threw all his energy into a life whose only connexion with his life at Oxford was that it required the same mental and moral qualities. The W.T.I.D. was an exceedingly interesting community of lawyers, historians, economists, dramatists, novelists, stock-brokers, and many other kinds of people whom Sir Henry Penson and his advisers gathered together. Among the dons Davis was easily supreme. He acted as vice-chairman, wrote daily minutes for the cabinet, represented the department on important committees. By sheer force of personality he acquired the sort of reputation—some of it, no doubt, mythical—which he had won in Balliol. As the routine of the department became more fixed and the work of each member more special-

---

[1] *English Hist. Rev.*, xxix (1914), 347-356.

ized, he was able to add to his duties the task of writing a history of the blockade at the time when records were easily accessible, personal memories fresh, and the blockade itself increasingly effective. What happened to this work I do not know. Indeed, the recollection of those strange years, spent in temporary wooden buildings in the bed of the lake in St. James's Park, is now very dim even in the minds of those who had most responsibility. The life which at the time seemed endless in its monotonous excitement is now a hazy memory. What Davis did only he could have described; what he was many recall with gratitude. The late Sir O. R. A. Simpkin wrote about him as follows:

> We worked together in the W.T.I.D. for about four years, but he was concerned primarily with the political and diplomatic side of the work, while I was concerned primarily with the evidential and secret service side of the work. Therefore, I did not come into direct contact with him so much as might have been expected. I did his work for him occasionally when he was ill or on holiday, just as he would help me with mine if need arose: but on the whole our relations were confined to occasional discussions about important questions of policy or administration and looking to each other for necessary information. He was certainly a splendid and inspiring colleague; absolutely methodical; scrupulously accurate, as indeed was only to be expected; quite indefatigable; full of resource and courage; never afraid of a difficult situation and never hesitating to take a view or express a definite opinion; full of patience both with men and with materials; and above all with a sense of humour. I think what struck me most about him was the extraordinary knack he seemed to possess both of finding suitable men to do work which was wanted and of producing information on any subject. As one of his "opposite numbers" at the War Office said to me the other day, "Davis was really wonderful. One never seemed to ask him a question that he could not answer."

Two years after his return to college work Davis accepted an invitation to the chair of modern history in the university of Manchester. He had literary plans and obligations which required more leisure than the heavy work of a college tutor after the war could afford. Professor Tout was still in general charge of the history school in Manchester, and others were able to help in the administration of the department; hence Davis was free to confine himself, so far as he wished, to his teaching and historical work. The years spent in Manchester were perhaps the quietest and some of the happiest of his academic life. Although his colleagues could not hope to keep him for long, and he had no hesitation in returning to Oxford when the regius professorship was offered to him, he would have been glad, had Oxford not claimed him, to identify himself with the Manchester school and to build up its modern side. He devoted himself in the main to advanced teaching of the subject which he was making his own: the political and social history of England after 1815, and especially the work of Sir Robert Peel. The most important result of his influence was Dr. Aspinall's study of Lord Brougham, but when he left he had set several other pupils to work on similar tasks. This side of his duties as professor was afterwards developed with much energy and success in Oxford while he was regius professor.

Another interest which absorbed him in Manchester was his work upon the *Dictionary of National Biography*. On his return to Oxford after the war the Delegates of the Clarendon Press had given him general charge of the *Dictionary*, both of the revision of the main book and of the preparation of the additional volume of 1902-21. The duty was onerous, and Davis was so fortunate as to secure the help of Mr. J. R. H. Weaver, of Trinity College, Oxford, an old friend whose remarkable gifts as an editor had been revealed in very exacting work entrusted to him in the War Trade Intelligence Department. After Davis's appointment to Manchester the main burden of the work naturally fell on Mr. Weaver, but the plan and contents of the additional volume had already been settled. In 1920 and 1921 an informal committee used to meet in the house of the late Dr. Hogarth. Lists of names were drawn up by this committee and were afterwards submitted for scrutiny to a number of persons eminent in their callings. The two editors then reduced the result to order, fixed a common standard, and assigned the articles to authors. Mr. Weaver states that Davis's wide acquaintance with persons in political circles was particularly helpful. While he was in Manchester he read all the articles in typescript and edited them with the scrupulous care natural to him. Moreover, he considered carefully the best way of approaching the problem of revising the main book. He accumulated a large stock of notes (in addition to the material collected by the Institute of Historical Research and others), and undertook a "systematic scrutiny of one or two categories of lives—in order to find out whether it will be possible to publish piecemeal revisions of this kind".

All this labour and much more have been suddenly interrupted. How much Davis did during the short tenure—less than three years—of his Oxford chair, only his Oxford colleagues know. They know also that he did too much. Fortunately some of his work in modern history, notably the revised Ford lectures, was nearly ready for publication. The objective scientific study of English democratic developments, for which he pleaded in his inaugural lecture, will not be without its witness, an example to others, and a further revelation of his gifts. And we have the Raleigh lecture, delivered for the British Academy, on "The Great Game in Asia". As has been truly said, "the man who could write thus of the old Indian political pioneers, of tragedy and indomitable journeyings on the high passes, had it within him to write of action. The action, it may be, of minorities and individualists rather than of whole peoples; for Davis's historical orthodoxy was shot through by an almost wayward impatience of the verdict of the crowd, and his severe intellectual serenity submitted to a native sympathy for men destined to bear the responsibility of life and death decision." The memory of that sympathy, the sympathy of the man who had found himself and was free from the entanglements of prejudice and convention, will long linger in the thoughts of his friends and companions. It was very unobtrusive, but it was always to be relied upon. It encouraged many who saw him but rarely, but whom he never forgot when the time for help or advice came. It was part of himself, like his pleasure in children and his fondness for dogs, and the happy moods of gentleness which came over him when he was at his ease. He died, in the height of his powers and reputation, as a man of his kind ought to die, at work. But he died more than twenty years too soon.

CHAPTER VI

THREE CAMBRIDGE SCHOLARS: C. W. PREVITÉ-ORTON, Z. N. BROOKE AND G. G. COULTON[1]

I have been invited to write something about three friends of mine who, each in his own way, helped to maintain and advance medieval studies in Cambridge during the last generation. Two of them, Charles William Previté-Orton and Zachary Nugent Brooke were bulwarks of the history school as teachers and lecturers, the one for twenty-six, the other for thirty-four years. Both were scholars of St. John's College and, although Brooke was six years younger than his friend, were contemporaries as undergraduates; both were editors of the *Cambridge Medieval History*; each in succession was Professor of Medieval History. It was not easy to think of one without passing on in thought to the other, as a man might take the short walk from St. John's to Caius. The third scholar, who survived both the others, was George Gordon Coulton. Born in October, 1858, a fortnight before Queen Victoria's proclamation of 1 November announced to the people of India that the territories, possessions and executive powers of the East India Company had been transferred to the Crown, he lived to know that the end of British rule in India would come within a year or two. He was the last survivor of a noble company of medievalists, to whose society, it must be confessed, he owed but a casual, though in general a respectful, allegiance. He was four and a half years younger than John Horace Round, three years younger than Thomas Frederick Tout, eighteen months younger than Reginald Lane Poole, four months younger than Hastings Rashdall, the scholar and friend whom he especially revered. He was five years older

[1] From *The Cambridge Historical Journal*, ix (1947), 106-116.

than Andrew George Little, the scholar for whom, I think, he felt the deepest affection. He outlived them all. It is strange to reflect that when Coulton was born the great Maitland, always in his eyes the model of what a scholar should be, was only eight years old, and that he did not settle in Cambridge until some years after Maitland's death. Coulton was, indeed, a link with the past; not a past of compact traditions, such as we, with all our infinite variety, have enjoyed in Oxford since the days of Stubbs, nor a coherent Cambridge past, but rather the kind of past suggested by Lord Acton when he spoke of "our three Cambridge historians, Maine, Lightfoot, Maitland", though even this does not fully convey the diffuseness of Coulton's attachments or the abruptness of his flights to independence. His was a searching, roaming spirit, yet always *somewhere*, never in the vague. One had only to hear him speak about Renan to realize this. And I remember, when he took me to his window in St. John's to show me the view, how he was careful to point out a secluded spot in Trinity where he had been wont to walk and talk with McTaggart. It is only right to add that he aroused in others either the same quick sense of attachment or the impulse to be free from his spell. On the few occasions when we met, he was kind and friendly, but, just as he was, so to speak, sampling me, so I, in my turn, though I admired him greatly, could never surrender. I wanted to be free. I used to envy A. G. Little's quiet, lightsome, affectionate yet detached and slightly amused feelings about Coulton; but Little was Coulton's contemporary and had the spiritual hospitality of a saint.

However, I must return to Coulton later. Previté-Orton and Brooke are much easier to estimate. I have said that it was natural to think of them together, but it would be wrong to stress a companionship which was due to circumstance, mutual regard and co-operation in common tasks, both in the History School and in the preparation of the *Cambridge Medieval History*. They were not twin souls. Both were humane, but, whereas Previté-Orton's humanity met one at every point, Brooke's was less expansive, either held in reserve behind his intellectual activity or finding outlet in times of leisure, in the pleasures of every-day life or of holidays in the country. "Previté", even in the anxious years when his eyesight almost failed, always seemed to be maintained by an inner life so cultivated and serene that it did not seek though it welcomed sympathy. "Zachary" was more like a boy. Beneath his seriousness, he was ardent and affectionate, easily depressed, sensitive to opinion, eager for appreciation. One loved him and at the same time wanted to "rag" him, for he could be so dreadfully solemn. Both were good men, sincere, kind, warm-hearted, and quite innocent of guile. Their inaugural lectures show very well what they were like, but Brooke's, though a characteristic utterance, fails to convey the charm of the man.

I am not competent to write of them as lecturers and teachers, and only a colleague could appraise the place which each of them had in the work and administration of the History School. Moreover, to do this one would need to know more than I do about the medieval side of the School as the home of a tradition. Cambridge had some fine medievalists in the splendid age which began with Archbishop Parker, whose collections are in Corpus Christi College, and ended with the publication of John Smith's edition of Bede's *Ecclesiastical History* in 1722. In the nineteenth century it contained a splendid galaxy of scholars, who, while not what are sometimes called "straight" historians, promoted the study of medieval life in all sorts of ways: the University registraries H. E. Luard and J. W. Clark, the librarian Henry Bradshaw, the professor of applied mechanics, Robert Willis (probably the greatest English student of architecture), J. Bass Mullinger and M. R. James. Then came the great days of F. W. Maitland and Mary Bateson. Maitland is one of the immortals. He transcends all boundaries. It would, I imagine, be hard to say how far the others whom I have named imparted a living tradition to the Cambridge History School. Miss Bateson was an historical teacher at Newnham, but she was a woman and women are only just coming into their own in Cambridge. The rest were not teachers in a Faculty of History, but in a sense free-lances, deriving from the classics and the sciences. Their influence upon the systematic teaching of history in a new faculty of history must have been negligible; but they wrote books which set new standards of scholarship in the editing or interpretation of texts and the description of monuments. Some of their writings are classics. Did the fact that they had lived and worked in Cambridge add weight and confidence to the work of historical teachers, or enlarge their ideas about historical study or foster a habit of co-operation between scholars within and without the new history school? And if it did these things, what share had the three men with whom I have been charged to concern myself in the gracious work of comprehension?

The question after all may be beside the mark. Maitland's greatness may have put every other influence in the shade and created a fresh tradition. I do not know, though I may observe that fine work of any sort can have an uncanny persistence in quiet and unexpected ways. It is obvious that Maitland's inspiring contributions to our legal and constitutional history, to the study of the relations between Church and State and to the development of political thought must have affected the interests of such men as Gaillard Lapsley, William John Corbett, Z. N. Brooke and C. W. Previté-Orton. I was once present at a lunch party given by Professor Hazeltine in Downing College and Lapsley, who was sitting by me, explained that we were lunching in the room which had been Maitland's study: he pointed to a place on the wall and said, with some emotion, "Domesday Book stood *there*". Lapsley, as lecturer and tutor, was, I believe, for many years the outstanding exponent of medieval English history in Cambridge but after his return to the United States and perhaps before, Brooke and Previté-Orton were presumably the leading medievalists in the School, and, with Miss Cam, undoubtedly a stalwart disciple of Maitland, and the well-beloved Bernard Manning bore the brunt of the teaching in medieval history.

Their duties as teachers and academic administrators did not prevent them in their determination to advance the understanding of history by their own researches. Here we come to influences in Cambridge to which I have not yet referred. These worked outside that of Maitland and mingled with it in the aspirations of Brooke and Previté-Orton. They were derived from the long and varied tradition of broad and liberal historical interests maintained by Seeley, Acton, Ward, Bury, Cunningham, Creighton (the Oxonian) and his successors in the Dixie Chair of Ecclesiastical History, Gwatkin and Whitney. This tradition (unless I am mistaken) was on the whole more in line with the general course of Cambridge interests than the work of Maitland, just as it expressed the wider tendencies in historical learning in Europe as distinct from the more specialized or antiquarian studies of Bradshaw, J. W. Clark and M. R. James. If professorial contacts in Cambridge are like those we know in Oxford, this tradition was diffused along personal rather than definite academic channels, as was the influence here of Stubbs and Firth; but it was powerful, impressive and sometimes almost incredibly learned. And, much though Brooke and Previté-Orton owed to Maitland, it was to this tradition that they belonged. Indeed, I am inclined to think that the significance of their work is especially to be seen in their efforts to express and maintain this tradition in the more humdrum and everyday life of the History School. They tried to do for medieval history what, with more obvious results, Clapham and Temperley did for later history. I must confess to strong feelings of sympathy with them.

The strain to which they were subjected was severe. They were not physically strong, were sensitive to distractions, and had those meticulous and delicate standards of scholarship which, if they are to be satisfied without any sense of frustration, need leisure and peace of mind. In addition to their college work, they were increasingly answerable for the volumes of the *Cambridge Medieval History* and, as scholars, were always and rightly impelled to continue the investigations in which they found their deepest satisfaction. In addition, Previté-Orton, who was not elected to his Chair until 1937, was, from 1926 to 1938, sole editor of the *English Historical Review*, originally founded by Creighton, and a very good editor he was. The legacy of Creighton, Acton and Bury was indeed charged with heavy responsibilities, the editorial succession to Reginald Lane Poole and G. N. Clark, to Gwatkin and Whitney and Tanner no sinecure. The *Medieval History*, it is true, was finished in 1936, and Previté-Orton gave up the editorship of the *Review* in 1938, the year in which he temporarily lost his sight at Rome. Also both men were able to find some relief from teaching after their election, the one in succession to the other, to the new Chair of Medieval History; but the war broke into their plans of life. Both died suddenly, in harness; Brooke in the early autumn of 1946 at the age of sixty-three, Previté-Orton in the early spring of 1947 at the age of seventy. It is pleasant to think of the happiness which after the war they gave and found around them, Brooke in the companionship of his sons, Previté-Orton in the visits of his daughter and his little grandsons, upon whom he could lavish his affection for children and his gifts as a teller of stories.

On the whole Cambridge men have tended to concentrate more than Oxford men upon foreign history, though we do not forget here in Oxford H. A. L. Fisher, Richard Lodge, Edward Armstrong, C. W. C. Oman and others who are still with us. After all, Cambridge has become the home of composite histories of ancient, medieval and modern times. Previté-Orton's services in the preparation of the third volume of the *Cambridge Medieval History* were handsomely acknowledged by Whitney in 1921; and from this time he and Brooke were primarily responsible for the continuation of the work, though J. R. Tanner, who had helped to edit vol. III, was senior editor of the next four volumes (IV-VII) and, a few days before his death in 1931, was at work upon the proofs of vol. VII (1932). The introductions which attempted to add coherence to the chapters written by the various contributors begin in vol. III with an essay by Whitney. Bury, who had planned the whole work, naturally wrote the introduction to vol. IV and Brooke that to vol. V. The introductions to vols. VI and VII and the epilogue with which the *History* was brought to a close in vol VIII (1936) were written by Previté-Orton. These three short essays, and notably the last, reveal him at his best. The breadth of view and the sensitive sagacity which give such distinction to the Epilogue are the culmination of the mental discipline which, a quarter of a century earlier, had gone to the compilation of his first historical work, *The Early History of the House of Savoy* (1912). In this book, deliberately modelled on the German *Jahrbücher* devoted to the reigns of the Holy Roman Emperors, he appears as the master of a rigid scientific method. His aim here was to disentangle and present in stark simplicity the available evidence relating to a dark and intricate subject. "I have put aside", he writes in his preface, "the idea of writing a history of the strictly literary kind. . . . I have gone plainly on discussing events and problems as the time brought them to light, and endeavouring to be complete and omit nothing." The patient and inexorable learning revealed by the book is indeed astonishing. The humility which could subdue, in the interests of a task of precision, the philosophical and poetical instincts which always gave life to the thoughts and spirit of the man, deserves an acknowledgement which it has never fully received. One has only to think of the country between Lake Geneva, the Rhone and Turin where the counts of Savoy built up their lordship, of the traditions into which they entered, of the events in their vigorous and adventurous lives, to realize that such a man as Previté-Orton must have been thrilled again and again by the exciting impulse to let himself go; but he held himself in restraint because he wished to get the facts right once for all. He had his reward in the conscious mastery of his craft and in the gratitude of scholars who could see what he had done. Thereafter, however widely he might cast his net, and however freely he might give rein to his imagination, his scholarship could be taken for granted, and his judgement trusted. His useful and widely read text-book on medieval European history, his *History of Europe,* 1198-1378, in Methuen's *History of Medieval and Modern Europe* (1938) and his fine chapters in the *Cambridge History* are firmly based and contain some memorable writing. At the same time he dug deep into the intellectual history of the fourteenth century, with a rare understanding of the circumstances in which the political thought of Occam and Marsiglio of Padua found its expression. His essays on Marsiglio and his critical edition of the *Defensor Pacis* are perhaps the most important of his works. He began to found a little school of studies in Cambridge, broken too soon by the deaths of Bernard Manning and J. G. Sikes, and by the failure of his eyesight, but still alive. Hence, when he wrote the Epilogue he did not write a line which he could not have substantiated with a wealth of learning; and how well he could write in the manner of a great historian is revealed in every page of this brief essay.

Brooke's particular interests were precisely focused on the relations between the secular and ecclesiastical powers in the eleventh and twelfth centuries. His work was broadly based, but not so expansive as Previté-Orton's, and came to a finer and perhaps a sharper point. At its best, his mind was like a powerful engine working a drill. While Previté-Orton rarely talked about his own studies, Brooke, with a nice touch of boyish *naïveté*, liked to talk about his, and would reveal in conversation a wider acquaintance with current literature than appears in his printed work, which is clear, concise and direct. He gave more time and care to his *History of Europe, 911–1198*, in the Methuen *History*, than a casual reader might think and never wrote without deliberate reflection and accurate knowledge. Although this book appeared in the later years of his life (1938), it was the outcome of a long acquaintance with the texts. When, by way of his studies on the movement which culminated in the "investiture conflict", he came to his most important work, *The English Church and the Papacy from the Conquest to the Reign of John* (1931), he did what Previté-Orton, with all his learning and insight, never did: he reopened a big subject in an exciting way. This book, made possible by a year's leave of absence, and clarified by its preliminary expression in lectures, is one of the half-dozen critical studies which are fundamental to our appreciation of the history of England in the times of the Norman and Angevin kings. It is a masterly piece of work, whether we regard it as an example of historical method or as an exposition. It made its readers think, stirred them up, and added a lively and stimulating impulse to current tendencies in historical investigation. It gave to the study of canon law a new sense of value and social significance. Brooke's conclusions have not escaped criticism, but this does not matter, or rather is significant just because they were so interesting and arresting as to provoke independent minds and set them to work. He had, so to speak, reopened the archives, and, since his book appeared some sixteen years ago, a score of busy scholars have seen to it that the dust shall not be allowed to settle on them again.

As we recall this outburst of disciplined enthusiasm, we may well wonder whether Brooke and others need have been so troubled by the future of medieval studies in Cambridge. It is true, I suppose, that Oxford can draw on deeper and more spacious reservoirs, and that Cambridge interests in medieval studies are more remote from tradition and less conscious of a common purpose than ours in Oxford. I can well understand how sensitive Brooke must have been to any movement of opinion which questioned the claim of medieval history to a place in the curriculum of all candidates in the history school, for its relegation to a distinct course of study would rob later history of much of its meaning and deprive undergraduates of an experience which has often opened their minds to a congenial world. All of us have our "specialisms", but in these days the traditional distinction between a pre- and a post-Reformation civilization, especially as objects of educational discipline, has become an absurdity. If a date *must* be found for a break in the history of the West it can more reasonably be found in the last decades of the eighteenth century. On the other hand, the healthy pursuit of medieval as of any other kind of study cannot be assured by academic regulations; a curriculum can provide opportunity, but performance must depend upon those intangible influences which play upon the student from all sides and carry with them their own compulsion. Brooke, who had a rigid streak in him, did not always give due weight to this truth. He himself had done much to maintain the right atmosphere. He had helped to keep medieval studies at Cambridge in contact with medieval studies elsewhere at home and abroad. He and Previté-Orton had, more or less consciously, paid homage to the tradition which I tried to describe at the beginning of this paper. The tradition of Luard, Bradshaw, Maitland, Bury and the rest is still alive, diffuse perhaps, but active. One has only to think of Professor Chadwick's great works, of F. C. Burkitt's brilliant studies in the sources for the life of St. Francis, of the purposeful attempt made by Dr. Chaytor to give medieval literature a social setting. And within the history school, a new generation of medievalists, learned, original and purposeful, is at work. Some of Previté-Orton's and Brooke's pupils are to be found among them.

And so we come to the attractive, formidable, cultivated, downright, quixotic figure, G. G. Coulton, the doughtiest free-lance of all the Cambridge historians. I was bold enough in my youth to stand up to him, and we became friends. That usually happened, I believe, unless he suspected his adversary of deceit. Once I quarrelled with him, for I thought he had been unfair—and his impulsive gallantry could make him unfair—but that is a private matter and we had made our peace with each other long before he died. No historical scholar in our time has so fluttered the dovecots. His enthusiasm was quite different from the impersonal intensity of the scientific investigator, nor was it quite the same as the indignant or ironical or fervent rationalism of the scientist who has made his scientific certainties the measure of the follies and illusions of his fellow-men. It was the zest of the man who is in the thick of the fray. He decided to take holy orders and found that he should not. He became a schoolmaster and, as a matter of course, an educational reformer. He realized as a citizen the dangers of wishful thinking and indolent acquiescence and found the remedy in the Swiss system of national service. As one reads his autobiography, one cannot but feel that his interest in history may have saved him from a life of frustration. The cultivated, courteous, well-informed but ineffective agitator is a well-known, if uncommon type. Nearly always right, wiser than those whom he tends to weary, he fails for one reason or another to carry conviction. Coulton managed to escape this danger. His decision to settle in Cambridge, his university lectureship in English and his fellowship at St. John's gave him a settled purpose in life, the means to pursue it, and recognition of its achievement. He remained a stubborn and impenitent controversialist, but he became a distinguished historian as he garnered the fruit of his devotion to the records and monuments of the medieval way of life. An accomplished linguist, he travelled widely and read voraciously. He did not turn himself into a medievalist. Since his boyhood in King's Lynn he had been a medievalist. I think of him as an inverted monk who could not shake himself free of the holy glamour of the regular life, as an inverted knight always on the look out for a tussle in the lists, as an inverted scholastic happiest in the exercise of his dialectical powers, or as an inverted preacher, primed with *exempla* and moral applications. He was inquisitive, original and encyclopaedic just as Roger Bacon was in his day. He was as discursive as a medieval romancer and as fond of the colourful as a medieval chronicler. And as he turned his tasks into hobbies, he said in *Who's Who* what a man of the Middle Ages might have said, that his recreation was "vegetating".

I have sometimes heard it said that, if he had lived in the later Middle Ages, Coulton would have been burnt as a heretic. I am disposed to doubt this judgement. He might very well have been a conscientious inquisitor. For, while he stood out among his fellows as a man of fearless, pungent, clear-cut speech—and hundreds of men in the Middle Ages were the same—his ideas were anything but revolutionary. He was frugal, austere and unconventional in his ways, but he was conventional enough in his ideas. A good party man is not the less conventional because he can express his views in a vivid and unusual way; and Coulton belonged to a school of reverent agnostics well established in his time. It is impossible to imagine him without ideas, or as timid or cautious in the expression of them. He was no hedger; but he was neither a rebel nor a visionary. He was a bit of a Puritan, and in his desire to see things done right, without equivocation, he was a perfectionist. He was tolerant, for he believed in liberty, was curious about other people's points of view, and kind-hearted;

but he could not stand casuistry in any form and was shocked by those whose professions were more precise than their practice, just as any monk who had not observed the details of the Rule was, in his eyes, a bad monk. In this he would have been quite at home in medieval Europe. He would have been surrounded by people who, as masters of invective, could leave him far behind. To say that, after all, he refused to become a priest is beside the point. It never occurred to him to leave England because he did not like some people and things in England; and in the Middle Ages he would have felt the same about the Christian society of the West which was then the Church.

Coulton's numerous writings have been so much discussed and are so hard to classify that I shall not try to deal with them in detail. Most of them I have not read; for although I doubt if he wrote anything, however short or controversial, which did not contain some interesting fact or suggestive observation, I have always been conscious—perhaps too conscious—of dominant notes and themes which recur like the phrases of a fugue in the setting of a riotous wealth of sound. The recognition of a familiar "kind of thing" arrested the desire to read everything that he wrote for the sake of what I could find. Many, I know, felt quite differently; a new book or paper by Coulton was for them an event, an experience not to be missed; and a formal appreciation of his work can best be done by the more learned and discerning among his votaries. It is a more congenial and, in this present context, a more useful duty to attempt a concise statement of the ways in which Coulton advanced the study of history in Cambridge and, indeed, throughout the English-speaking world. I doubt if he exercised much influence outside this world.

First of all, I would put his scholarship, I use the word in the narrower sense, of sureness of touch and the punctilious concern for detail, to whatever use he might put it. He had a feeling for the meaning of technical words and took great trouble about them. He could read a text as a master of it and sense errors in transcription whether he had access to the manuscripts or not. He once sent to me, as I knew he was wont to send to others, a list of *errata* in a text which I had edited, and I think that he was right in every point. And recently, while I was going through some of A. G. Little's papers, I came upon notes by Coulton on Little's edition of Eccleston's *Tractatus de adventu fratrum minorum in Angliam* (Paris, 1909). In one of the manuscripts a later hand added a list of the first sixty-seven Franciscan lectors at Oxford. The entry about William of Alnwick, the forty-second master, reads: "qui postea apud montem Bononiae Neapoly legit" (p. 69). The meaning of *montem* has been much discussed. Obviously it has no relation to Bologna and Naples, but does it refer to the "mount" at Paris or to some other place? The problem was solved a few years ago by V. Doucet, who discovered an entry in an old printed catalogue of manuscripts, then (1778) existing in the Dominican house at Venice, about a codex with the colophon "explicit primum Quodlibet disputatum et determinatum in Monte Pessulano a fra Ghilielmo de Alvellwic Anglico"—a disputation determined at Monpellier by brother William of Alnwick the Englishman. The reference to William's lectures *apud montem* in the manuscript of Eccleston was to his teaching at Montpellier. But, years before, Coulton, in his notes, had quietly added "Pessulanum" after "montem", with the comment: "in view of the evident corruptions this might not be too rash". Little either overlooked Coulton's addition or, more probably, did not accept it; but Coulton was right. This was characteristic. Some of Coulton's critics, when they engaged in debate with him, did not always realize that they were dealing with a fine scholar. They did not distinguish between the scholarship and the opinions of their formidable adversary, and they fell. I do not suggest, of course, that Coulton was impeccable, but it must have been a revelation to his pupils, as it gives a sense of safety to his readers, to realize the familiarity with which he approached and interpreted medieval texts.

Secondly, Coulton did more than any historical scholar of his time to bring important but forgotten books within the mental range of his fellow-students; not because he happened to be a bibliophile but because he had pursued his own literary plans so remorselessly and widely, without any conventional inhibitions, and had found in this neglected literature fundamental texts. As we all know, he did not possess a big library of his own. In the more stringent years he accumulated an enormous mass of notes, to which he later made frequent additions, and these collections were the main source of his writings. Gradually, I think, he came to look at the Middle Ages through this satisfying medium, and his absorption in it tended to cramp his judgement. This was natural enough. I prefer to stress here the advantage which his freedom and freshness of outlook gave him and the astonishing insight and energy which enabled him first to see the significance of this literature and then to exploit it. Caesarius of Heisterbach, Odo Rigaud, Berthold of Regensburg, Bromyard and many more medieval writers are well-known names now; through Coulton's work they have come to symbolize and point the way to a vast field of study, just as recent work on saints' lives, on scholastic texts and on the canonists and civilians has familiarized us with ways of approach to medieval problems, from which we had been inclined, in some trepidation, to avert our eyes.

Lastly, Coulton, from the students of History and English Literature and others attracted to Cambridge by his reputation, made a school of his own. To what extent his pupils have been able to maintain the union so natural to him between historical and literary studies and to carry on his work, I cannot say. One or two, I know, are carrying on, and there may be more. The volumes in the series which he edited of English Studies in Medieval Life and Thought are the finest memorial of his work in Cambridge. Professor Deanesly's *Lollard Bible*, Eileen Power's *Medieval English Nunneries*, Professor Owst's volumes on medieval preaching, Mr. H. S. Bennett's *Life on the English Manor*, Miss Wood-Legh's *Church Life in England under Edward III*, with the editor's own great book, *Five Centuries of Religion*, unhappily not finished, and *The Medieval Village*, make a notable book-shelf. They remind us that Coulton's circle was wide. He attracted and inspired scholars of strong and independent minds who did not all look at things as he did, just as he had a peculiar influence over his Catholic pupils. And this is but half the story. Hundreds of students listened eagerly to the lectures which, in their finished form, appeared in *Five Centuries of Religion* and some of his other works. I remember vividly the crowds which flocked to hear him when he delivered the Ford lectures in Oxford. He made medieval life real and delightful to thousands of readers.

I find that it was much easier to express my disagreements with him when he was alive than it is now. I remember too well his fine head, his gracious and courteous bearing, the eagerness of his talk, and the humility which, especially in his later years, and most of all while he was writing in Canada the beautiful recollections of his boyhood, endeared him to those who knew him well. The tiresome strain in him no longer matters. He stood out in every society. He was at home with the best things, never petty, never bored, and a great gentleman.

CHAPTER VII

LEOPOLD DELISLE AND ANGLO-FRENCH HISTORY[1]

Delisle owed his European reputation to his work in bibliography and diplomatic. Yet in one sense he was always an historian first and a bibliophile afterwards; he never ceased to bring the weight of his wide learning to bear upon his work, with the result that his most technical studies are a real contribution to history. It may be said of him, as Lord Acton said of Boehmer, that he raised drudgery to the rank of a fine art. However minute the problem might be, however limited its scope, Delisle saw it in relation to the whole field of medieval knowledge. Hence his work is always to the point. There is no waste, so that the distinction between big work and little work ceases to exist; all is informed with a peculiar quality, like the work of a great surgeon, who is neat and unflurried without pettiness. Enthusiasm gave direction to this method. Delisle was never a mere antiquary. The portrait prefixed by M. Lacombe to his bibliography of the scholar's writings has something of the strength and alertness of Victor Hugo; it shows the face of a vigorous man of letters, who might easily have been either a poet or a man of business.

Yet no antiquary of the most limited interests ever allowed himself so few distractions. After the interruption of his studies at the École des Chartes, he worked steadily through the years of the Second Republic and the *coup d'état;* and he continued to pour out articles and reviews during 1870 and 1871. The excitement of the period was a brief glimpse, "for a short

[1] This short essay is taken, with some slight changes, from the latter part of an article on Delisle in the *Quarterly Review* for April, 1911. The earlier part of the article was written by the late Reginald Lane Poole. Delisle, who was of Norman origin, was director of the Bibliothèque Nationale from 1874 to 1905. From 1852 to 1874 he had served the library in the department of manuscripts.

half-hour", of "a magnificent psalter which, I discovered, had been made for Ingeborg of Denmark". But, if his interests were in the Middle Ages, they were none the less organized and controlled. The boy who had been stupefied by the encyclopaedic vastness of the "Speculum Naturale" was possessed by no parochial passion.

Delisle was a great historian who wrote no great history. His knowledge was for him an instrument in the interpretation of manuscripts. All his chief historical work, in the stricter sense, belongs to his earlier years; and, with the exception of his thesis on the Norman revenues, it is not his most successful writing. The well-known study on the Norman peasantry [1] is, for example, an excellent preliminary sifting of the evidence, but is not, and was not intended to be, a good piece of economic history. It is overburdened, lacks chronological sequence, and is not determined by a regard for economic problems. It was in the presentation of historical material that Delisle excelled; he was less interested in the use to which the material could be put. His style was brief, clear, emphatic, or occasionally gravely whimsical, as in the early essay on the *rouleaux des morts;* it sometimes possesses a dry charm, as in the "Souvenirs de jeunesse" which he prefixed to one of his latest books, the beautiful "Recherches sur la librairie de Charles V" (1907). It was always virile, convincing, courteous, without a trace of pedantry. The introductions to his collections of charters or other documents especially useful to historians are models of their kind; and the work itself was at once accepted even in Germany as an example of what such work should be.

The "Cartulaire Normand" (1852), the "Catalogue des Actes de Philippe-Auguste" (1856), the unfinished "Recueil des Actes de Henri II" (1909), are, like an increasing amount of similar work in France, of final authority. So far as labour of this kind can accomplish the task, the ground has been swept clean. The gleaners will have little to do. The work is, of course, not flawless. Mr. Howlett has rightly questioned the

[1] "Etudes sur la condition de la classe agricole et l'état de l'agriculture en Normandie au moyen âge" (1851, reissued 1903).

complete accuracy of Delisle's analysis of the library used by the Norman chronicler, Robert of Torigny; Mr. Round has been able to correct a few blunders in the criticism of Henry II's charters. And doubtless there are other blemishes in this output of sixty-three years.

When Delisle, at the age of thirty-one, was elected a member of the Academy of Inscriptions (1857), he had already made a place for himself as the future historian of medieval Normandy and of the reign of Philip Augustus. His work at the Bibliothèque Nationale prevented the fulfilment of the hopes which his friends had formed. In 1864 he published the collection of thirteenth century judgments delivered at the Norman Exchequer; forty years later, in 1904, appeared the edition of St. Louis's inquests, with a remarkable introduction upon the administrative divisions of Normandy after the French conquest; finally the old man was able in 1909 to redeem the promise of a lifetime by the publication of the introductory volume of his work on Henry II's charters, to which we have already referred.

All this work is of the same order as the careful studies of French and Norman documents which appeared before 1857. Delisle left it to others to build upon the foundations so laboriously laid. Yet, just as the student desirous of solving a problem of English medieval history would begin by reading what Stubbs had to say about it, so, if his interests lie in French or Norman sources of the twelfth and thirteenth centuries, he would turn first of all to the bibliography of Delisle's writings. It is unwise to presume that he has left any point untouched. Two or three years ago a local antiquary took the trouble to copy some Furness charters from the chartulary of Savigny, now in the Bibliothèque Nationale, ignorant of the fact that Delisle had communicated them to the British Archaeological Association in 1851. The extraordinary labours of these early years are indeed a link between the revival of Norman studies after the Napoleonic wars and the recent collaboration of French, English and American scholarship.

Maitland described in 1904 how forgotten discoveries of Spelman and Selden were taken up and extended after two centuries by German scholars. The closely-connected studies in Anglo-Norman institutions have had a still less continuous history. The work of German scholars was carried forward by Stubbs and, in the great field of law, by Maitland; but, with a few exceptions, English and French students have worked in unnatural isolation. Nothing seems more obvious than the necessity for the comparative study of Norman and Anglo-Norman law, of English, Norman and Gascon records, of French and Norman and Angevin institutions. For more than a century the Norman conquerors of England had continued to regard Normandy as their home; under the guidance of Angevin counts their dominions had been welded into a federation of feudal states in which Bordeaux, Poitiers, Dublin were cardinal points. Yet, for lack of material of a more concrete kind, the historical imagination, even in the great mind of Stubbs, hardly got a glimpse of this fruitful field of inquiry.

The problem of Norman origins seemed (as it still seems) insoluble; the Norman and Angevin chroniclers were unsatisfactory and elusive in comparison with such an official annalist as Roger of Howden; at first sight the machinery of the Norman Exchequer and of Angevin administration did not correspond to that of the English Exchequer and of Anglo-Norman administration. The narratives of the numerous writers upon Norman history who lived at the beginning of last century—Goube, Licquet, Duncan and others—were not very helpful. Even Lappenberg and Palgrave had to rely in the main upon chroniclers whose value is still contested, and some of whom have not yet been adequately edited. Hence scholars passed over Norman history after 1066 in silence, and leaped from Frankish charters and capitularies to the pages of Glanvil and Bracton in their interpretation of Anglo-Norman feudalism. Only two men perceived what a comparative study of English and Norman records could teach. One of these was the English antiquary, Thomas Stapleton, whose "Observations on the Great Rolls of the Exchequer in Normandy" were published in 1840 and 1844. The other was young Delisle.

After the Napoleonic war the literary interests of the French were largely directed to England. The liberal revival found poetic material in the career of Cromwell and political lessons in English institutions. The work of the historian Thierry anticipated the greater work of Palgrave and Freeman. Englishmen, on the other hand, felt the curiosity of the antiquary. Travel in France was resumed with an energy which was intensified by previous restraint. Anderson, Cotman and Dibdin directed the attention of French, and especially of Norman, scholars to the archaeological treasures all about them.[1] The Abbé de la Rue, Auguste le Prévost, and Charles de Gerville, the last of whom had spent a youth of exile in England, took the lead in a revival of Norman studies. Le Prévost was undoubtedly the greatest of these scholars; his edition of Ordericus Vitalis, completed by Delisle, will long continue to be one of the main sources of Norman and Anglo-Norman history in the eleventh and twelfth centuries. It was a Norman again, M. de Gerville, who, as we have noted above, had the distinction of introducing Delisle to the world of letters, and making him acquainted with Guérard and the chief medievalists of the Paris of that day.

Delisle's historical interests, no less than his duties at the Bibliothèque, brought him into touch with English records and English scholars. Other French scholars, also, were leading the way. At this time, Francisque Michel was commencing those long, if at times inaccurate and ill-directed labours which made him familiar to Scottish and English students half a century ago[2]; it is also worthy of note that Delpit and Champollion-Figeac were describing the fruits of old and new researches among English records. In the middle of the eighteenth century the scientific study of French history, of which we have such noble monuments in the "Recueil des historiens de France", and in the official edition of the Ordonnances,

[1] Passy, in "Bulletin de la Société des antiquaires de Normandie", xxii, 163; Prentout, in "Revue de synthèse historique", xix, 67.

[2] The following publications by Francisque Michel may be mentioned in this connexion: "Rapports sur les anciens monuments de l'histoire et de la littérature de la France, qui se trouvent dans les bibliothèques de l'Angleterre et de l'Ecosse" (1838); "Chroniques Anglo-Normandes, recueil d'extraits d'ecrits relatifs a l'histoire de Normandie et d'Angleterre pendant les xie et xiie siècles" (Rouen, 1836); the first volume of the Gascon Rolls (1885).

received encouragement from the ministers of Louis XV, Machault and Bertin. The work upon the Ordonnances involved a search in English archives for the French records which, it was supposed, had been captured during the struggle between Philip Augustus and Richard I, and especially during the great wars of the fourteenth and fifteenth centuries. With this object the distinguished scholar Bréquigny was sent to England in 1764.[1] Bréquigny did not succeed in his quest, but he brought back with him a rich collection of extracts from other sources. After lying neglected for seventy years, much of this material was published by Champollion-Figeac between 1838 and 1847. During the same period, between 1843 and 1847, Delpit was at work upon his "Documents français conservés en Angleterre", the result of an inquiry similar to that entrusted to Bréquigny.

These publications had no very special bearing upon the subjects which were beginning to interest Delisle, but they may well have helped to direct his attention to the more important work of Stapleton and Duffus Hardy, which had recently appeared in England. In his report upon the results of his mission, Bréquigny had dwelt upon the riches of the great collection of Norman, Gascon and "French" Rolls upon which the clerks of the Anglo-Norman and later English chancery had transcribed the official acts of the English kings. The genealogical material contained in these rolls had long been legal evidence in the French courts; but an account of their contents was available only in the very defective catalogue edited by Thomas Carte in 1743. Here again Bréquigny's observations bore no fruit for more than seventy years. Then in 1835 Duffus Hardy made a start in the publication of these invaluable records, and edited some of the Norman Rolls. Five years later Stapleton issued for the Society of Antiquaries the first volume of the extant rolls of the Norman Exchequer, with his preliminary observations. The work was finished in

---

[1] For Bréquigny's mission see the preface to Champollion-Figeac's "Lettres des rois, reines et autres personnages" (1839), vol. i, and Hardy's preface to the "Rotuli Normanniae" (1835), vol. i. Compare also Wolf, "Einführung in das Studium der neueren Geschichte" (1910), pp. 683, 684.

1844. Delisle fastened upon it, and chose, as the subject of his thesis for the diploma of *archiviste paléographe* at the École des Chartes, the public revenues of Normandy in the twelfth century. The greater part of this essay was published between 1849 and 1852; and other studies of French and Norman history, of much importance for the criticism of English records and institutions, appeared rapidly during the next few years.

The work of Stapleton and Delisle seems to have received little attention in England. When, a few years later, scientific inquiry into the history of English institutions was resumed, it was directed, as we have seen, by German influences. The inconsequent method adopted by Stapleton in his learned introductions was, no doubt, partly to blame for this neglect; but the real cause lay in the uncertainty of the subject. The records edited by Hardy and Stapleton were confined to a few scattered years between 1180 and 1203; the history of Norman administration before the reign of Henry II was still a blank; and the scientific study of charters, by which the casual indications of later rolls could be interpreted, was hardly understood in England. If the work of Stapleton had little influence upon English historical studies, the obscure labours of an unknown Norman scholar were doomed to lie unnoticed from the outset. The fame which Delisle acquired later in England as a palaeographer and bibliophile was more than bright enough to dim the importance of his work as an historian.

During the last twenty years, French scholars have done much to continue the work of Delisle. The close comparative study of those events and forms of government which were common to the medieval history of France and of England was resumed by M. Charles Bémont in his biography of Simon de Montfort (1884). The Earl of Leicester was, in a sense, the centre of Anglo-French relations in the Middle Ages. By birth he linked the society of France to that of England; his political career influenced the history of Gascony hardly less than it influenced the history of England; he stands midway in time between the Angevin Empire and the Hundred Years' War; and his administration of the remnant of the great duchy which Eleanor of Aquitaine had brought to Henry II had much to do with the disaffection which first encouraged France in the long struggle against England. Thus M. Bémont's book, which treated a familiar subject from this point of view, broke new ground. It has been followed by many important studies of similar value to the English student, such as M. Petit-Dutaillis's book on the reign of Louis VIII (1894), M. Berger's life of Blanche of Castile (1895), M. Gavvrilovitch's study of the Treaty of Paris (1899), and M. Déprez's study of the causes of the Hundred Years' War (1902). Above all, M. Bémont has been inspired to take up the work commenced by Francisque Michel in 1885, and, in a more scholarly manner, to edit the Gascon Rolls (1896–1906).

With this classical achievement we are brought back to labours similar to those of Delisle. Years ago, a Poitevin scholar, Bardonnet, sought in vain for official memorials of Richard's and John's government in Aquitaine; if any documents corresponding to the Norman Rolls ever existed,[1] they have been lost. Their disappearance adds to the value of the Gascon Rolls; and thanks to M. Bémont, it is possible to reconstruct the life of Gascony in the thirteenth century, as Stapleton and Delisle, with their successors, enable us to reconstruct the life of the Duchy of Normandy.[2] Finally, a little crowd of specialists, since Delisle began his studies on Normandy, has begun to restore the picture of the English occupation in France during the early fifteenth century.

The results of these manifold labours are not yet clear; but English scholarship and English history have already felt their influence in a hundred ways. The habit of comparison has been formed.

[1] The inquiries made at the command of Alphonse of Poitiers in the middle of the thirteenth century seem to point to the existence of Exchequer records in Poitiers during the Angevin period.

[2] For these successors, since the date of this paper (1911) see above pp. 111-112. for Charles Haskins, and the note in my *Loss of Normandy* (1913), pp. 1-7. Much more has been done since then.

CHAPTER VIII

SIR CHARLES FIRTH[1]

Sir Charles Firth was Regius Professor of Modern History for twenty-one years (1904–1925). He had mastered his subject during the twenty-one years of comparative leisure, which had preceded his appointment. He aged so slowly that one hardly noticed the passage of time in him, and it needed an effort to realize that he was in his seventy-ninth year when he died. It might seem to be an easy thing to write about him, for he had lived in Oxford almost continuously, since he entered Balliol sixty years ago, he was always the same, and "his life was the study of history". In reality it is not at all easy to write about this big and lovable man, and one feels rather ashamed to say anything about him when others who knew him better and were firmly bound to him by ties of affection feel that they cannot write. Yet the effort should be made, for many who did not know him at all have the right, and perhaps the duty, to learn something about him.

Firth was a kind, genial and friendly man, and also a very strong man. Chronic asthma and bronchitis made him deliberate in action and quiet in speech, but one could not meet him without being made conscious of his strength. He abhorred fuss and rhetoric, and there was a stoical quality in his quietness. He had great courage and a power of whimsical endurance. He looked like a big administrator, slow moving, firm and sagacious. The alertness of his eyes was emphasized by the somewhat drowsy and meditative aspect of his face. To imagine that massive head and pointed beard above a ruff was to see one of Queen Elizabeth's wiser counsellors. And, indeed, he liked the preparation of memoranda and the intimate, allusive discussion of the council chamber, just as he loved desultory and knowing talk with his cronies, while he

[1] From *The Oxford Magazine*, 12 March, 1936.

crouched over his fire or smoked at ease in his garden. Probably he was at his very best as a member of the last Royal Commission on the Public Records, where he was *facile princeps*.

He wrote one short sentence by way of autobiography: "engaged in literary work and historical teaching at Oxford since 1883." That is the literal truth. His teaching was never confined to formal instruction, and he was still the teacher after his retirement. Although he was so responsive and enjoyed the give and take of talk, I doubt if any younger man ever had the impertinence to feel that he could do anything but learn from him. He was always reading and learning. Three or four years ago, when the desire to write was failing in him, he said to me: "I have spent so much time in writing; now I must learn some history," and he added that he was trying to learn something about the time of Queen Anne. And not long ago, when talking to another friend, he deplored the fact that his memory was not so good as it was, but added, "I think it is as good as ever it was for the seventeenth century". His exactness of memory was not the uncanny and embarrassing faculty of the man who cannot forget; it was more disciplined and purposeful than the casual ease with which his great friend and predecessor, York Powell, tumbled out the rich spoils won by his buccaneering mind; it was the certainty of quiet possession. Firth talked about the seventeenth century as he chatted about everyday matters in the common room at Oriel or All Souls. He knew it as he knew the Banbury Road, so that his conversation was, as it were, a genial emanation from his great store of books, and yet more from his experience as he brooded over the past. He would have talked like that with Ben Jonson or John Selden, in short pithy sentences, with an occasional sidelong look as he waited for the reply of happy understanding which he was sure would come. When one knows a thing so well and feels about the poets and statesmen of a past age as one feels about one's intimate friends, it would be silly to wrap it up in abstractions or to orate about it. Short, pregnant, allusive speech is the best. And just because Firth could talk about history in this way, history became more real; one felt somehow that one was there.

Behind Firth's spacious and unprejudiced outlook on past and present, there was a good deal of the Puritan and the radical. He was downright, and could be very severe. For example, he took an austere view of the obligations which the privileges of living in Oxford imply. He loved Oxford, but he never surrendered to the fashion of easy-going service into which her charms can beguile us. He was quite free from all pretentiousness and snobbery, quite immune against the insidious temptation to feel that in the direction of our studies we in Oxford have nothing to learn from elsewhere and are better than other people because we happen to be here. Ideas of this kind seemed to him to be grotesque. He welcomed the new universities and made it his business to understand what they were trying to do. He recognized the good everywhere, however unexpected its source might be. His encouragement went out to help any man or woman, old or young, cultivated or callow, who was doing honest work. And in the same spirit he was quick to see the value of new movements in Oxford. He championed with vigour the School of Modern Languages and was one of the founders of the English School. He supported them for their own sake, and also because he believed in the unity of historical study, political, literary, philological; and, no doubt, he was glad to see the establishment, alongside the older schools controlled by the Colleges, of University departments which might help to create fresh traditions of teaching and research. With the same freedom from prejudice, he was a friend to the women and their claim to enter the University on the same terms as the men.

He had his difficulties and disappointments, of which I need not speak here. He must have learned all the lessons that the history of the Commonwealth and Protectorate can teach, yet he never quite realized that forms of government, unless they are maintained by brute force, cannot outrun opinion, and that the voice of reason is not necessarily sufficient in itself. Sometimes he may have under-rated the good intentions on the other side. But we see now, when so much that he stood for is gradually coming to pass, how good it was for Oxford to have this stalwart man. He loved Oxford and gave her of his best, and Oxford, with dainty assurance, picked and chose from what he gave; but long before he died she had taken him to herself, and numbered him with gratitude among the greatest of her sons.

CHAPTER IX

REGINALD LANE POOLE[1]

Reginald Lane Poole was the last of a group of great scholars who had been at Balliol and had known Stubbs in the seventies; and, among these, he was the most characteristic Oxonian, adapted to the congenial conventions of the place, and finding in them a stimulus to the busy exercise of a very independent mind. A man of profound and accurate scholarship, with a gift of precise and pithy speech, he combined, as has often been the case in Oxford, a cultivated love for music with an intimate acquaintance with the history of the University and with a punctilious regard for its traditions. He gave the impression of sensitive alertness, as Strang's portrait of him suggests, and he had in Magdalen a peculiarly appropriate setting for his treasured personality. There he was on easy terms of learned fellowship with C. H. Turner, F. E. Brightman, and his friends Dr. H. E. Salter and Dr. Clement Webb. But he was very much more than an Oxford figure. He was a man of international repute, one of the few who satisfied the exacting standards of critical scholars in all parts of the world, especially, perhaps, in the Paris of Delisle and Langlois. It is right that this should be remembered and said with emphasis, at a time when Dr. Poole's work might so easily be overlooked, yet at a time also when, if England is to be a sure refuge of sound learning, his high standards should never be forgotten. He never condescended to a popular utterance, yet no scholar of our age has had more far-reaching influence. As the editor of *The English Historical Review* he was the trusted guide of all his contributors, from his friend and admirer Maitland to the humblest beginner. His willingness to put his learning at the disposal of his fellow-students never failed, and some of them

[1] *The Times*, 3 Nov., 1939. See G. N. Clark in the *English Historical Review* for January, 1940, and C. C. J. Webb in the *Procedings* of the British Academy, vol. xxv.

remember how he gave them far more attention than they deserved. When I attended his lectures on diplomatic, I was generally his only auditor, and I recall how, after he had amused me with a little mordant gossip, he would proceed to his discourse with as much care and gravity as he would have regarded a class of twenty persons.

Others will write in due time of his published work, so ample in range, so beautiful and exact in texture. Here in Oxford his friends go back in mind to the years before 1914, when he was at the height of his powers, and his fame, among those who did not know him, acquired an almost legendary quality from his own seclusion. And in many places, as well as in Oxford, there are those who think of him with respect and gratitude, of the incisive criticism which chastised them, and the wisdom which steadied them, and the interest in whatever was good in them, making them happy with the happiness which a truly great scholar has the power to give.

CHAPTER X

JAMES F. WILLARD[1]

The sight of this volume brings back memories of the scholar who planned it, brooded over it, spent great labour on it and died five years before it appeared. James Field Willard died at the age of fifty-eight on 21 November, 1935. For nearly thirty years he had been head of the Department of History in the University of Colorado, established at Boulder under the Rockies. He had been attracted to medieval history at the universities of Pennsylvania and Wisconsin, and it was his chief delight to come to London, settle down in Bloomsbury, and work at the Public Record Office. He came as often as he could, though, in spite of some generous periods when he had leave of absence, not so often as he would have liked to come. In Boulder he built up a sound school of history and, as the *University of Colorado Historical Collections,* which he edited, remain to show, he did much to promote the study of local history. As time went on he gradually became one of the leading men among American medievalists, and notably in the Medieval Academy. The bulletin on *Progress of Medieval Studies in the United States of America,* which he began to edit in 1923, and which has been continued by his successor, Professor Harrison Thomson, is one of the most helpful bibliographies at the disposal of medieval scholars. Yet I like to think that he felt at home in England, where he had won instant recognition from those engaged in historical research. His particular interests brought him most closely in touch with Charles Johnson and G. C. Crump and the little group of experts who understood the mysteries of the medieval exchequer, and with Professor Tout and his circle at Manchester,

[1] An extract from a review in *History,* xxvi (1942) of *The English Government at Work, 1327-1336. Volume I: Central and Prerogative Administration.* Edited by James F. Willard and William A. Morris. The Mediaeval Academy of America, 1940.

where I first met him; but his sympathies were wide and his friendship was very generous. His first published work is an essay on *The Royal Authority and the Early English Universities*, a thesis presented to the Faculty of Philosophy of the university of Pennsylvania (Philadelphia, 1902), and among his last bits of work is a careful and detailed little paper, "Occupations of the Months in Medieval Calendars" (*Bodleian Quarterly Record*, vii, 1932, pp. 33–9). I well remember how this came to be written. He had come to a pause in his work at the Record Office, and felt the need for a change. Most men would have taken a holiday and wandered about England. Willard, with boyish eagerness, went to the Bodleian Library and spent a few happy weeks studying the miniatures in Psalters and Books of Hours.

Professor Willard was a strongly built man who had to endure frequent bouts of physical pain. He suffered with great courage and was one of the most cheerful men that I have ever met. Patient, hard-working and humble-minded, he sometimes misled others on a first acquaintance and gave the impression of being a laborious plodder. One young historian once carefully explained to him a well-known practice of, I think, the central exchequer, under the impression that he was enlightening this simple American about a custom peculiar to an English shire. Certainly Willard did not indulge in speculation. His object was the understanding of complicated facts, and his refusal to be hurried could stir feelings of affectionate impatience in his friends. But he had a searching, lucid and incisive mind, and very little of his work will ever need to be done again. He isolated detail, so far as he did isolate detail, in the manner of the scientist, not because he regarded detail as an end in itself; and few men have ever obtained so wide and firm a grasp of the working of medieval administration in England, whether central or local. The outcome of his prolonged investigations was his definitive book, published by the Medieval Academy of America in the year before he died, on parliamentary taxes on personal property, 1290–1334. This book has the appropriate sub-title, "A Study in Medieval English Financial Administration". And it was while he was working on this subject that he planned the co-operative enterprise whose first volume is the occasion of this tribute to his memory.

CHAPTER XI

HISTORY LESSONS AND THE LEAGUE[1]

In the "London Letter" of the *Manchester Guardian*, in the course of a statement on the programme of the League of Nations Union, it was recently mentioned that "another interesting scheme is the preparation of text-books in which for the first time the international value of history will be put before the young. This work will be done in co-operation with the leaders of the teachers' organizations. This is a plucky enterprise. The current history books, as everyone knows, are the chief instrument of nationalist propaganda". The suggestion will be received by teachers of history with very mixed feelings. The scheme, as stated, is vague yet full of contentious implications. It is confined, we may presume, to a series of text-books for use in British schools. But what is meant by the international value of history? What teachers' organizations are to co-operate, who are their leaders, and what qualifications do they possess? Is it true that the current history books are instruments of propaganda? What sort of nationalism do they teach? Is it so pernicious as to justify their ejection in the interests of rival propaganda? How does the Union propose to substitute its text-books for those now used in British schools? These questions require the most serious consideration, and until they are answered historical teachers, however ardent believers in the League of Nations they may be, should refuse to commit themselves to support of the scheme.

Clearly there can be no objection to national history as such. Even if, in spite of Lord Robert Cecil's repeated warnings, the League of Nations became a super-State, the sense of more intimate understanding with which we regard our own history as compared with the history of other lands would be

[1] From the *Manchester Guardian*, 12 March, 1921.

as fitting as it is inevitable. The ordinary man can no more feel objectively about his own country than he can read Gray's "Elegy" with the detachment with which he can read, let us say, Lamartine's "La Cloche du Village". And no one who feels about his country and its history as Gray, Blake, Keats, Meredith, Hardy feel about them is in the least danger of taking a Philistine's view of other countries and their history. By nationalist propaganda the critics, of course, mean teaching of a blatantly insular or selfishly imperialistic type. The suggestion that our text-books—defective though they doubtless are—have transmitted teaching of this kind is ridiculous. The most popular books have been written by scholars who have reputations to maintain. They have their limitations, which are revealed, as the books are used, to the intelligent teacher; but no teacher worthy of the name could find any difficulty in adjusting the contents to any point of view from which he chose to teach.

The League of Nations Union would be more justified in pointing out that the international aspects of history are not always treated clearly and intelligently. The study of foreign history both in British and in American schools has made striking advances during the last twenty-five years, and after the events of the last seven years the text-books in any case need revision. But the worst way to effect an improvement would be the way of organized propaganda. Propaganda would be immoral, because it would imply that historical teaching should be subordinated to external considerations. It would be unwise, because it would interfere with the natural response of all intelligent teachers to the tendencies of their time. Historians, as Dean Inge has remarked with a good deal of truth, are natural snobs. They are only too apt to accept what has happened as a step forward, simply because it has happened. They often forget Lord Morley's remark about the frequency of the *pis aller* in history. This responsiveness, however, has its good side. It facilitates the passage of ideas. Not so very long ago our historical text-books entirely failed to show how the British Empire grew and how its growth was related to the history of our foreign policy. The defect was remedied, not by the energy of any Imperial associations, which would have been quite incompetent for the task, but by Sir John Seeley and his disciples. Similarly, not the Navy League but Mahan's books on sea-power and the scholarship of the men who run the Navy Records Society have woven the exploits of the British navy into the texture of our history. Teachers of history and the writers of text-books can safely listen to the scholar, and be indifferent to the causes which originally prompted him so long as he bases his conclusions on a patient study of the facts; they will turn a deaf ear to him if they suspect him of selecting his evidence in support of a theory; they will actively resist him if he tries to advance a political cause, however noble, while professing to give impartial instruction about the past.

The historical literature of modern Germany is full of apposite examples of the distinction between legitimate and illegitimate theorising on history. When Haüsser, Sybel, and Droysen left Ranke's seminar they had all been impressed with the idea that public opinion was going wrong on the subject of the nature and the influence of the French Revolution. In other words, they were satisfied as historical students that there was less of a breach in continuity than was usually supposed. The result was a series of remarkable books on French and Prussian history. No doubt they were tendentious, but they expounded ideas quite honestly and legitimately acquired —ideas which have to be reckoned with as the ideas of Taine, Acton, or Aulard must be reckoned with. But we reach a more dangerous stage with the generalization of another German scholar of repute, Maurenbrecher, who wrote: "Revolution is a break with the historical traditions of a people, and no good can ever come of it." This view imposes a moral judgment upon history which would make a large part of history a breach with itself. The splendid historical aptitude of German scholars was too often given to the service of the German State in the form of specious generalizations of this kind. Nothing is easier than the depression, or even the elimination, of portions of history when history is written in the interests of a political dogma.

If we turn to the United States, where for a long time scholarship was much less informed or balanced and patriotic history much more blatantly taught in the schools than was the case in Germany, we may find in the activity of the American Historical Association a valuable lesson in the art of exercising the right sort of influence. The effective intervention of the American Association began about 1890. At that time historical writing and historical teaching were haphazard. There was no common purpose, no sense of proportion, small regard for impartiality. Little or no teaching was given in foreign history, and in many places the children either became little Jingoes or developed a violent distaste for the history of their country. The standard histories, upon which the text-books relied, neglected the most important aspects of the American past. The Association saw that it must organize a systematic revision of the evidence. It was not content with committees and conferences on the teaching of history in schools and universities. It appointed an Historical Manuscripts Commission, which since 1896 has issued a series of valuable reports and printed several volumes of original papers. In 1900 the first report of a Public Archives Commission appeared, describing the contents of the various State and Federal archives. All the while the Association has, through its meetings and reported proceedings, encouraged the scholars who were rewriting the history of the United States to make their influence felt. One group tried to exorcise the evil spirit of prejudice by showing how the history of the American people, and especially of the extension to the Pacific of the State system, was full of value for the comparative study of economic and social development. Another group set to work on the causes of the American Revolution. They broke the hard shell of provincial conceit. The results of all this activity can be seen in the revised text-books and the wider and more intelligent syllabuses of the American schools.

One can well understand the gesture of impatience with which historical teaching in English schools, and especially in primary schools, is frequently dismissed. But changes are more rapid than we are apt to think, and the fit instruments for effecting them, particularly our own historical associations, are now in being. It is permissible to point out that the League of Nations Union was not first in the field. The scientific study of international relations and of what Freeman called comparative politics is well known in this country, and has not been without influence upon the text-books. Even the conceptions of world-unity—from that still flowing fount St. Augustine's "City of God" onwards—have received careful attention. One of the earliest fruits of the agitation which ultimately developed into the proposals for a League of Nations was Mr. L. S. Woolf's admirable book on "International Government" (1916), which is essentially a piece of history as well as a forecast of future possibilities, and may safely be left to exercise its own influence. It is only a question of time before those aspects of history which are dear to the League of Nations Union receive adequate recognition. If the text-books lag a little behind the teachers, it is not altogether a bad thing. Historical writing is not a branch of modern politics, and must be allowed to take its time.

CHAPTER XII

HISTORICAL STUDY IN OXFORD[1]

In coming together this afternoon we all have one thought in common. We think of the teacher who was so suddenly taken from us, and, in our gratitude for all that he did, of the things which we had hoped that he would do. Everything else seems insignificant in the presence of these memories. I do not wish to intrude upon them. Elsewhere I have tried to say something of what I feel and believe you to feel about the work and influence of Mr. Davis. Some of you can claim a closer, a more constant companionship with him than I can; and this very fact encourages me to make upon you the claim which dwells in my own acquaintance with him. I also was his pupil, his colleague, his friend. Our future association together will have this common bond to strengthen it, to give us confidence as we face the work ahead of us, and to atone, I trust, in some measure for my own weakness. We share the inspiration of a fine example.

The appointment of Mr. Davis as Regius Professor in one respect marked an epoch in the history of his chair. He had behind him a long and distinguished period of service as a college tutor. None of his predecessors had been so intimately concerned with the teacher's daily task. He succeeded a great scholar who has always made the welfare of the Oxford School of History one of the first interests in his life, and within the school itself he found at work tendencies, largely the outcome of his own influence, which were full of promise of still closer and more systematic co-operation between the teachers of history. You know in how fine a spirit of companionship, yet with what deliberate and detached impartiality, Mr. Davis did his work. His successor, although he is returning to a second home and to many friends, must depend, if he has anything

[1] Inaugural lecture at Oxford, 8 February, 1929 (Clarendon Press, 1929).

helpful to contribute, upon experience acquired elsewhere. Yet I do not wish to exaggerate the significance of the change. Mr. Davis himself came back to Oxford after four years in Manchester, and my own coming is not an isolated fact, but an incident in a wider movement, in which two vigorous schools of history have been brought more closely together. When Freeman died, his books were bought and presented to the Owens College, and since that time the Freeman Library has been a centre for historical work in Manchester. I began to study history among these books, and after four years in Balliol, I returned to them; to them and to the others which were being gathered about the Althorp collection in the John Rylands Library. But, in Manchester as in Oxford, the teachers were more than the books. In Manchester I had two great teachers, both of them Balliol men, both Fellows of Pembroke, both masters in the study of English history. In Oxford I found three men as unlike each other as they were united in their power to inspire—the late Master of Balliol, Dr. Reginald Lane Poole, and Professor York Powell. And later, while the same two masters held me there, I came under new influences here, in the friendly guidance of Sir Charles Firth and Sir Paul Vinogradoff. I owe a twofold allegiance.

One's thoughts naturally linger over the Oxford History School as it was thirty years ago, and the changes which have since occurred. It was a genial, spacious period in the life of the school, when we read in the traditions of Ranke and Stubbs and were pleasantly excited by the latest work from the hand of Maitland. We had tutors of generous mind, undisturbed by any resounding movements in the historical world, yet keenly interested in what was going on, and eager to tell us about the best work. I seem to remember that Heinrich Zimmer's essay on the Celtic Church caused a brief sensation in some quarters. Of that notable band, Mr. Armstrong, Mr. Owen Edwards, Mr. Fletcher, Mr. Hassall, Mr. Hutton, Mr. Arthur Johnson, Mr. Oman (as he then was), and Mr. A. L. Smith were at the height of their vigour. Mr. Lodge had recently gone, Mr. Medley was just going,

Mr. Fisher and Mr. Grant Robertson had arrived, Mr. Barker and Mr. Davis were arriving. Behind them the quiet penetrating influence of York Powell and W. P. Ker was at work. If we meditate on the force of character and the variety of intellectual interests which lived in this group of men, we realize how much England, no less than Oxford, owed and still owes to them. They gave coherence to the School of History as the home of humane study and the training ground of administrators, politicians, men of letters, journalists. Some of them, notably Mr. Armstrong and Mr. Fisher, gave a powerful direction to learning, while the belief, which they all shared, in historical study as a serious discipline and as the revelation of a world with wide horizons, has kept the men whom they trained fresh and productive. We have entered upon a more strenuous time, when schools of history are less isolated, when here and everywhere the opportunities for congenial employment and serviceable leisure are not frequent. We sometimes tend to look backwards and forwards in perplexity, to move uncertainly between humane and professional views of history, not seeing how they are to be reconciled. We can still learn much from the more serene certainties of our predecessors. We can always remember, for example, that it is better for our pupils to have read Macaulay and Stubbs and Freeman and Froude before they learn all about the things in which these famous historians are said to err.

The history taught in those days was firmly rooted in medieval studies. Stubbs's *Constitutional History* was finished in 1878, the year in which William Bright published his *Chapters of early English Church History* and Haddan the last volume of *Councils and Ecclesiastical Documents*. The last volume of Freeman's *Norman Conquest* appeared in 1879, his *William Rufus* came in 1882. Vigfusson and York Powell's *Corpus Poeticum Boreale* belongs to 1883, Dr. Poole's *Illustrations of Medieval Thought* to 1884. In the 'nineties we had J. H. Round's early work, Charles Plummer's *Bede* and *Anglo-Saxon Chronicle*, Rashdall's *Universities*, W. P. Ker's *Epic and Romance*, A. G. Little's *Grey Friars in Oxford*. The work of Henry Bradley and W. H. Stevenson, which was to have such fruitful results through its influence on younger men, had begun. And this brief list omits the earlier work of Maitland, Seebohm, Vinogradoff, and Mary Bateson, work which Oxford cannot claim. While the school of history was taking the form with which we are familiar, it was provided with new material for reflection and study. Indeed, if we remember that the traditions beginning with Maine and Bryce and T. H. Green were combined with those of Stubbs and Freeman and Froude, the Oxford of thirty years ago would seem to have been the natural home of those more philosophical studies of our national life in which the influences of history, jurisprudence, and political thought are combined. The great work done in Oxford during the previous half century suggested a history of England, or a series of studies, in which the various academic traditions would help to elucidate the development of modern English society since the Reformation. The publication of the *Clarke Papers* by Sir Charles Firth, on the one hand, and of Professor Dicey's *Law and Public Opinion*, on the other, seemed in different ways to invite work in this direction. But the wind bloweth as it listeth. The influence of a great teacher or scholar, of a Savigny or Ranke, a Renan or Fustel de Coulanges, penetrates far and wide, and so it has been with the great Oxford teachers, but a home of learning rarely keeps an identical spirit for more than a generation. The old work, if it is continued, is more often than not continued elsewhere. Two busy publicists have laid the foundations of the history of modern local government. A Frenchman has given us the philosophical history of England in the nineteenth century. The successor of Maine and Stubbs in Oxford was a Russian; but he was the successor of so many other people as well, his range was almost too wide, his outlook too cosmopolitan, to allow his influence to be focused quite successfully. Yet in those last lectures of Vinogradoff, delivered in America, I am not sure that we cannot trace the effects of his long residence in England and Oxford and hear a kind of prophecy of the work which Oxford may do. Difficult, powerful, suffused with dusky light, they bring to bear upon the political and legal tendencies of to-day the historical method which is required for the study of a Year Book or a roll of Parliament. If contemporary history can be submitted to this treatment, so can the history of England in the days of the Stuarts and Hanoverians.

Historical scholarship in Oxford during the last thirty years has revealed a variety of individual taste rather than the unity of an academic tradition. The work of Sir Charles Firth, Sir Charles Oman's big book on the Peninsular War, Mr. Armstrong's *Charles V*, Mr. Fisher's Napoleonic studies, Mr. Stevenson's edition of Asser, Mr. Davis's *Regesta*, the series edited by Sir Paul Vinogradoff, the activity in colonial, economic, and American history, could not be brought within the terms of a single description. It is worthy of note that, with the exception of Sir Charles Oman's book, the long sustained works written in Oxford have lain rather outside the range of our political interests and have not come from scholars who are mainly preoccupied by the demands of the schools. Professor Holdsworth's *History of English Law*, Dr. Carlyle's *Medieval Political Theory in the West*, and the noble edition of the letters of Erasmus by which the President of Corpus recalls us to the spacious learning of an earlier age, are all in the wider Oxford tradition, but, while they touch, they do not belong to the school of history. Yet they are as significant of the historical movement in Oxford as is the variety of work produced within the school. Here, as elsewhere, we are in the middle of a gradual adjustment of the outlook, implied by the demands of a busy tutorial system, to other points of view. A process of this kind is in its earlier stages inevitably hesitating and unsteady. It involves a deepening no less than a widening of interests. Our knowledge not only comes under the inspiring influence of scholars who are applying the historical method to related subjects of study, it also is challenged, within as well as without its own range, by the revelation of unexplored archives. Prevailing tendencies are naturally arrested by the vision of new opportunity and more exacting claims. One interest gets in the way of another or curiosity finds vent in a monograph. We take a long time to settle down. I imagine that the great influence of York Powell, already a hero in our academic legends, was both the most stimulating and the most disturbing factor in this movement. Like Vinogradoff, but with a lighter and more detached play of ideas, he seemed to be aware of everything that was being said in all languages. But I must pay my tribute to the steadier guidance of Sir Charles Firth and Dr. Poole. The little band of Oxford teachers who are doing such fruitful work upon the history of England and of English foreign policy during the century after the Restoration know better than I can how much we owe to Sir Charles Firth, and our debt is but part of the obligation of students of history and literature throughout the English-speaking world. Of Dr. Poole's place in the development of historical studies I can speak with more knowledge. He was early in the field, and while the influence of his work has always been considerable, its significance is only now being realized. His was pioneer work, appealing at first to scholars with special interests, such as the late Dr. Rashdall, Professor Clement Webb, and Dr. Carlyle; but, as we become more familiar with the movements of continental learning, the importance of work like his for the interpretation of medieval society is made increasingly clear. Even if this were not the case, Dr. Poole's patient and faithful dealing with many young people who were beginning to write history will never be forgotten. To pass the ordeal of his editorship of the *English Historical Review* was a disciplinary experience for which they cannot be too thankful.

There has been a wider, more obvious movement, during the past generation, in which Oxford can take a legitimate pride. I refer to the work done by Oxford men outside the University. Through these men the Oxford History School has played a large part in the development of English academic life and in the renaissance of historical study. Moreover, some of the most valuable results of the influence of Oxford scholars have been reached through co-operation with them. The movement has been made possible by and has reacted upon several developments—the rise of new universities, the organization of the historical school in the University of London, the publications directed by the Deputy Keeper of the Public Records, the co-operation in a kind of historical fellowship between historical scholars and the learned assistant Keepers in the Public Record Office, the opportunity for service offered by the *Dictionary of National Biography*, the *Victoria County Histories*, and the Historical Manuscripts Commission. Some of our best-known historians learned their craft while working for these publications. They were compelled to explore the contents of our archives, central and local, private and ecclesiastical. Two or three of them, in the course of or after a discipline which opened new fields to them and formed new associations, were able to use their experience in the work of teaching. The movement thus made possible can be estimated from two points of view, as it found expression in new historical studies or in the creation of local schools of history. As an example of the former, I cannot do better than give the revolution in the study of local history and remind you of the contrast between this study as it was thirty years ago and as it is today. The way to the right appreciation of local history was pointed out many years ago by Freeman and J. R. Green, and before the end of last century Round, Maitland, Miss Bateson, Vinogradoff, and others had written some of their epoch-making studies in the interpretation of national in the light of local history. But since then this method of interpretation has spread far and wide; it has made wide breaches in the defences of our local antiquarian societies; and Oxford men have taken a large part in the good work. Professor Tait's little classic on Lancashire and Manchester, for example, Mr. Salter's and Canon Foster's illuminating researches into the history of Oxford and Lincolnshire, and Dr. Craster's contributions to Northumbrian history have helped to give us new standards. We are gradually being given an authoritative survey of England and English society in the eleventh and twelfth centuries, and Oxford men have been to the fore in this work also. Others have done much—William Farrer, Canon Wilson of Carlisle, W. J. Corbett among the dead, the Dean of Wells, Mr. G. J. Turner, Professor Hamilton Thompson among the living. But, in the direct line of succession to Round, Tait, and W. H. Stevenson, Oxford can claim Mr. Stenton, who, standing out among a little group of other Oxford men, has, more than any one else, given a new impetus to the study of local history as the basis of the intimate understanding of social change.

Many other examples could be given. Professor Pollard's stimulating work upon the evolution of Parliament and Tudor politics has already led to developments in the study of the fifteenth and sixteenth centuries which must have surpassed even his expectations; and I am especially bound to mention the Franciscan studies for which, by example and precept, Dr. Little is responsible, and the school of thought founded by the late George Unwin and the massive labours of Professor Tout and his pupils upon administrative history. The mention of these names, particularly the names of Tout and Pollard, brings us to the other form of activity which has characterized the work of Oxford men outside the University. Both Mr. Tout and Mr. Pollard are identified with schools of history. Both began their work as scholars by extensive contributions to the *Dictionary of National Biography*. They are men of vision, of vigorous, distinctive and formidable personality, inspiring teachers, bold and successful administrators. Of Mr. Tout's achievement in Manchester I need not speak. Mr. Pollard saw what use could be made of the unique opportunities which London affords. He not only saw, he achieved, and the Institute of Historical Research, full of splendid promise, is his memorial.

In attempting this rough sketch of developments during the last thirty years, I have had a practical object. The work in all its variety and vigour is going on about us. Oxford historians, as I have tried to show, have been largely responsible for it. We cannot afford to forget it in the consideration of our own academic problems. In particular, it raises the issue of the organization of advanced or post-graduate work, and I now wish to say something, not about the details of organization, but about the point of view from which, as it seems to me, we can most profitably approach the task of incorporating advanced study within the Oxford School of History. I am not concerned with regulations and details of policy, but with a general principle, an attitude of mind. I take the existing system and present tendencies for granted; the system in which perhaps one in fifty of the undergraduates is likely to proceed to serious advanced study. I accept the view that the main purpose of the Oxford school is to educate a man to understand modern civilization, that the study of history cannot be dissociated from concern with political and wider ethical problems. With more hesitation and in general terms, I will accept the statement that the training of the undergraduate is not primarily concerned with erudition. To sum the matter up in a few words, let us agree that the teaching of history is concerned with human activities which have and will continue to have real significance, with the spirit and intention even more than with the forms of conduct. For this very reason I suggest that we should avoid the assumption that the undergraduate and the post-graduate student of history belong to two distinct schools. The health of a school of history depends upon mutual appreciation by all its elements of the various ways in which the sense of values finds expression. For the quality which distinguishes the historical from other forms of the study of civilization is surely the fact that the historian is seeking for closer and ever closer approximation to an understanding of the past activities of mankind. The man who is going out from Oxford into public life has had in the history school a particular kind of discipline of which the realization of the search for historical truth is the essential basis. He recognizes in historical erudition a development as natural as his own, of the work which he has done, and of the interests which he himself proposes to turn to public use. On the other hand, the man who is driven by some inner compulsion to more advanced work, if he is to study with profit, must not regard himself as in a class apart; he should not feel that he is entering upon an adventure in a world hitherto entirely closed to him and leaving behind the citizenship which inspires his fellows. It should be impossible for a sixth year man to feel that he is not as much at home within the school as he was in his third year. This was not the way in the days when Balliol and Merton were founded for men proceeding to the degree of master in arts or theology. One of the reasons why personally I should welcome the division of the undergraduate course into two parts is that it would in some measure reduce the significance of the "Schools" as a kind of crisis. When a man has taken his schools, he has hardly begun to be an historian; when he takes his doctorate, he has presumably mastered the rudiments. And I should welcome the division still more because it would enable us to weld together in the third year of study the two kinds of experience which historical study can provide and which should not be separated, namely, the lessons suggested by the historical treatment of political science and by general historical developments, and the discipline implied in the careful intensive study of a special historical subject. Each kind is required by the student especially interested in the other, the future man of affairs learning that his understanding of the modern world must be grounded in a love of truth, the future historian learning that his researches must be inspired by a regard for the things which matter most. Further, just as we have our traditions of public service, so we should have our traditions of scholarship. An historian does not equip himself for his work by suddenly donning the vesture of erudition as a man in a laboratory puts on an overall. His decision should come earlier and his way be prepared for him. And lastly, the tendency to draw a sharp distinction between the undergraduate and the post-graduate student aggravates a real, if small, social problem. It encourages professionalism in research, the illogical idea that, because proficiency in advanced work (I do not say elaborate achievement) is generally regarded as a necessary qualification of the university teacher, anybody who engages in it can legitimately look forward to an academic career. A little body of the unemployed already exists, a tiny market in researches which may well grow to the dimensions of the market in the United States. The spirit of professionalism would in course of time play havoc with the ideal which is the best justification for encouraging and organizing advanced work. It substitutes the hope of a job for the inward compulsion, and makes it more difficult to pick out the man or woman who might profitably spend a few more years in study before settling down in life, the kind of person who is capable of doing fine literary work, or has a flair for investigation, the future writers of our best local history or collaborators in tasks which require a number of helpers. I have learned how much a group of people can get out of work, in itself rather dull or seeming to lead nowhere, when they are conscious of working towards a common goal. If one spirit prevails in all the elements of a school of history, there need be no limits to the interest in history. We want more country gentry and clergy, more ecclesiastical dignitaries, more school-masters and mistresses, more lawyers, more public servants, more persons of leisure to be engaged in historical work. Hence, while I hope to see a systematic organization of advanced study, within the scope of the existing statutes and regulations, I venture to suggest that we should avoid the tendency to regard advanced students as constituting a separate post-graduate school, and should strive for the strengthening of one school in which there is room for all kinds of interest, and a mutual respect for all kinds of good work. In such a school the post-graduate workers, whether we have trained them from the first or they have come to us from elsewhere, would regard themselves and be regarded as an integral element, and by contributing to its health, would be conscious of their unity with each other.

The craving for an interpretation of history is so deep-rooted that, unless we have a constructive outlook over the past, we are drawn either to mysticism or to cynicism. A man who feels no sense of correspondence between his experience and the object of his study, and has no idea of values proper to it, may become a dilettante, a lounger in the wake of philosophy or science. Philosophies of history have been more powerful than history, for, in one form or another, from the system of St. Augustine to those of Hegel and Karl Marx, they appeal to man's sense of destiny. Yet there can be no doubt that the study of history as history, and not as the instrument of a single conception or theory, has steadily undermined the influence of the philosophies of history, while it has given new force to what is enduring in them. Despite his great range of knowledge, I doubt if Spengler in the twentieth century will have as much influence as Joachim of Flora had in the thirteenth. History could not do this if it had no value of its own, if there were no correspondences which, in every age, are suggested by some dominating interest or need, but whose form is dictated by the material of history, not imposed upon it. Their form of expression changes with the growth of the knowledge which the interest in them brings about. To take a well-known example: interest in the problem of the regulation of trade by the state suggested that the economic history of England in the fourteenth and sixteenth century had peculiar significance; the policy of Edward III and of Elizabeth was studied, the history of their times made more coherent, and, so to speak, put into shape; but the conclusions ultimately reached about Edward III and the Merchant Adventurers were very different indeed from the first impressions—the shape changed. The material has a controlling interest in the expression of our sense of correspondence although this latter itself changes with our own needs and interests. When Voltaire undertook to show that modern history can be made as interesting as ancient history, he was influenced by a strong belief in the value of modern culture as a means of self-expression. His ideal was civil and religious liberty in an ordered, humane, polished world, and he studied the developments of history from this point of view. Its value to him lay there. In the nineteenth century, history was studied from the point of view of the national state, and, within this conception, of political liberty or political strength, as the case might be. Hence the profound investigations into the nature of law, the growth of political forms, the types of statecraft, the development of foreign policy. Modifying these interests was the influence of geological and biological investigation, the influence which provoked York Powell's epigram that Lyall and Darwin were the chief modern historians. The study of history could no longer be confined to a few kinds of human activity, for the conventional framework of human life had been shattered.

The war seemed to dislocate all our outlook on life. It has loosened many old allegiances, while it has given an impetus to the interest in history, and this at a time when the marvellous development in the physical sciences has brought still more fundamental conceptions in question. Confidence in these is shaken, while we are hesitating again about the idea of sovereignty and the meaning of the state. All kinds of interests, suggesting new values, are playing upon or with history. Corresponding to the romantic movement of a century ago, though very different in its metallic certainties, is the movement for which the Germans have already found the name, "historische Belletristik", the application to history of psychological analysis in a finished literary form. Many people, uncertain of the old values and dispirited by an ever accumulating mass of intractable material, find something positive and interesting in this. But the constructive impulse cannot be checked. The sense of order, the faculty of judgement will assert themselves. They are asserting themselves before our eyes, and I believe that the immediate concerted attack upon the innumerable records of world history since 1914 will be regarded in the future as one of the finest achievements in historical scholarship. It would not have been possible thirty years ago. The energy which can face a task like this will not fail to express itself elsewhere. For this expression of energy is part of a general constructive idealism which gives new meaning to history. Two or three years ago an eminent German historian, in the last work of his life, urged that if the danger of "positivism" and the attendant danger of romanticism are to be avoided, the study of history must have a constructive purpose, a criterion of judgement; and, perhaps naturally, he argued that the historian should test the movements of history by their value as contributions to the fabric of national life.[1] The worth of the criterion depends upon the idea of a healthy national life, and for my part I believe that our historians will find themselves drawn to a wider outlook. I am disposed to think that

[1] George v. Below, *Die italienische Kaiserpolitik des deutschen Mittelalters*, 1927, pp. 13-19.

the constructive idea will be the search for the forces which have confirmed in mankind the sense of fair dealing and mutual understanding. It will be a search for equity. I do not mean to suggest that the sense of equity is prevalent, still less that the interpretations of historical development with which we are familiar were beside the mark. What I would suggest is that, in a constantly narrowing world, the old constructive impulses, such as the sense of race, of nationalism, of class, or the organization of the State on the basis of force, have become so incompatible with each other that we cannot take them as our guide without reducing ourselves to the scepticism from which these same impulses, when they were fresh and young, rescued our forefathers. Even the conception of political liberty in a democratic community can no longer satisfy us if we do not merge it in a wider outlook. And in this wider outlook the dominant conception is the need of mutual understanding and equitable behaviour between man and man, nation and nation, race and race. If this be so, the study of history will be pursued under the influence of the larger conceptions, not as a duty, but as a matter of course. How the material of history will respond, how it will shape itself to dictate our historical judgements, is known only to history itself. The persons who go about urging us to revise our teaching of history in the light of the League of Nations do not appear to realize that, in so far as they are historians and are not trying to force historical study into the service of politics, they are not controlling, and cannot control, the stream of thought, but are, like bits of wood, being carried along by it. At present only the widest and most tentative generalizations are possible. If equity is to be the criterion, historical judgements will be fundamental and ethical indeed —wanton cruelty and destructiveness, for example, will be condemned—but they will not be narrow, for they will involve a patient consideration of circumstance, of the personal factor, of contemporary ideas. In tracing the relations between individual, social, and national rights, the history of law and of associations will have to be comprehended; the history of the Church will acquire new meaning; and the significance of the old conception of justice as righteousness will be appreciated.

If historians are sometimes slow to acknowledge the stimulus of constructive ideas it is because they would not have us forget that the study of history has its own method or discipline. History has no disciplinary or independent value if it is used with an easy and indifferent familiarity to point a moral and adorn a tale. Whatever our object, it must be taken seriously. We must learn how history is written and how to distinguish the good from the bad work. The effort required to trace correctly the course of a development or to take the measure of an historical character is as great as the effort required to comprehend the value of the result or achievement—a truth which is overlooked by those who teach that the only value of history is in its applications. We cannot in the long run separate the lessons from the discipline of historical study, and it is as absurd to attempt psychological analysis or ethical judgements without an appreciation of the facts and of the evidence for the facts as it would be to make a delicate scientific experiment in a moving motor-lorry. At this point one is sure to be reminded of the personal or subjective element in the observer. Here I can only offer a brief confession of faith. Clio is a goddess to be venerated, not a suitable victim of marriage by capture. She is not to be bullied in a mood of boisterous pessimism nor caressed in smug complacency. She has no high priests, and flees from the pontifically-minded. She has, it is true, her heavy-laden veterans, but if we are not of the calibre of a Mommsen or an Acton, we shall do well to travel light in her service, avoid equipment which is too burdensome for us, and, keeping our eyes open and our tools sharp, trust first and foremost in her and in our own integrity of purpose. She will not respond to pompous service nor pour her gifts into ready-made receptacles. She has no use for professional tricks and artifices, and belongs to no school. But patience, thoroughness, fidelity, and honest intelligence she will welcome, transforming their efforts "as fire converts to fire the thing it burns". There is then no Subjective and Objective; they disappear, with Synthesis and Analysis,

Dry-as-dust and Anti-dry-as-dust and all the other idols of the market-place, like Milton's Apollo, "with hollow shreik the steep of Delphos leaving".

Just as the prevailing interests of an age offer a way of approach to history and reveal some of its hidden shapes, so the true scholar finds strength and insight in reliance upon the things which mean most to him. They are the incentives to disinterested service and safeguards against alien enticements. I do not refer to set opinions or prejudices, which the true scholar will set on one side, but to the traditions, the varying associations of memory, sight, and sound in whose company we are most conscious of inward freedom and satisfaction. I imagine that most of us are aware of these incalculable aids to reflection,

> of affinities
> In objects where no brotherhood exists
> To passive minds.

It may be some overmastering idea, or some kinds of poetry or music, in contact with which, with all its associations, we find the unfettered energy to see more clearly into the mysteries of our task. If a man does not possess the advantages of cosmopolitan or of great civic traditions, he frequently finds the source of his strength in the associations of a countryside, his native place or made his own by adoption, where every name and line and colour evoke mysterious memories and associations, which, for all he knows, may be as nearly related to the object of his study, as much a part of history, as the documents which he has to use. All that is best in him and most real to him is bound up with them; and if he does not constantly turn to them, as to old loyalties, his strength is abated, and his vision grows dim. "If I forget thee, O Jerusalem, may my right hand forget her cunning."

The student of history may allow himself to be influenced by the ideas and moods of his time, or he may be repelled by them. He can welcome the guidance of his deepest self, but he may also distrust it. One thing he cannot avoid: he must begin somewhere; and, if he is honest with himself and means business, he will find himself, somehow or other, in a subject. When one considers the various motives and external compulsions which may drive a man to a particular subject, it would be foolish to suggest that there is anything inevitable about his decision. I know of no process by which a man and his theme come to be brought together with unerring fitness. Yet, sooner or later, a harmony is reached, and, to repeat, if the student is honest with himself, he will find his powers engaged in something suitable.

I was brought up in a tradition of medieval studies, and I have no intention of deserting it. I make no extravagant or exclusive claims on behalf of this tradition, although I think that earnest attention to medieval history is the best preparation for the specialist in any field of later history, not because it offers a picturesque invitation to the dormant historical faculty, but by reason of its austere disciplinary value and its penetrating over-present influence upon our modern life. I am not sure that since the war the nearness of the Middle Ages has not been more apparent. The outlook of Dante is in some ways more natural to us than the outlook of Hobbes. But, quite apart from the mental and spiritual results of recent events, there is no doubt that during the last generation the medieval world has become much more real and intelligible to us. For one thing, the setting of medieval history is different to-day. It is one thing to reveal the vast stretches of time during which human life was struggling to order itself before Rome was founded, to reduce the thousand years of the medieval societies to a mere episode in the history of mankind; it is another to fill in the background. It is one thing to insist upon the continuity of history and the organic treatment of the development of national institutions; it is another to trace the influences which played upon the medieval world, and the persistent survivals of medieval habits of life and outlook into later centuries. Thirty years ago we were familiar enough with the former processes of scholarship, and I should be the last to underestimate their significance. Sir Francis Palgrave's wise preface to his *History of Normandy and England,* written in 1851, and much in Guizot's fine work, and Freeman's teaching, and the spirit as well as most of the letter of Stubbs, are as true to-day as they were then. But the scholarship of the last forty or fifty years has gradually given life and meaning to principles, and bridged the gap between the historical imagination and historical truth. We are prepared to find a greater variety in medieval life, to see medieval society as we see our own, more as self-conscious, constructive, receptive, complex, less as the half-awake creature of habit. We can regard the Middle Ages more in the manner of Tocqueville, not so much in the manner of Maine. The change in the setting has led to a revision of the contents.

Take, for example, the development of Byzantine studies. For about eight hundred years the Eastern Empire was not merely the chief Christian state in the world; it was the only state comparable to Persia, and later to the Caliphate, able to profit on equal terms by intercourse with them. While by its existence it protected the western communities, it was a clearing-house in which they could become acquainted with the treasures of the East. So far from being a moribund society of decadent voluptuaries and half-imbecile theologians, it was the greatest, most active and most enduring political organism that the world has yet seen, giving for centuries that opportunity for living which we associate with the spacious but transitory peace of Augustus or Hadrian. The recognition of all this has been the result of the scholarship of the last half-century, so that with some exaggeration we tend now to give to the Empire the sort of significance in the development of the West as we give to Venice in the story of medieval trade or to Glasgow in the life of the Scottish Highlands. The indirect results of restatements of this kind are even more important. We realize that medieval peoples could be taken out of themselves. Their absorption in their own beliefs and customs, their efforts to reconcile the teaching of Christian missionaries with their own traditions, were disturbed by visions of material and artistic splendour and influenced by fresh movements of the mind. They became more sophisticated and in course of time creative. And in adopting this point of view we are led on to find new values in activities of the schools, of men of letters, of the workshops, which were at one time regarded as somewhat remote from the normal course of medieval political life.

All the same, we shall never cease to argue about the meaning and the value of things in the Middle Ages. Amidst so much that seems familiar to us, there is something which escapes us, and which we feel must always escape us. This aloofness is felt most in that central period—the Middle Ages proper—which passes into a more friendly age in the middle of the fourteenth century. Just when they are most expressive, they are most withdrawn, and as it were most indifferent to us. It was a wonderful, but to us it appears as an uncomfortable, time. I should be more at ease listening to Dr. Johnson for an hour than sitting in the classroom of Aquinas. I once heard a well-known novelist say, at the end of a paper on Dante, that if the poet were to enter the room, he would go out of it. This perhaps was excessive, but I at any rate should withdraw into a corner. What is it that draws us to such an age, quite apart from the lessons which can be derived from it? Why should a man be more thrilled by the Paris of Abelard than by the Paris of Molière, more moved by the career of Simon de Montfort than by the exploits of Nelson? Shepherds have kept their sheep in all ages: why am I stirred so deeply because I can trace the very sheepwalks of the monks of Furness? Why is there a remote, yet strangely familiar, music about the names of places—Beverley, Gainsborough, Thrapston, Tewkesbury—a music in which it is impossible to distinguish the call of authentic English speech from the echoes of a hundred insistent associations? This is more than an obstinate survival of the splendid, if ignorant, excitement of the romantic movement. It is unprovoked, with no heat or enthusiasm driving us beside ourselves. It grows with knowledge, as the familiar becomes more accessible, and the remote more sharply defined in its aloofness from us. It is the sense of the past which comes to us from the Middle Ages as it came to the young American in Henry James's story, as he wandered about his eighteenth-century house in London—the sense of a "conscious past, recognising no less than recognisable". The place was a museum, "but a museum of held reverberations". So long as we are conscious of these "held reverberations", history will continue to entice us. So long as their mystery endures, and it will always endure, the past will continue to escape us.

CHAPTER XIII

THE COLLECTION AND CRITICISM OF ORIGINAL TEXTS[1]

Nearly all the present tendencies in the study of the Middle Ages are forms of one fruitful interest—the collection and criticism of original texts. It would be easy to discuss a number of subjects with which medievalists are especially preoccupied, and to say that these represent the trend of present learning. There is, for example, administrative history. There is the scattered work, which as it increases is gradually finding a unity of its own, upon the development of medieval thought and learning, revealed by scores of forgotten theologians, canonists, preachers and moralists. There is the investigation, of which the work of Konrad Burdach and his school is a fine example, into the relations between chancery practice, political and ecclesiastical propaganda and the art of writing: the work which shows how poets and dreamers, humanists and political thinkers made themselves felt by way of the notarial art.[2] There is the analysis of economic forces, the growth of credit, the use of instruments of exchange, the elaborate social expedients devised to meet the dangers of shipping and overseas trade, the effects of papal finance, the interplay of money payments and payments in kind. All these express tendencies in modern scholarship, and other examples could be given from the history of art and literature. It is possible to go further and to deduce from these tendencies some broad generalizations about the reactions of the modern or contemporary mind against traditional methods of regarding history. Yet, for every man or woman who is influenced by reactions of

[1] A paper read before the Medieval Section of the Anglo-American Historical Conference, London, on 16 July, 1931. Printed in *History*, April, 1932.

[2] See the *Burdach-Bibliographie*, 1880-1930, presented by Burdach's friends and pupils (Berlin, 1930), 47 pages.

this kind, there is always another man or woman who is not. Beyond all these, and underlying all the work most characteristic of our time, is the interest in texts.[1] When historical students get together they tend to talk about texts and the problems suggested by the study of texts: where are they, what is happening to the manuscripts, what provision should be made for their safe-keeping, how ought we to edit them, what is the bearing of the unpublished upon the published texts, is the record or the literary text the more valuable? and so on. The old subjects of discussion tend to be left to debating societies, college essays and examination papers.

It would be foolish to suggest that the interest in texts is a new phenomenon. A noble tradition lies behind the greatest enterprises: behind the work of the Berlin Commission, for example, or of the French school at Rome, the publications of our English Record Office, and of our societies, such as the revived Pipe Roll Society or the Canterbury and York Society or our best local societies. Joint enterprise in the collection and edition of texts began in the sixteenth century, when Flacius Illyricus organized his history of the Church[2] and Archbishop Parker gathered Elizabethan scholars about him. The work of the Benedictines of St. Maur and the Bollandists[3] is in one form or another still as active as it ever was. The inspiration of our English work on records came over a century ago. Yet to-day the preoccupation with texts is more widespread, continuous and anxious than it has ever been. It produces our most fruitful work. Also, it carries with it dangers of its own.

However continuous our traditions may be, the study of texts has naturally produced work so fresh or authoritative that it provides criteria for the testing of other labours, and

[1] An extreme instance is the discussion, into which psychological considerations enter, about the problems involved in the translation of early medieval texts, *e.g.*, the exact meaning of such words as *nobilis* and *ingenuus*. The latest contribution is Philipp Heck, *Uebersetzungsprobleme im frühen Mittelalter* (Tübingen, Mohr, 1931).

[2] For the work of Flacius Illyricus (d. 1575) and the *Centuriators* of Magdeburg, see P. Polman in the *Revue d'histoire ecclésiastique*, Jan., 1931, xxvii 27-73.

[3] H. Delehaye *L'oeuvre des Bollandistes*, 1615-1915 (Brussels, 1920).

throws light upon the needs and tendencies of recent scholarship. Some of us are old enough to realize, as young scholars cannot, how important some of Horace Round's studies of charters were, and Maitland's edition of the *Memoranda* of the parliament of 1305 in the Rolls Series, and the line of approach suggested in Professor Chadwick's books. Or, to take a different field of study, we know how our outlook upon medieval thought and feeling as, so to speak, organic parts— even functions—of social life was cleared by the writings of Denifle, Gaston Paris, Paul Meyer—and, in our own time, of Mandonnet, Bédier and Duhem. Work of a rather different kind has affected us by its finality. It is so clear-cut and authoritative that it satisfies us. The writings of Paul Fournier and Ch.-V. Langlois in France affect one in this way, or of Professor Haskins in the United States, or of Dr. R. L. Poole in this country. Some books, again, though not quite so original as Round's nor so definite as the writings which I have just mentioned, carry us into a wider world because of their range and ground and a penetrating quality in them. They are big and new, yet in the tradition. The books of H. C. Lea in the last generation were of this kind, and among more recent work I should include that of Bresslau and Dopsch, Tout's Administrative Studies, Davidssohn's Florence, Olivier Martin's history of the customs of Paris, Grabmann's history of and studies in scholastic method. All of it is directed by a critical appreciation of texts.

Now a characteristic quality in the best work upon texts is its regard for the relation between the texts and general history. Here is our criterion. Texts are no longer flung out as the useful Hearne flung them out. The days of the indiscriminate *thesaurus* or *anecdota* or *miscellanea* are gone. We demand an intelligent purpose, even though it can only be revealed in an index. The subject indexes of the *Curia Regis Rolls* of John and the *Close Rolls* of Henry III show their compilers arranging references as contributions to history. However minute or detached the work may be, we expect it to be intelligently related to existing knowledge, to be presented in such a way that we can grasp its significance. "Books, Medicines and

Laws," wrote Thomas Powell in the reign of James I, "should never be publisht or prescribed, but as Obiters, to meet with Evils imminent; ever applyed and ever complying with the present necessitie." This counsel of perfection was directed against the scribblers of Powell's own time. I wonder what he would have thought of our modern publishers. His standard was an austere one, but it remains true that the study of history for its own sake can only be reconciled with the necessity for order and direction in historical work if we have a definite purpose in our writing. We can only fall into step with the tendencies of modern scholarship if we have this ideal before us.

I would distinguish two tendencies suggested by the best work. The first is the growing appreciation of the bearing of various kinds of texts upon each other. The second is the desire to appropriate for our new learning the literary tradition.

Intense and fruitful appreciation has grown with a more intelligent realization of the unity of knowledge. I refer not to the unity of history, as it was taught by Arnold and Freeman, for this fundamental truth becomes more obvious every year. I refer to the unity of our knowledge of history at any particular time, to the cross sections which we can cut through the whole body of contemporary evidence. Just as the study in combination of sculptural design, illuminated manuscripts, jewel work and literary symbolism has broken new ground in the history of art and architecture, so the comparative study of texts, brought together with an intelligent (not a capricious) disregard of the limits set by artificial divisions, is throwing fresh light upon medieval society. It does not matter whether the text directly under consideration is a Pipe Roll or a passage in Geoffrey of Monmouth, a charter or a lecture in moral theology. The relevant texts, required in elucidation, may be few or many, but the alert appreciation of them must be there. We profit from a competent editor of an Assize Roll just as we profit from, let us say, M. Lot's analysis of the prose Lancelot. That distinguished scholar, Paul Kehr, has published this year a short study of the reign of the Emperor Henry III. It is a model in its kind. Starting with the highly technical scholarship inherited from Sickel and Bresslau, he has, by the study of Henry's scattered *diplomata*, reconstructed the history of the reign and conveyed a more convincing impression of its significance than one could get from volumes of narrative history whose writers did not possess his critical imagination.[1]

One cause of the success of good work is that, consciously or unconsciously, our masters have recaptured the secret of the old scholars. The appreciation of texts is a much higher thing than the reliance on technique. The great scholars of the seventeenth century were *familiar* with manuscripts. They were forced to use them, and they acquired an everyday knowledge of them. However casually or incompletely, they lived among them. As the chief texts became more accessible in print, later scholars lost this sense of familiarity. Either they relied entirely upon printed sources, neglecting to refresh their minds and verify their arguments by turning to the manuscripts, or, as editors, they were not thorough. Two results followed. In the first place, many learned arguments were vitiated at the source. A good example is the mystification which the excellent Riley introduced into his editions of the later chronicals of St. Albans.[2] In the second place, they failed to see how much they could learn by using different kinds of manuscripts together. The beneficial effect of familiarity is far-reaching. Nowadays we are learning to reconstruct medieval libraries, to see the connexion between what a man wrote and what he read, to realize the bearing of one kind of evidence upon another. A pretty example is the reconstruction, begun by Hauréau and completed by Professor Haskins, of the story of Echard the baker, the heretic of Rheims.[3]

The other tendency which I noted is the desire to appropriate the literary tradition in historical writing for the service and conveyance of the new learning. While we learn from the old scholars, we must beware of the chaos of the old learning.

[1] P. Kehr, "Vierkapitel aus der Geschichte Kaiser Heinrichs III", off-print from the *Abhandlungen der Preussischen Akademie der Wissenschaften*, 1930: Phil.-hist. Klasse, no. 3 (Berlin, 1931), 61 pages.

[2] I owed this example to Mr. V. H. Galbraith, who has since published a study of the subject: see *The English Historical Review*, January, 1932.

[3] C. H. Haskins, *Studies in Mediaeval Culture* (Oxford, 1929), pp. 245-55.

Historiographers are now agreed, I think, that the literary tradition in historical writing was a reaction, inspired by the success of the great writers of contemporary history, against the dangers of unregulated learning. The result was a gap which, in spite of the work of great men like Giesebrecht and Stubbs, has not yet been closed. The literary generalization is still cut off from the sources of truth. Even the learned find it hard, as they try to write continuous and reasoned history, to avoid the false emphasis which the enlightened scholar who lives among texts and manuscripts, and who keeps his head, so easily avoids. A pupil of the late Maurice Prou has recently described how Prou used to insist upon the dangers latent in current generalizations about medieval society. He made his pupils master Championnière's treatise on the ownership of running waters, with its refrain, "fief and jurisdiction have nothing in common," for he saw in this book the right kind of emphasis, due to the right appreciation of texts.[1] Now—whether Prou was right or not in this particular case—it seems clear to me that the reconciliation between the literary tradition and true learning, which is one of the needs of our day, must be sought in this spirit. We should all strive after generalizations and we should strive to phrase them as clearly as we can, as well and as simply as we can; but we must refuse with passionate resolution to impose our generalizations upon the facts, and we must set no limits to the possibility of the relevant fact. May I give you a slight illustration? Miss Hope Allen has written a masterly and definitive book upon Richard Rolle.[2] Naturally enough she has at times allowed her imagination to wander. After showing that Rolle was probably born at Thornton-le-dale, near Pickering, she gives a little picture of the place:

> The stream comes curving down into the village from the high wooded moors which closely overhang the settlement at the back. The appearance of the stream and moors can hardly

[1] George Tessier's inaugural lecture as Prou's successor in the chair of diplomatic in the École des Chartes, 8 Dec., 1930, printed in the *Bibliothèque de l'École des Chartes*, xci, 242-63: especially p. 245.

[2] See review in *History*, xiv, 251 (Oct., 1929).

have changed since Rolle's time, and a short distance up the course of the stream on the moor is a very primitive small church.

Then a local historian comes along in the person of Mr. R. W. Jeffrey. He takes the passage which I have cited, and pulls it to pieces.

> The present stream through the village is known to have had a different course in 1729, and altered again since 1830. The high woods closely overhanging Thornton were planted in 1797, and "the moors beyond" were in Rolle's time covered in parts with oak, and not, as when Miss Allen wrote, with heather and bracken. Nor can anyone who knows describe the "primitive small church" as "on the moor," for it is nothing of the kind, nor is there any reason to think that since the Norman Conquest Ellerburne Church was on the moor. It certainly was not in Rolle's day, when the village had its bleaching mill and was surrounded by cultivated land.[1]

As this illustration shows, it is not easy to bridge the gap between the facts and literary tradition. But we must make the bridge, or rather we must close the gap, if only in self-defence. Periodically, the big narrative study, comprising new aspects of history as they are revealed to us, is required to focus all the work done; to show us how best to arrange the co-operative work which is becoming more and more essential, but which, if history is to be human, must always be kept in its place. The great human books clear the air and we need more of them.

We need them all the more because, while the specialists are at work, the philosophical writers lose patience. They are students of life, and they want to know and to tell others what all the new history means. Here we come upon a tendency, to

---

[1] R. W. Jeffery, *Thornton-le-Dale* (Wakefield, 1931), p. 26. Needless to say, I give this illustration simply to show the kind of error to which all of us are liable, and with no desire to reflect upon Miss Allen's book. On the more important point at issue, whether Rolle was or was not born at Thornton-le-Dale, she has a great deal to say for herself. See her letter in the *Times Literary Supplement* for 10 September, 1931.

which I have not yet alluded and which is only incidentally concerned with the criticism of texts. It is especially active in Germany, where, just as we see a political cleavage between the parties which wish to make the best of the new democracy and the parties which wish to impose a government more consonant, they think, with Teutonic traditions, so we see a cleavage between the steady-going scholars and the seekers after historical categories. I am thinking of students of history who are restive under the discipline of the academic tradition. It is true, of course, that German scholars have always had to spend a good deal of time in breaking up each other's categories, as Professor Dopsch of Vienna is now carefully engaged in breaking up the categories of the economic historians. Yet anyone who observes the trend of German writing to-day knows that the historical category is especially attractive to the new generation which has seen the old Germany shattered and wishes to find moral support in history. In the preface to his interesting book, *Sacrum Imperium* (Munich, 1929), Alois Dempf tells how, after trying to understand the processes of medieval thought by a study of its characteristic form, the *Summa*, he felt the need for something more realistic and humane. And so he seeks in his new book to appropriate the whole range of medieval experience. He does not realize that the *Summa* disappointed him just because he did not let it lead him into the recesses of medieval life. He does not wish to be led, he wishes to explain. And the quick and ready way to explain is to impose categories of one's own upon the material collected by others. But, if one is not very careful, one can so easily forget that every coherent happening, every social unit, has its own form and *tempo*. When all is said and done, what we call history is more than the texts and monuments which lead us to it, more than our rules of method, and our generalizations. It gives rather than receives. Otherwise it is mere flotsam and jetsam.[1]

[1] For this "theory of history", see Mr. R. G. Collingwood's penetrating remarks on the work of the late Professor Bury in the *English Historical Review*, July, 1931, xlvi, 461-5. One of the most stimulating discussions known to me is to be found in the second volume of Professor A. E. Taylor's *Faith of a Moralist* (1929).

To sum up; underlying all the present activity we can see an ardent preoccupation with texts. The best work teaches us that, through the study of texts and familiarity with manuscripts, we can realize the unity of knowledge. The various sources throw light upon each other, and so they strengthen our perception of the activities and relations of medieval life. But if we are to express this, and to avoid hasty and artificial generalization, we must appropriate the great narrative tradition, and adapt it to the service of our complicated material. I have spoken, not of literary achievement, but of desire, as one of the tendencies of our time. Perhaps even this is too bold a claim. At any rate, I am quite sure of the need. Dangers beset the new historical learning: the arid professionalism which regards history as made for the historian, the absence of vision which can make historical research "a pedantic chase after the insignificant," the generalizations which disregard the inner significances of human experience and do violence to history. We must find a way of escape.

CHAPTER XIV

MODERN METHODS OF MEDIEVAL RESEARCH[1]

If our discussion this afternoon is to be helpful, the scope of our subject must be clearly defined. I take it that, by "Modern Methods in Medieval Historical Research," we mean especially the various kinds of co-operative study which have grown so rapidly in recent years. If this be so, let me say at once, on behalf, I am sure, of my fellow medievalists no less than myself, that we do not imply, by the limitation of our subject, any lack of faith in the supreme value of private and individual investigation. The best and finest work must always be done in solitude. It may not be the most useful work, if by this we mean the work whose every-day value as an aid to study is most apparent, but it must always be the finest work, the most satisfying and the most stimulating. "Have salt in yourselves and be at peace one with another" is a golden rule in scholarship as well as in life; and in the world of scholarship I am not sure that it is not better to have salt in oneself, to have something clear and definite to do with the intention and ability to do it, than to be at peace one with another. But this afternoon we are mainly concerned with the second part of the precept, with that positive kind of peace which we call co-operation. If you say that co-operators can and do fight as bitterly as isolated persons do, I can only reply that I am assuming, for the sake of our subject, that they will not.

Three tendencies seem to me to be at work in the modern developments of co-operative study:

(a) The relations between master and pupil in advanced work;

[1] A short paper read before the Royal Historical Society on 8 December, 1932, to open a discussion. Printed in the *Transactions* of the Society, Fourth Series, xvi (1933), 45-53.

(b) The necessity, felt in local, national and international societies, of some attempt to give order and purpose to the active, but somewhat chaotic, interest in historical work;

(c) The realization that some kinds of work, although it might perhaps best be done by individuals, is never likely to be done save in co-operation.

These tendencies, of course, cut across each other, and I distinguish them for the sake of clarity.

A teacher who has the responsible duty of advising graduate students is inevitably forced to consider the existing range of studies, his own particular opportunities for effective guidance and the possibilities of future publication. He must not get in the way of others, he must concentrate his own energies so far as he can, and he must keep clear of subjects which, however useful they may be as exercises, could not help the promotion of learning. Hence, during the last twenty years or so, our graduate schools have tended—slowly and uneasily, no doubt, but quite definitely—to adjust their work to the work and views of others, and to find stimulus in the interests of particular teachers. In this, as in other movements, Manchester led the way. Perhaps I may give one example. In three or four years the British Academy will, I hope, publish the texts and kindred documents relating to the judicial proceedings and settlements under the Dictum of Kenilworth.[1] The book will be based upon co-ordinated work done by Manchester graduates who were working for their Ph.D. or M.A. degrees. Most of you, I imagine, could give other examples. I can think of two or three which illustrate the links which can be forged between our Universities and the local historical and record societies—of a chronicle published in the Surrey Archaeological Collections, a little cartulary published by the Yorkshire Archaeological Society, town records now being edited for the Oxfordshire Record Society—all of them work done for higher degrees. And more of it is on the way. Graduate work of this kind can also be directed to help big

[1] Nothing came of this, but work upon an edition of the rolls, with a view to publication, has recently been resumed.

enterprises, such as the volumes of the Pipe Roll Society or the scheme for continuing Haddan and Stubbs.

The concentration of purpose in local, national and international activities presents more difficult problems. Here self-restraint is almost as important as a spirit of adventure. Here also it is sometimes wiser to use resources in order to help particular scholars than to promote co-operative work. We have only to think of the fine thing which Professor Tait made, during many years, of the Chetham Society, of Mr. Salter's work for the Oxford Historical Society, of Mr. Jenkinson's searching and skilful use of the Surrey Record Society, of Canon Foster at Lincoln, Mr. G. H. Fowler at Bedford, Miss Wake at Northampton, each with his or her Record Society, or of Mrs. Stenton's quiet, but forceful control of the Pipe Roll Society, Dr. Rose Graham's steady influence in the Canterbury and York Society, Dr. Little's in the Society of Franciscan Studies and the great work of the Provost of University College and Professor Stenton for the English Place Name Society; or, in international enterprises, of some of the projects sponsored by the Union Académique, such as Dr. Lowe's *corpus* of early Western manuscripts. In all these cases corporate revenues have been wisely and economically spent because someone who knew exactly what could and should be done has been there to give a lead and encouraged to give it, or take it. The drawback is that such people do not live for ever. Even if the Pipe Rolls are not thought deserving of publication beyond, let us say, the reign of Edward II, Mrs. Stenton would be required to maintain her interest and her faculties unimpaired until she was somewhere about 160 years of age.[1] And what, in the meanwhile, of the Memoranda Rolls which become increasingly the more important record? It is just here, in the planning of simple, straightforward schemes for a long period that the difficulties of co-operation are so great. Our healthy Record Societies may lapse into amateurish ineffectiveness, the Pipe Roll and Canterbury and York Societies may collapse, as for a time even the wonderful Society of the Bollandists collapsed or as the old Pipe Roll Society, the old English

[1] In this paragraph I retain the words as I spoke them twenty-two years ago.

Historical Society, and many more have collapsed. The difficulty of finding the right people to carry on a tradition is complicated by the difficulty of finance, a difficulty before which even the Record Commission, and the Historical Manuscripts Commission, have had to bow, and to which, if it had not been for the courage and pertinacity of Dr. William Page, the Victoria County Histories would have been forced to surrender. And there are other difficulties. Anyone who has had to attend meetings of the Union Académique and the International Historical Committee is soon made alive to the delicate diplomacy required in the maintenance of their important undertakings. It is essential that our younger scholars, as they come along, should be encouraged to understand these activities—local, national and international—and to take their share of responsibility for them, although their interest may involve the loss of some personal freedom; for the historians of the future will depend on the results of these activities just as our predecessors depended upon Ducange and the Benedictines, Muratori and Mansi, Dugdale, Prynne, Madox, Wilkins, Rymer and the rest.

I have already trespassed on the third section of my subject, the co-operation of scholars for the execution of some definite task which is an end in itself. I hope that, in the discussion which is to follow, spokesmen may be found for the new *Concilia* and the new Ducange. The new Ducange, though an international enterprise, is, so far as it is concerned with English records and writers, a distinct task with a definite aim, needing English help. And I hope that we shall hear something about the policy of the English Place Name Society.

And now what about our Society, with its house, its library, its considerable funds? How is it related to all these recent developments? What is it going to do about them? I can merely ask the question, for it would be unwise to attempt an answer until we had paid far more attention to the problem than we have. Moreover, it is a question which concerns modern no less than medieval history.

There is, however, no harm in elaborating the question.

In the first place, can members of the Royal Historical Society, as individuals, do something to aid some at least of the enterprises? I venture to mention one, a child of the International Historical Committee, which I think many of our members might assist. This, modestly described as an inquiry on the revision of Chronological Lists, has been entrusted to a Special Commission. It is really a project for a new and up-to-date *Trésor de Chronologie*, a modern revision of the great work done by the Benedictines and, since them, in the big volume compiled by Mas Latrie. Recently, at the request of our British National Committee, Mr. Charles Johnson and I suggested to the Commission the lines which a British contribution to the project might follow.[1] We consider that, in a big general chronological work, British contributions should comprise

- A. Lists of Kings, including the rulers of Saxon Kingdoms, Scotland and Wales, giving the important dates (birth, succession, death), notes on relationships to previous rulers, marriages, children, long absences from the Kingdom and so forth.
- B. Lists of Bishops, with family names, dates of election and consecration, death or translation.
- C. Lists of Earls and superior ranks to about A.D. 1600, and I would include the more important barons before 1300. These lists would include genealogical notes.
- D. Lists of Chancellors and Treasurers to A.D. 1700; of Principal Secretaries of State from Elizabeth's time and of Prime Minister's from Walpole's time.
- E. A geographical alphabet of ecclesiastical and civil Councils, with dates.
- F. The Saints' Days, including those of local saints, observed especially in Britain, and a list of local feasts and phrases, such as Relic Sunday and Plough Mon-

[1] The outcome was the *Handbook of British Chronology*, published by the Royal Historical Society in 1939. A new edition is being prepared (1954).

day, used in England. Also notes on the various kinds of year, the regnal year, as calculated in the Chancery and Exchequer, with the various usages of chronicles and records in beginning the year, dates of legal memory, terms, Scottish "quarter-days" and the like.

Most of the material is readily accessible, and, if a few people interested in or attracted by these matters would help, it should not be hard for us to see that the British section is worthy of such an important work, and worthy of our historical scholarship. Here I mention the suggestion both by way of invitation and as an illustration of the kind of help which Fellows of the Society may well be expected to give.

A second form of the general question which I am raising is the relation of this Society to other societies or organizations for historical study. We are naturally expected to take a leading place in the historical world. On particular occasions we give receptions or we co-operate in particular discussions, as for example, the committee on the relations between history and geography. But ought the Society to have a deliberate, permanent policy, by which it is prepared to stand, and to advance which it is prepared, if necessary, to modify its constitution or to depart from its traditions? For example, how should we stand in relation to the various record societies? I rule out the historical and archaeological societies in their general, more discursive activities, for I imagine that, from this point of view, their activities will be focused in the existing federations and possibly in the new British Records Association. I am not thinking so much of the persons generally interested in local history, nor of the preservation of Records, but of the people actively concerned to promote the edition of records, whether purely local, or national (such as Feet of Fines and Assize Rolls), in their local manifestations. Would it be possible, if I may venture on a definite suggestion, to make our library, not only a centre, but *the* centre and home of local record publications, and to have it recognized as such by the Institute of Historical Research and other libraries outside the British Museum and some of the greater libraries? Could we become the centre for the student as distinct from the organizer and preserver of such records? As we are inclined to raise the qualifications required for election as a fellow of the Society, could we strengthen our position and enlarge our membership by erecting a class of Associates, some of whom would be drawn from the more active members of local record societies, and others from clergy, teachers and persons who were actively interested in historical study?

And, finally, to take a third form or mode of my general question, what about the distribution of our funds between our more casual semi-social activities and the most important and valuable part of all our work, our publications? Or, to put the question in a different and perhaps a better way, how can we best relate our normal traditional activities, particularly as publishers, to the learned world about us? Is it possible to make our Society the national and generally accepted vehicle or patron of certain kinds of historical work, such as the "major research enterprises" of the Medieval Academy of America? A great deal has been done already, largely through the efforts and devotion of Dr. Hubert Hall and through the Publication Committee of the Council which supervises his work; but is it possible to offer both of them the best of all tributes, by trying to organize and generalize their work; to enlarge it and diffuse the generous spirit of their labours through a permanent, carefully wrought plan of action?

These are very important issues. I cannot pretend to deal with them here, and I do not think that any of us at this stage should do more than take sympathetic cognisance of them. If you are eagerly inclined, restrain your ardour and work for careful inquiry. If you feel hostile, ask yourselves if it is not right to see what is in them. I can only in all deference, but with real earnestness, submit them to you as worthy of the Society's consideration.

CHAPTER XV

THE LIMITS OF EFFECTIVE CO-OPERATION IN THE SYNTHESIS OF HISTORY[1]

The important words in this phrase are *effective* and *synthesis*. What are the limits of *effective* co-operation in the *synthesis* of history? The ideas implied by these significant words are to be connected. They must not be considered apart from each other. When we are speaking of co-operation we have in mind the *synthesis* of history, and when we are speaking of history we must not forget that co-operation is to be *effective*. We are not concerned to-day with co-operation, however effective, in some special historical task, such as the elucidation of place-names or an edition of the medieval translations of Aristotle; nor are we concerned with co-operative history, however synthetic, which is not effective. Finally, the words before us turn our thoughts to the border-line, the *limitations*, of our subject. We are asked to consider especially how far effective co-operation can go, and we need only consider effective co-operation in so far as it helps us to understand the nature of these limitations. We are to be like a child, holding on tightly to its father's hand, as it looks down over the edge of a dangerous cliff.

Co-operation implies deliberate effort by each of the co-operators. This is an important point, for it distinguishes our subject from the historical synthesis which depends upon the work of others, yet is the deliberate act of only one man. Gibbon's *Decline and Fall* is, I suppose, the most effective piece of historical synthesis ever written, and it could not have been written without the work of hundreds of others who

[1] Printed in the *Bulletin* of the Institute of Historical Research for November, 1933 (vol. xi, pp. 75-9).

were, so to speak, unconscious co-operators with the author. The first deliberate effort of a group of historians to compile a synthesis of history was that made by the Centuriators of Magdeburg in 1554, under the direction of Flacius Illyricus. Their famous *Ecclesiastica Historia* was planned by Flacius, who joined four other scholars with him as a directorate of five. Two of these directors or *gubernatores* undertook the business part of the concern. Under the five were two *architectes* and seven *studiosi*. The syndicate was able to extend the scope of annalistic history by comprising within it some account of the developments of doctrine and of non-Christian religions. Moreover, they made it easier for later scholars, notably Baronius, to work over the same ground singlehanded. We get near the edge of our precipice if we compare their work with that of Gibbon.

The first and most obvious reflection suggested by this comparison is that the *Decline and Fall* is a real book, and the work of the Centuriators is not. We are immediately faced by the question; "Can an effective piece of synthetic history be written by a group of people?" Gibbon's work was the outcome of one powerful mind and is written in a uniform style. It has force and unity, and is readable. It lives, while the *Ecclesiastica Historia* is as dead as mutton. The Centuriators were remarkable people who did work of much consequence, but they did not write effective history. Suppose we take a fairer example to compare with Gibbon—the Cambridge Histories, Ancient, Indian, Medieval, Modern, Imperial. Many of us in this room have contributed to these Histories. With a secret preference for the chapters which we have written ourselves, we all find the big volumes incredibly useful. If we cannot find what we want, the bibliographies will generally put us on the right track to the discovery of it. We are made to realize the enormity and perplexity of our subject—a humbling process of great value—we read some of the contributions with pleasure and profit and others with profit, and we use them with frank unscrupulousness. But, if we compare the Histories with the *Decline and Fall*, can we say that they are a more effective effort in the synthesis of history? I doubt it. Lord Acton's own historical views and instincts give us some explanation of one's sense of doubt. First, it is only the barest outline that can be quite objective; secondly, the historian requires the honesty of mind which "throws itself into the mind of one's opponents", an impartiality which is not invertebrate, a style which represents the ideals of the writer and impresses by the inward intensity of which it is the symbol. These qualities may and often do appear in parts of a co-operative work, but they do not appear in the synthesis as a whole, or if by some miracle they do, the total effect is the effect conveyed by a kaleidoscope. There is no single far-reaching source of light which makes every detail significant, as luminous as the stonework in the High Street at Oxford on a clear evening in June.

We have looked down this cliff long enough here. A railing should be erected at this place. I hope that the Cambridge Histories will be brought up to date and re-issued every fifty years or so, for scholars and many others need them; but I hope also that they will not be regarded as a tentative exploration in a direction where there are further possibilities; for there are no further possibilities. The Histories can doubtless be improved, but only within the limits already imposed by their editors. They stand half-way between real history and the encyclopaedias. And to cut the whole matter short, all effective co-operation in the synthesis of history must be content to be a half-way house—it is none the less useful for that. Since the days of Gibbon the range of history which any single man or woman can hope to compass has narrowed very much. I doubt if any man, dealing with any period of European history or world history since the eleventh century, could write a really great book which covered more than fifty years, or, if he attempted a complete history of one country or one important aspect of social life, more than a century.[1] And, to do this well, he would require to have behind him the work of

[1] By a "complete history", I mean, of course, a history in the Gibbonian sense, based upon the available material, original, secondary and critical. I do not deny that suggestive, and important books even, on world history are within the capacity of some rare people. Whether books of this kind should be regarded as history is a debatable and arid question. I should prefer to call them essays about history.

others who had co-operated effectively in historical synthesis. Our historian would do his task all the better if he had himself taken part in co-operative work, or at least, like Charles Lea of Philadelphia, had adopted a preliminary co-operative system of his own. For, if the days of Gibbon have gone, the days of the free-lance who is unwilling to join others while he is writing his histories are numbered. The great men who carried on the work of the Maurists in France and organized the "Monumenta" in Germany chose the right way. Their history, written in solitude, with deep searchings of mind and spirit, was all the better because they were also taking the lead in big co-operative tasks. Any amount of co-operation in the synthesis of history remains to be done. How can it be made most effective?

Two criteria suggest themselves. Co-operative work should aim at saving time and at giving confidence. The fact that every historian worthy of the name must learn, as my old master Tout used to say, "to fetch and carry for himself", makes it all the more important that he should be saved unnecessary labour. More assistance of this kind can be found in bibliographies, topographical and biographical dictionaries, lists of bishops and abbots and officials, well-informed encyclopaedias compiled with a definite purpose, systematic and scholarly calendars of documents, authoritative genealogies, and trustworthy catalogues than in all the synthetic narratives put together. The Benedictines of the Maurist Congregation in the seventeenth century, in their various memoranda, pointed the right way once for all, and it is no exaggeration to say that nearly everything which is most worth doing in co-operative work goes back to their inspiration. What remains to be done should be done in the same tradition. I will give an example, taken from my own subject. We now possess hundreds of good catalogues of the manuscript collections in hundreds of libraries. These are scattered, have been published in various places and languages, and no scholar who is not an ardent specialist can keep track of them. Corrections of their contents abound in learned periodicals and specialized monographs. A few catalogues of the first importance, notably of the Cotton

MSS., have yet to be compiled. Yet it is quite time that some great effort was made to conflate all this work, to "pot" it in a few handy volumes with good indices and lists of *incipits*.[1] The modernists, I understand, feel a similar need with regard to state papers of all kinds.

The other criterion is confidence. This is largely a psychological matter. I would begin with the big libraries and the free access to aids to study—not to all the books in a subject, as at Harvard, but to aids to study, including the more important periodicals. I should like to see a little volume containing an agreed list of works, carefully arranged and explained, where the student could discover what is open to him in the great libraries of America and Britain. An authoritative book of this kind, frequently revised and reissued, would give confidence. It would be effective, synthetic, historical, have definite limits, and it would require much co-operation. It would be the *vade mecum* of the investigator. I should prefer to see no limitation in this book of subjects or periods—its scope would be its own limitation—and for this reason. Such a book should keep before the scholar's mind the whole range of history and remind him, as other co-operative work should remind him so far as it can, that there is a proportion, a scale of relative values, in historical matters. Nothing helps to give confidence more than the feeling that one is a member of a great society, that the isolation and sense of oppression which we all have to face at times are disciplinary means to a great end, that one is constantly being warned against the allurements of what has been called the biggest of all the sciences, the science of the things which are not worth knowing.

If the organizers of historical co-operation keep these guiding principles in mind and set up a strong fence on the edge of what I have called the precipice, I see no limit to the amount of effective co-operation. It would be unwise, I think, to lay much stress on synthesis, for all effective historical study, co-operative or not, makes for synthesis. And, if I have laid too much stress upon what, for want of a better word, I have

[1] I am told that this work is in hand.

called psychology, it is because I believe that, in the end, we are more likely to advance successfully by getting together to deal with particular needs as they arise than by planning ambitious schemes. The danger which lurks in ambitious schemes is the incalculable personal element. To put it bluntly, we can so easily let each other down. Hence I should prefer to begin at the other end, and make sure of mutual understanding and confidence between the co-operators before anything else.[1] In nine cases out of ten the brunt of the work will fall upon the few; it is the part of the many to organize so effectively that the few can go forward in their particular task without unnecessary anxiety.

[1] Professor Webster, urging that it will become increasingly possible to "pool" brains and historical imagination and to write really synthetic history, suggested that here I was giving counsel of despair. I did not intend to do this. I am sceptical about the truth of his prophecy, but I should also argue that, if it is fulfilled, it will be fulfilled by people who have "mutual understanding and confidence", and are thereby made bold enough to "pool" their knowledge, brains and imagination. I believe that Mr. Webster would agree.

CHAPTER XVI

A PRESIDENTIAL ADDRESS[1]

On previous occasions I have chosen as the subject of my address at the annual meeting of this Society a historical theme suggested by my studies. Three historical addresses, each of which involved careful preparation, are, I venture to think, as many as a President of the Society need feel it his duty to deliver. Yet I think that I should have inflicted a fourth upon the Society if some special considerations had not combined to divert me from what is certainly the safer, and is perhaps the more profitable course. Moreover, it so happens that the period of my presidency has been a time of significant development in the organization of historical study in this country. The history of this Society has been affected by the general movement. We have tried deliberately to adjust ourselves to it, and to take a leading part in it. I decided, therefore, to make my last appearance in the chair an occasion for a review of current developments and for some reflections upon them.

As we look round this room to-day and remember how it has looked on similar occasions in the last decade, we might well feel that, in an unstable world, the Royal Historical Society is one of the few fixed points. Old faces go, new faces come, slight changes can be traced in the faces which remain, but our procedure is the same, and the physical and mental atmosphere is the same. I imagine that, in its new quarters—so appropriately hallowed by dignified historical tradition, and so beautiful and dignified themselves—the Society will retain its own traditions of Victorian decorum, and sedate self-possession. As the years go by, the most obvious change in its life is one which, in its remorseless recurrence, is the most

---

[1] Delivered 11 February, 1937; printed in *Transactions* of the Royal Historical Society, Fourth Series, xx (1937), 1-12.

insistent of all testimonies to the unchanging nature of things. Year by year, death takes from us honourable, useful and learned men and women, almost as many as the new fellows who are elected to our Society. According to the Report presented four years ago, there were 888 Fellows of this Society; the Report presented to us to-day gives the number 915. During this time it has lost 84 Fellows through death. I am especially bound to recall the name of my predecessor, Sir Richard Lodge, who in his last years renewed his youth in the service of history. Then Sir Charles Firth, also a former President, has gone, nearly the last of a noble group of scholars, for the like of which we have to look back to the days of Madox and Tanner and Wanley. Among others who served this Society we remember Sir John Fortescue, President, Eleanor Lodge, J. E. Morris, C. W. Foster and Maude Clarke, whom I am privileged to number among the first and most brilliant of my pupils. Lord Fitzmaurice, Sir Frederick Pollock, T. Rice Holmes, Sir Robert Rait and J. F. Willard, a dear friend to many of us—all Honorary Vice-Presidents—have gone during the last four years. William Page, who has left the Victoria County Histories as his monument, audited our accounts from 1917 to 1928. Lady Burgclere, Sir George Cory, Sir Vincent Evans, F. C. Montague, F. S. Oliver, Cecil Headlam, D. C. Munro and that amazing polymath, J. K. Fotheringham, were Fellows of this Society. Sir Arthur C. Doughty, whose work as archivist in Ottawa marked an epoch in colonial history, was a corresponding member; as were those great European scholars, Émile Bourgeois, Henri Pirenne and Alfred Stern. The mere recital of these names helps us to realize the range and vitality of the learning represented by the Society. And we would also remember two other names of two warm friends of the Society, Sir Cato Worsfold, a Fellow, who served us so long and so ably as Honorary Solicitor, and Lady Prothero, who, though she was not in name one of us, retained to the last the eager interest in our affairs which she had shared so long with her husband, our greatest benefactor.

These recollections, some of which give us a link with the earlier days of the Society, almost with the age of Earl Russell himself, recall us to a sense of our continuous life in the midst of death. Yet, as I have suggested, the Society, with no forgetfulness of its past but, rather, in a spirit of service to its traditions, has found itself affected by the more self-conscious historical movement of our own day. During the last four years an older tendency towards orderliness and co-operation in the historical world seems to me to have become more rapid, and more carefully directed. We are aware of its possibilities. The activity of the Historical Association and the Anglo-American conferences arranged by the Institute of Historical Research have undoubtedly helped to hasten the process by breaking through old barriers and by awakening widespread interest in the problems of teaching and research. The British Academy, by giving countenance and financial support to the Place Name Society and other learned enterprises, has done a service which goes beyond the limits of its practical help. The steady and growing passage to and fro of students and teachers between the Universities, the British Museum, the Public Record Office and the Institute implies much more than the additions to knowledge which may be its result. Moreover, as the Universities take a more active share in the encouragement of advanced study and its teachers become better acquainted, by travel and personal friendships as well as by reading, with the movements of learning outside this country, the beginner is better able to feel at home in the wide world of learning than he was when I was young. He responds more quickly and naturally. Both as a teacher and as a student of history I am conscious of a change in the academic atmosphere and I imagine that the impulse towards co-ordination, which has of late years been so widely felt, owes much of its vigour to the influence of this change. On all sides historians are taking stock, improving their tools and making arrangements with each other. Field archaeology has become a widespread scientific adventure, and has ceased to be the desultory interest of an unco-ordinated band of specialists and amateurs. The new *Complete Peerage* is more than a safe work of reference; it is a sign of the victory of organized genealogical research over the doubtful antecedents which have hampered the subject for so long. Again, the formation of and response to the Council for the Preservation of Business Archives illustrates the wider and more confident interest in history taken by the business man no less than the alertness of our economic historians.

Three developments of major significance can be seen in the activities of the Institute of Historical Research, the rapid growth of the British Records Association and the part played by British scholars, through the British National Committee, in international historical enterprise. During the last four years the Institute has given a sharper edge to its policy and taken a lead in the adjustment of its work to the work of others. Its library policy has as its aim careful provision for the studies in which it specializes and helpful regard to the ways in which the Institute can co-operate with other libraries. Its great task of completing the Victoria County Histories has been organized with astonishing rapidity and, *inter alia*, has helped to focus the interest of Oxford and Cambridge in their own antiquity. The function of the Institute as a national clearing house is admirably performed by various publications in and supplementary to its Bulletin: the reports on the work of societies, the detailed description of the accessions to collections of manuscripts and on the migrations of manuscripts, the annual lists of theses completed and in progress, and the guide to the historical publications of the societies of England and Wales. I should like here to express the formal thanks of this Society for the helpful co-operation of the Institute with us in the preparation of our annual Bibliography, to which I shall refer later. If you look at Mr. Parsloe's introduction to the last issue of his Guide[1] you will see that he has agreed to provide us with material from the publications of non-historical societies (whose occasional historical papers are so easily overlooked) and has so arranged his own work in the Guide as to adjust it to our plan.

The British Records Association came into existence shortly before I took office. Its remarkable development is therefore as good an illustration as we could have of the cul-

[1] Bulletin: Supplement no. 7, November, 1936.

mination of tendencies in resolute and conscious effort. The Association has already succeeded in bringing together local record societies, libraries, county and municipal authorities, and even the custodians of private and ecclesiastical archives. The local repositories entitled to take charge of historical documents under the direction of the Master of the Rolls have been supplemented by a central clearing house in Lincoln's Inn where the Records Preservation Section has its office. At the same time the various Committees of the Association have been engaged in a survey and classification of archives of all kinds and in work on the regulations which affect the custody of local archives. The sense of unity and confidence which has resulted from these and other activities of the Association will undoubtedly strengthen the desire for a common policy and will encourage further effort in the collection, preservation, study and publication of historical documents.

The work of the British National Committee—one of many national committees which co-operate in carrying through the enterprises of the International Historical Congress and its various commissions—is not so easily appreciated. I can best illustrate its value by reminding you that, through its action, several international commissions have been able to enlist the support of our own Society, the Historical Association and the Institute of Historical Research. The British contribution to the commission concerned with teaching is made by the Historical Association. Our Society undertook the work required by the commission engaged in the compilation of chronological lists. The Institute has agreed to provide the information required by the commission on abbreviations. But we can receive as well as give; and I venture here to remind you of the International Bibliography to which English helpers contribute year by year, and of the useful articles, generally of a bibliographical nature, which appear from time to time in the Bulletin of the International Committee. The last issue, for example, is devoted to a preliminary world-list of historical reviews. These publications are not so well known in this country as they deserve to be.

In the course of this brief survey I have already had occasion to refer to the co-operation of this Society in the historical movements about us. It is time to speak more directly of our recent history.

You will, I am sure, forgive me if at this point I recall a discussion which we had here in December, 1932,[1] during the last year of Sir Richard Lodge's presidency. On that occasion I was speaking as a free lance, and could not even be certain that my suggestions had any practical value at all. Events have shown, however, that the conclusions which we reached during that discussion could find a place in our programme. May I read a few sentences?

1. "In the first place, can members of the Royal Historical Society, as individuals, do something to aid some at least of [current] enterprises? I venture to mention one, a child of the International Historical Committee."
2. "Ought the Society to have a deliberate, permanent policy, by which it is prepared to stand, and to advance which it is prepared, if necessary, to modify its constitution or to depart from its traditions?" I proceeded to suggest the reorganization of the Library and the creation of a class of Associates.
3. "What about the distribution of our funds between our more casual semi-social activities and the most important and valuable part of all our work, our publications?"

The subject of the discussion in December, 1932, was modern methods of studying medieval history, and it is important to remember that, in later consideration of the issues raised, the obligation of the Society to promote the study of all English history, whether medieval or modern, had also to be kept in mind. It was, in fact, kept in mind, and I am not sure that the result of our attempt to enforce the policy outlined in 1932 will not prove to be even more helpful to the students of modern than to the students of medieval history. Needless to say, this Society, except for purposes of convenience, does not recognize the distinction and admits no cleavage, other than

[1] See above, pp. 193-198.

that of convenience, between the periods into which our history is customarily divided.

It will be agreed, I think, that the Society is well on the way to the formulation of a "definite policy". The Council, in view of problems which would arise in the near future and of the general developments which I have tried to illustrate, gradually "cleared the decks", if you will allow a nautical metaphor. The constitution of Council and of its committees was revised; its procedure, by the circulation of minutes and careful memoranda and other expedients, was made more effective; it devised a pension scheme for its full-time paid officers; it examined the relation between the financial claims of the library, the publications and establishment, and instituted separate and accruing accounts for the two former; it was able to secure the services as honorary secretary of Professor Bellot, to whom the Council is already very greatly indebted. The two proposals made in 1932 have been adopted. We now have a library of English history, strengthened by most of the late Sir George Prothero's books, and specializing in the more general texts and in the publications of our local societies. And we have our class of Associates. Here, though we have made a good start, we have much to do. We are not satisfied by the present condition of either change. The Library should be used more and the class of Associates should be much larger. In my view, the best way to effect both aims is to link them together; and I suggest that this can be done if we enter into closer relations with the British Records Association, and with the graduate schools in our universities. Every society and interest affiliated with the Records Association and every teacher of advanced students should know about the facilities which our Library provides. I see no insuperable obstacle in the way of a formal concordat with the Association which would make our Library a centre of its historical work. We might, for example, offer facilities in return either for a small fee or for publications. We might even reduce the qualifications and subscriptions required from Associates and confine their privileges to the use of the library and the purchase of the *Transactions* at half-price.

What I want to make clear is this. When we overhauled the library and instituted the class of Associates we did not wish merely to make the former more useful to ourselves and the latter a kind of minor decoration. We wished to enter the arena, to widen our bounds and increase our usefulness as a party in the organization throughout this country of the facilities for historical study. We shall not do this if we think that we have completed our task and that further effort, even at "the expense of our traditions", is not required. There ought to be hundreds of Associates, coming to our meetings and using our books while they are in London, as so many local workers and university graduates now frequently are. If, as the Report presented to you to-day says, the Society is "the principal organization representing English historical scholarship", the Society must adjust itself to a changing world. I venture to commend this problem to the consideration of Council and of my successors.

The Camden Series of publications—and we should never allow ourselves to forget that we use the name of a great man who helped to open the way to the study of English history—the Camden Series, especially in these stringent days, gives an opportunity to competent scholars who desire to edit texts. Periodically our Publications Committee compiles a programme of future publications. We have some difficulty in maintaining a balance between the various periods of English history and should welcome expert advice or suggestions. As you are aware, the project of an independent series of volumes which will contain materials helpful to the student of history is now well advanced. This series, like our latest adventure, the annual bibliography of "writings in English history", is a real attempt to take a part, in a way consonant with our traditions, in the contemporary efforts to equip our historians and to save them from bewilderment as historical material grows or is made accessible. The Bibliography, which has long been needed, has been made possible by the Prothero bequest. This use of the Prothero fund, originally suggested by the Honorary Secretary, has been made effective by the prompt energy of our new officer, Mr. Milne. Indeed, the task of putting through, as well as of planning, our publications, never a light task, is becoming very heavy. How the Director, that most faithful friend and servant of the Society, Dr. Hubert Hall, manages to do all he does, is something of a mystery to me and I feel that something should be done to relieve him of part of the secretarial strain upon him. As our activities increase, as they should, the task of publishing is bound up more and more closely with the other work done by the Society. Some of our books, for example, are not presented to us from outside as finished or rather professedly finished works of art; they have to be planned and contrived within our walls, and I foresee in this direction developments which will involve closer co-operation and even more careful organization. It is natural and right that the Council should be asked, from time to time, to co-operate with other bodies by undertaking definite tasks. The volume on chronology, to which I referred by anticipation in 1932, is in some degree due to the initiation of the British National Committee, whose duty it was to provide an English contribution to the international scheme of one of the commissions of the International Historical Committee. Recently another commission has been formed for the study of the origins and development of assemblies of estates. I cannot imagine a better centre than this Society for the execution of this task. M. Coville has asked for critical bibliographies, including information about unprinted material. The Italian scholar, Professor Leicht, wants us to study, in contemporary literature and documents, the points of view, at different periods, about the legal rights of systems of estates and their relations with the sovereign power—a demand not unlike that made last summer by Mr. H. G. Richardson in the Anglo-American Conference. M. Olivier-Martin feels that we must have a chronological study of assemblies in the formative periods—here, again, he has been anticipated by Mr. Richardson and Dr. Sayles. Now personally I feel that here is a great opportunity for co-operative study and publication which this Society might well seize. We have among our Fellows nearly all the experts in the history of Parliament. We want, and they want, to get down to and to gather together the actual texts in exactly the ways suggested by the international commission. This is the second suggestion which I venture to make, this time to the Publications Committee. It would meet new contemporary needs and opportunities, and it is in the tradition of the great statesman who sponsored the foundation of the Society.

The foregoing considerations are suggested by circumstances which this Society cannot afford to disregard. To some of us, I know, they may be repugnant, for they seem to imply a more mechanical and professional attitude to the study of history than we like to adopt. Personally, I dislike professionalism. At the same time ours is a society which has to co-operate with other societies, and so long as we do not confuse the means with the ends, the instruments with the music, we have little to fear and something to gain by deliberate attention to problems of policy or organization. Indeed, our habits of social intercourse and meeting for the discussion of historical problems give us an advantage over other societies. We are more likely to remember the object of historical study and to give play to the impulses which cannot be defined by rules or directed by policy. Moreover, we can try to encourage a clear, simple, well-expressed presentation of historical truth with no temptation to stray from the evidence. The best answer to the cry for popular and literary history is to let people know what we are doing. The most effective way to meet the undiscriminating idea that, so long as a historical book is pleasant to read, it is as good as any other historical book, is to show, as clearly as possible, how we arrive at our conclusions, and why we think some things are right and others are wrong. In other words, those who know, or are most likely to know, should be asked to speak about their work. They cannot and should not be expected to waste their time by competing for popular favour, with all its caprices, but from such platforms as ours, they can properly be invited to explain the nature of the problems on which they are at work and either to draw conclusions or say why conclusions cannot yet be drawn. The Royal Historical Society can be the clearing-house for work of this kind, a meeting-place of scholars of all ages with those who are intelligently interested, and our *Transactions* can be the means of transmitting their contributions to the world. This does not imply that those who read papers here must have attained the age of fifty or that detailed erudition, because it is detailed, is to be banned. It means that we should give preference to the significant, from whatever quarter it may come. A man should not be encouraged to talk about his work unless he can say why he thinks it *is significant*, in other words unless he is a historian.

In conclusion, I wish to thank the Fellows, Associates and guests of this Society, for the unfailing kindness and indulgence which they have shown to me throughout the past four years. They have been very happy years. The duty has sometimes been onerous, but the companionship never. In Council and committees we have been informal and friendly, but businesslike, and united in the pursuit of a common aim—the well-being of the Society. I have formed friendships here which, I trust, will last as long as I live.

CHAPTER XVII

RECENT WORK ON THE ORIGIN OF THE ENGLISH PARLIAMENT[1]

It is happily unnecessary to interpret my subject as a critical study in bibliography. Mr. Lapsley has written about present-day tendencies in the investigation of English parliamentary history, and in December, 1937, in the *Bulletin of the International Committee,* Miss Helen Cam published a careful survey of recent literature. I propose this afternoon to concentrate upon the different ways of approach, which in some degree imply different attitudes to historical method, to the study of the subject. Some years ago M. Lousse urged the importance of taking a wider view than that which is implied in the rigid and accurate scholarship of contemporary research upon the origin of "estates" in medieval Europe. In England we do not much care to emphasize the differences between schools of historical thought. We have always distrusted them and I hope that we may long be free to distrust them. English history sometimes exasperates the European by its intractable indifference to "ideologies", and English historical study thrives and takes pleasure in this very circumstance. Yet, within a narrow range of ideas and against a spacious background of general agreement, the issue, even in England, is becoming clear between the scholars who wish to see every step clearly in the mist, and those who think more about clearing away the mist, and are prepared to take the steps for granted. Mr. Lapsley, in a recent review of Mr. Jolliffe's *Constitutional History,* has called attention to this difference of outlook. Other writers have been less urbane. Here is a sentence from a review of the late Miss Clarke's book on *Medieval*

[1] Address given at Zurich in the Eighth International Historical Congress (August, 1938) to the Commission Internationale pour l'Histoire des Assemblées d'Etats; published University of Louvain, 1939.

representation and consent: "It is the last infirmity of historical minds to give precision to primeval slime and form to what is void."

The reference is not to the palaeolithic age but to the century of Bracton, Hostiensis and St. Thomas Aquinas. The implication is that, even in the thirteenth century, no argument is safe unless it is deduced from clearcut isolated facts, that what we term circumstance, or tendency, or influence is as slippery and formless as mud. That issue should be joined in such a way within the classical tradition of English scholarship, on the central problems of the origins of parliament is very significant. For the classical tradition, represented in the last decades by Stubbs and Maitland, is solidly based on the conceptions of law and precedent. It has been immune against the infection of abstract theorising or teleological schemes of history. The issue does not lie there, between the abstract and concrete ideas and facts, but here, within the framework of law and precedent. It concerns the limits within which observation and deduction are permissible. It raises the question of interpretation: are we or are we not justified in discussing the problem of parliament in the light of any general apprehension—of intelligent vision rather than of ideas—of what England was like in the thirteenth century? Stubbs, I suppose, thought that we are justified; other scholars on the contrary appear to think that any such apprehension is an illusion, however carefully it may have been reached, and has, therefore, no validity in historical discussion.

Some of those who are most emphatic in their repudiation of the view that the early history of parliament should be studied in its relation to the nature of English society are influenced, I think, by their own ideas about English history. Their denial that we can find any trustworthy basis for discussion in the nature of English society, in reality starts from views that English society in the thirteenth century was very like French society. Their view is coloured by their conception of French society. This might be regarded as a "debating" point, and I do not wish to lay any stress upon it. It serves, however, to remind us that recent discussion of parliamentary origins has been greatly influenced by French scholarship and French historical method.

In the paper to which I have already referred, M. Lousse pointed out the widespread influence of the French historical schools. As one of those who felt it at an early age and have never ceased to profit by it, I should be the last to deny its healthy and clarifying effect upon English scholarship. If this were the proper occasion on which to enlarge on the theme of the influence of French upon English scholarship, I should like to avail myself of the opportunity. Yet there can be no doubt, I think, that one result of this influence has been a tendency to concentrate upon aspects of English life which were common to the West and are most familiar to French scholars; and also to interpret the more insular rather too rigidly in terms of the continental. Closely related to this influence, indeed an expression of it, has been the insistence upon what is now called administrative history. I say "what is called administrative history", because our most distinguished exponent of administrative history, the late Professor Tout, never, I think, attached to it the independent significance with which the term is now invested. The study of administration is part of the classic tradition. Spelman, Selden, Madox and other famous scholars relaid its foundations in the seventeenth century; English interest in it reaches back to the *Dialogus de Scaccario* and earlier still. Tout, availing himself of a hint given by a French scholar, was moved to rewrite two centuries of English history from this point of view, but he was far too sagacious and comprehensive a scholar to seek in the development of medieval institutions, in any specialized sense, an interpretation of English history, to give an unduly bureaucratic twist to classic interpretations. Lastly, the amazing wealth of our English records has had an almost hypnotic effect in recent years upon the minds of English students. Already disposed to find the answer to historical problems exactly here or exactly there they have felt that, if only all the mass of chancery, exchequer, and judicial records could be searched, everything would become clear.

We speak of recent work on parliament, but in fact the

new work began forty-five years ago, when in 1893 Maitland published the *Memoranda* of the Parliament of 1305. Maitland was the greatest master of descriptive analysis that we have ever had in England. As all his work shows—and particularly, I think, his chapter on *Ownership and possession* in the *History of English Law* (first edition 1895)—he had a deep distrust of clearcut explanations of legal and social developments. And, so far as I can see, the value of subsequent work on parliament lies, not in explanation, but in description; not in its flat denials but in its positive contributions to a survey of complicated life. As a result of this work we feel safer. We could not say now things which we said too glibly before we knew—or perhaps I should rather say felt—what the king's court and household and the relations between court and country were like and what they involved. Behind every entry on a plea roll, a liberate roll, a close roll, we know and feel that there was a complex of relations, emerging as naturally and freely as the various acts by means of which we became aware of this Congress, made arrangement for our tickets and accommodation, and then assembled in this room—acts which imply the conscious or unconscious share in our life for the time being of postal systems, shipping and railway companies, hotels and so on, as well as of the machinery of the Congress.

For example, when the king tells a petitioner, or a bishop writes to a friend that he will go into a certain matter at the time of the next parliament, we do not think of a strange and revolutionary experiment on a *tabula rasa,* but of a series of relations within a wider series of relations. We think of a coming concentration of activity within the king's court. And just because this was the case, I, at least, have never been able to see the gradual emergence of the parliamentary process, and the knights and burgesses, as active elements in it, as the outcome of clearcut administrative acts, like the invention of a new chancery writ, and, even if I could, I at least, should still wish to know why the administrative mind responded in these particular ways. In English public life parliament was rather like "that wonderful calculus of estates" in land which, in the words of Maitland, "is perhaps the most distinctive feature of English private law". And we may say of parliament as Maitland, giving precision, perhaps, to primeval slime, said of the doctrine of possession, by which estates in land were maintained—"at different times and in different measures every conceivable reason for protecting possession has been felt as a weighty argument and has had its influence upon rights and remedies. At first we find the several principles working together in harmonious concert; they will work together because as yet they are not sharply defined." History, in short, is the interplay of thought and action, and the sense of obscurity and vagueness which we may feel in our contemplation of any particular process during a particular period is due not to the fact that men did not know or care what other men were doing, but that their own acts and thoughts were dictated by such an incalculable variety of circumstances and motives.

We are not looking for needles in a haystack, but at a stack of needles, capable of different degrees of magnetism. Hence we seem to be driven back to the environment of parliament, and, for my part, I see no reason why we should object. For the work of this last half century has been quite as detailed and penetrating in its investigation of English society as in its search for parliamentary origins. Apart from his notorious connection with parliament, the knight of the shire is now much better known to us, so well known, indeed, that his appearance in parliament comes to be the most natural thing in the world. Historians have tried hard to discover when and how the "commons" became a significant or an essential element in parliament. I doubt very much if any answer can be given to such questions. Knights and burgesses might play a significant part without being essential; they might be essential and at the same time, insignificant. The important thing is that, during the century *c*. 1250 to 1350, the social and political character of a middle-class element was a fact. And the knight of the shire is the clearest expression of this fact. He was a knight of the shire: the one word "shire" is as important as—in some ways is more important than—the other word, "knight". Except possibly in Hungary, there was nothing like him in the rest of Europe. His gradual emergence reminds us of several interesting things, clearly visible, not vague, and certainly not abstractions of the mind.

The knights of the shire did not form a definite class; they were freemen, whose military character, though never lost or forgotten, was merged in a property qualification. Any country gentleman, of whomsoever he held his land, could be "distrained", forced to assume the dignity and obligations of knighthood if he possessed land of a certain annual value. A man who numbered freeholding peasants, even unfree tenants, among his kindred, might be or become a knight of the shire. The cadets of baronial houses might be knights of the shire. The knight might be the holder of a compact manorial estate which can be traced back to *Domesday Book*, but he as often as not held various parcels of land of various lords whom he might never see and to whom he owed rents and other dues which did nothing to shape his daily life; his daily life was passed in a social and administrative environment which in England we still term the life of the shire. The evidence of a great record, the Hundred Rolls, and of the vast body of private charters, shows that, in the heart of what is sometimes described as "manorial" England fifty per cent at least of the landholding population was free. The freeholder was not an exceptional figure in a compact manorial grouping of lords and villains. He was to be found wherever one turned. He disposed freely of his land, gathered and lost estates scattered in various places, had his own seal, engaged in litigation in the public courts, served on juries of all kinds, planned and built on his holdings, large or small, as he wished. Like everybody else, he was subject to manorial customs and feudal obligations, but customs and obligations were not a burden, they were incidents in his life, part of life's routine.

Now scholars talk sometimes as though this free element, of which the knights of the shire were the natural leaders, is a negligible factor in the development of English social and political history during the thirteenth century; it had administrative importance and in due course it was given political significance, but the development of parliament and of royal policy would have been just the same if this element in society had not existed. I must say that this attitude seems to me perverse in the extreme. I find it impossible to delay the appearance of the knight or burgess in political life until he clamours for recognition. I do not care whether he played an important or formative part in parliament or not before the year 1340 or the year 1376; but I do care to remember that he was an active and intelligent element in the social, economic and administrative life of the country. A man like Henry Bray of Harlestone, just beneath the rank of knight, could read and write and keep accounts in Latin and French, help to administer the affairs of a neighbouring religious house, sit on local commissions, and administer his small property with sagacity. It is quite incredible to me that men of his standing, but more active and experienced in local affairs, were in public matters only the playthings of the royal will and that when they were gathered together at the royal court were dumb.

The significance of parliament in medieval English history does not lie in the initiative of the commons—initiative, indeed, was not claimed as a matter of course until the seventeenth century and is not normally exercised today—but in the recognition that the range of conscious participation in the life of a closely knit political community had been widened to include a large and intelligent middle class. We have not to seek here and there for isolated signs of political assertiveness; we have rather to watch the gradual adjustment of this middle class to a political life which could not exist without it.

The background of parliament was concrete, not abstract. England was a small country, composed of shires and hundreds, administratively educated, so to speak, growing in well being, generally peaceful. Its unity under a strong yet distributed central authority excluded the difficulties which arise from feudal provincialism or isolated city life. Professor Taylor, of Harvard, has recently shown how the size of the French kingdom was an obstacle to the effective working of the representative system in France in the early fourteenth century. Quick co-operation between the court, the towns and their representatives was very difficult. In England the country was, for the most part, under the king's eye. Moreover, the widely diffused training in local affairs, and the absence of any hard and fast distinction between municipal and rural society, prevented the growth of distinct estates. Throughout the public documents of the century 1250–1350 runs the consciousness of community, which is both slower and firmer in texture than the sense of nationality. Finally in this realistic development, men learned to use but were not directed by theory. It did not occur to them, for example, to define "election" or to be worried by the implication of the term "elected". I imagine that in the shirecourts of England the German *"Folgepflicht"*, whose importance has been emphasized by Professor Mitteis in his latest work, was perfectly understood without being consciously expressed. Responsible and respected men gave a lead and others followed not because they were like sheep, but because the lead was felt to be a good one and was received with general approval. The ecclesiastical system had devised careful methods of voting and had consciously adopted the principle "what affects all must be approved by all", and in due course its ideas and practices helped to give precision, no doubt, to the thoughts and actions of laymen. But I do not think that we need look to the Church for inspiration in political thought and action. The clergy, rather, in their archidiaconal and diocesan assemblies were co-operators, more aware of themselves, but not guides, for the suitors of shire and hundred, and the burgesses in their courts and assemblies, had experience behind them. Hence the Englishman, just because he was so familiar with their application in practice, was almost untouched by contemporary discussions about corporations and fictitious persons and the like. He refused to separate the individual from the community. It was not an accident, I think, that, as M. de Lagarde has shown, the one great thinker of our period who deliberately refused to let the individual be lost in the *communitas* was William of Ockham. He knew too much about these things to surrender to the abstractions of the scholars.

CHAPTER XVIII

AFTER FIFTY YEARS [1]

The Council of the Historical Association has done me much honour. I welcome this opportunity to give the annual address. In the early days of the Association, when men like Sir Charles Firth, T. F. Tout, A. F. Pollard, A. J. Grant and others, some of whom are with us to-day, were helping to shape its policy and enlarge its membership, I had a small part in the formation of the Manchester Branch, and I suppose that since then I have done my share of lecturing to local branches and contributing to the Bulletin of annual literature and to *History*. To-day I have no intention to indulge in personal recollections nor to estimate the changes in half a century of historical work and historical teaching. To do the former would be trivial, to attempt the latter might seem pontifical. Yet I cannot resist the desire to take stock. In the year I was born Freeman published the last volume of his *Norman Conquest*; in the previous year Stubbs had brought his *Constitutional History* to a close. Fifty years ago, when I was still at school, S. R. Gardiner was somewhere in the middle of his history of England from 1603 to 1660. I was in my first year at college in Manchester when, in 1897, he lectured at Oxford, as the first Ford's lecturer, on Cromwell's place in history, and in this year Maitland's *Domesday Book and Beyond* appeared. I remember how I cut out Professor Tout's notice of Maitland's book in the *Manchester Guardian* and wondered if I should ever read the book itself. A boy who had been taught little or no history at school, and had soaked himself in Carlyle and Macaulay as great literature, approached the more technical sides of historical investigation with diffidence. The professor lived in a world far removed from his.

This diffidence, it may seem strange to say, did not affect

---

[1] An address given at the thirty-eighth Annual General Meeting of the Historical Association at Birkbeck College on New Year's Day, 1944; printed in *History*, xxix (1944), 2-16.

the sense of power which grew with the eagerness to learn, the sense that, if only time would stand still, all knowledge was attainable, and all truth was an object of knowledge. Indeed, time was in a sense going to stand still. Things were moving quietly and inevitably to a stationary state, such as Dante dreams of in his *Monarchia,* when the problem would be how men might best enjoy this vacancy of time. When I read John Stuart Mill, the part of his writing which fascinated me, as it may still fascinate all of us in his autobiography, was his reflections on the stationary state. It is true that once, inspired, if I remember correctly, by the discourses of a forgotten scholar,[1] I contributed to the college magazine some observations on the Armageddon which was to come; but, though they must have been the truest thing I wrote in those days, I am sure that I wrote, not in a genuine spirit of prophecy, but rather in the mood in which Macaulay described the New Zealander meditating on the ruins of London. How innocent, how ignorant, how safe a boy was then, as he sat and read and read in his father's library, and the chart of history, as he saw it, was unrolled! It was not his fault, for what tremendous fellows these historians were, how sure of themselves and of the world in which they lived! The confidence of the Marxist view of history was tremulous when compared with theirs. The historian was greater than history, just as for most of us the Peloponnesian war is still what Thucydides says about it. Historical criticism, it is true, was gradually undermining authority, and the introduction to it was exhilirating, but it swept aside one finality to put another in its place. Who could know the past if the historian did not know about it? Nor was this the fault of the historian, though perhaps he was inclined to bask in the radiance of the worship. The cause of this confidence was the belief that man had become adequate to his surroundings. That belief has been shattered, and with it the confidence in the historian. The movements of actual living history—not of the history in books—during the last fifty years transcend the changes in the pursuit of and reflection about history.

[1] A. J. Scott, *Discourses* (1866).

Like most things which bring us face to face with reality—and if this is not the aim of the historian and the historical teacher, what is?—the shock has been salutary. There is no room, and no need, for cynicism or scepticism. Historical criticism is our job, and, as the master to whom I owe most was never tired of saying, "a man should never despise his job". A man can never take his job too seriously, but he can very easily take himself too seriously, and so, if I may say so, can an association. Let us try to be frank and simple with each other.

It is often said that the dominating influence in modern thought during the last hundred years has been the historical method. This is *the* historical age. We are living in the middle or, it may be, at the end of the most systematic and thorough effort of the historical spirit ever exerted by the human mind. Now, I am by no means certain what this means. It may mean that the most significant and influential expression of what we call the scientific method, the search for truth regardless of any dogmas, creeds, sympathies or prejudices, is to be seen in the study of the course of human experience on this planet, and this for the simple reason that what affects man most is man, what interests man most is human affairs. If this is what the statement means, I think that, with some reservation, we may accept it as true. It does not divorce the historical from the scientific method as a whole, but recognizes the dependence of one upon the other, perhaps their mutual influence upon each other. It gives full weight to the realization that man is a historically minded animal, and does not claim that he has only recently become one; for one of the achievements of the historical method has been the revelation of the fact that man is essentially historically minded. Every country squire or parson, every village sexton, every man, woman or child, who likes to investigate or to talk or hear about the history of familiar things, has a mental ancestry which has no known beginning and, for all we know, may have existed among the primitive cave-dwellers. Every institution, every assertion of right, every formal act of justice depends upon respect for and the exercise of what, in our pompous way, we call the historical method. From one point of view the Christian religion is a daily invitation to the study of history. The appreciation of history has no break; it is a series of "historical revisions". You and I have no more right to claim a monopoly than the corporation of Blackpool or Brighton has to make a charge for ozone. Hence—and here I come to the reservation—we cannot allow any predominance in the scientific movement of modern times to the historical influence as something new and revolutionary in thought. Man is a historical animal, just as he is a political and generally an inquiring animal. Some people, it is true, have no historical interest and even no sense of chronology, but some people have no political interests and even no political sense, just as some seem to be entirely lacking in curiosity or even to have no common sense. Incidentally, I will add that, in my view, it is the duty of teachers to draw out the historical sense in those, the majority, who have it, and not to pump it into those who are devoid of it, just as the wise statesman tries to build up and clarify the minds of his politically minded compatriots, and does not worry himself about those whose interests lie elsewhere, unless their interests are harmful to the commonwealth. But to return to my argument. Just because man is historically minded, he is quick to see the bearing of scientific discovery upon his traditional conceptions of the past. Sometimes people talk as though the "higher criticism" of texts in recent times has had more influence upon the human mind than the higher criticism of nature. This seems to me to be nonsense. The higher criticism has been simply an application of an awakened critical faculty to a particular kind of material, and was encouraged by the achievement of this faculty to form its bold conclusions. If the biologists, the geologists, the astronomers, the physicists, the anthropologists had not been at work, I venture to think that the higher critics would have been either non-existent or a tiny minority in a world of fundamentalists.

Criticism has always been a prophylactic derived from disciplined common sense, against absurdity and extravagance and, when it is fully awakened, against error. It can be seen at work in Bede's writings about time, in the halt called by William of Newburgh to the new-fangled cult of King Arthur, in clerical efforts to curb the riotous allegorical exposition of Scripture, in Petrarch's insistent contrast between the beneficent features of the ancient Roman empire and the evils of his own age, in the determination of Cardinal Nicholas of Cusa to use only the actual texts of his authorities and to eschew elegant extracts. The examples might be multiplied from later times. On the other hand, historical criticism is naturally conservative and works within the limits of its subject matter and of accepted theories of the nature of things. Its vigour and boldness, and I may add, its occasional wildness, in our times are due to the influence of the natural sciences. And the reception given to it is due to that sense of enlargement which comes of the realization that the history of man, as a thinking animal, occupies a minute period of time on a tiny planet in an immeasurable universe. The higher criticism of our time began long before I was born, but the reception of it as a matter of course, as a thing which no longer disturbs us, has occurred in the last fifty years. Happily, familiarity has shorn criticism of its terrors, and it has in its turn become the target of the informed common sense from which it originally sprang. Man, because he is a historically minded animal, has refused to be thrown off his balance by its revelations. He has too much sense to be dominated by it. In the long run, he finds it easier to adjust his mind to the teaching of Copernicus and Newton and their illustrious successors than to any of the great explanations of history. European thought was guided for centuries by St. Augustine's conception of history, and in our time civilizations have been shaken under the influence of Karl Marx. Theirs was a higher criticism indeed, and a criticism rooted, not in abstract speculation, but in the profound experiences of human life, yet neither St. Augustine nor Marx captured the spirit of man in the way that modern physics has captured it.

At the same time, as we look back over the last fifty years, all of us must be conscious of the *malaise* or discomfort which oppresses the thoughtful study of history. The historical student, especially if he is also a teacher of history, has never been so conscious of the significance of his subject. He is convinced, and rightly, of its importance and is beset by a public eager to know what it is all about; yet he can give no clear answers. This, at any rate, is the impression, probably the strongest impression, left upon my own mind, as I reflect upon the movement of the last half-century, and a most uncomfortable impression it is. The main reason for it is the susceptibility of all of us, whether we are historical students or not, to the sense of inadequacy to which I have already referred. The old smooth generalizations do not seem to fit, and the effort to make new ones is so faltering. The spacious and cultivated ease of our predecessors is denied us, for the whole subject is in a state of constant flux. We can afford to accept so little without testing its accuracy. Interpretation has to wait on scholarship and scholarship has to avail itself of tentative explanations. If we look around for aid, we find that every cognate study or type of reflection is in the same case as ours, while each presses upon us as it never did before. How pleasant it would be if we could just adopt as established truth a body of accepted doctrine, like the Austinian view of sovereignty or the economic man of the old orthodox economists; or if we could afford to disregard, as outside our ken, the work in other fields. The sense of moving about in worlds not realized is so disturbing. And yet, I doubt if our discomfort would be so great, had we not during the last fifty years created a profession which stands in the sight of the world as the authority on history. We have turned history into a "subject." Throughout the schools and colleges of the land we have established a vested interest. We are expected, willingly or unwillingly, to speak with assurance about the most mysterious and most intimate problem that can engage the mind of man, the experience of man as a social being throughout the centuries. And we undertake to instil this lore into the minds of children from the age of 11 +, not in the manner of Scott's *Tales of a Grandfather* or of *Little Arthur's History of England,* but as graduates who have studied the last word on the subject. No wonder that sometimes we feel rather uncomfortable.

I wish to examine this situation more closely; and to relax the tension a little.

History is presented to children as a body of truth. The better they know it the better citizens they will be. What is this body of truth? How is it known? Can anybody *know* an historical fact? If he tries to establish or even to verify a fact, he finds himself faced by a long elaborate process, so long and so elaborate that, at every turn, he has to cut it short by reliance on the work of others. The establishment of a fact is an achievement in deduction, and all of us derive our "knowledge" of history, regarded as a whole, at second, third, fourth, up to nth hand. Moreover, the history which we read, though based on facts, is, strictly speaking, not facts, but a series of accepted judgements, and what we call historical generalizations are judgements about judgements. Yet, as a subject of systematic instruction, whose results in the pupil's mind are submitted to a hierarchy of tests by examination, it inevitably comes to be regarded as a body of objective truth, a sort of photograph of the past. The process of discovery and judgement is lost to view. If you analyse the meaning of the phrase, "I have done the Tudors", you will agree, I think, that this is a fair statement. To do the Tudors in this way may or may not be an enlightening process, but as a preparation for life through the appropriation of truth it compares very badly with the mastery of a language or the capacity to sail a boat. And yet a boy who *understood* the Tudor age would be a very remarkable boy indeed. He would have the wisdom of the ages.

I must not be misunderstood. I believe that, before a student tries to understand a historical subject, he ought to have firmly fixed in his mind a plan or chart of history, and I believe also that a child who has a sense of time and is interested in it can acquire and memorize such a plan, with outstanding dates and relief maps all complete. As I have said, most of the history which you and I know is this kind of history, and we cannot safely proceed without it; but it is not the understanding of history. Pictures and stories may give it life, but it is the alphabet, not the reading of history. It is a chart, not a photograph. And, for my part, I should not attempt to give formal instruction in class in anything more than this. I should take it very leisurely, never crowd it or rush it, and, above all, never philosophise about it; but I should have a very good library, and encourage every boy who wanted to know more about anything to read for himself. I should have class tests in what I had taught, but no examinations, in the usual sense of the term, of any kind. And for boys from the ages of sixteen to eighteen I should do no work in class, but gather about me small groups for discussion. I should give opportunities for the exercise of the historical judgement. All this guidance, formal or informal, I should give in what, for the lack of a better word, I am going to call the hours of leisure.

In short, history is not, in my view, a school subject in the sense that grammar and natural science are school subjects. I use the word grammar in the good old sense which survives in the term "grammar schools", the art of speaking and writing with intellectual mastery in one's own and other languages. By "natural science" I mean the elementary knowledge of the world about us in terms of mathematical abstractions (physics) and of biological processes. These are school subjects both because they have become essential as a preparation for life, and because they are rarely mastered instinctively. History, and its kindred, economics, politics, art and literature are concerned with the life with which boys and girls should be prepared to cope. They should be in the school, but not of it. Man is a historical, political, creative animal. From his earliest years he should be given leisure and opportunity to interest himself in his surroundings and to exercise his creative gifts in art and literature. Our schools should provide drilling—systematic drilling—in a few things, leisure to expatiate in other things, and teachers and friends are needed both to drill boys and girls and to guide their leisure. You may think this Utopian, but it seems to me to be common sense. At any rate it is better than "doing the Tudors". As I have gone so far, I will go farther. The greatest social virtue, it has been said, is consideration for others; and I should try so to staff, equip and manage my school that the hours of leisure could be passed in a spirit of mutual trust. Leisure and compulsion are incompatible. This also seems to me to be common sense. An interest in history is one of nature's gifts, capable of infinite growth. If it begins in joy, it will end, not in tears, but in sweat. It cannot be injected. I should never force a boy to learn history. This is counsel of prudence, for compulsion, when applied to such subjects as history, invites evasion, and evasion is easy. Compulsion is a boomerang which returns in the shape of the soft option, and this is not fair to the universities which have to suffer from the search for soft options. What the history schools in our universities need is not the historical specialist but the well-drilled man or woman who has a mastery of English, Latin and French and wants to read history more than anything else in the world.

This analysis of the discomfort which often afflicts us has so far led me to try to face the problem of the school and to plead for the isolation of well-ascertained and well-ordered facts without bothering, in the presentation of them, about the intellectual processes which the establishment and judgement of "facts" imply. I have suggested that the presentation should be spacious and leisurely, outside the compulsory drill of the curriculum, that the eagerness of the child to ask questions and use his mind should be fed and encouraged by the provision of good libraries and good advice, and that, after the period of presentation is over, the genuine interest in history should be stimulated by discussion; finally, that there should be no examinations. If you still say that this is Utopian, I reply that I am taking a long view, and that it seems to be Utopian only because we regard the machinery of the existing system as fixed, although in truth it is a constantly changing affair of trial and error, contrived by educational authorities and teachers during the last fifty years. I see the possibility of a state of things which, in current jargon, would be a teacher's charter no less than a children's charter. Teachers also need and should have leisure. There is no reason, for example, why teachers in our schools should not give us some of our best historians, scholars like J. E. Morris and half a dozen others, still living, whom I could name. What a relief it would be to have to prepare but the simplest of time-tables, syllabuses and tests and to have to mark no exercises at all! I can never understand why we all acquiesce so easily in the assumption that professors and dons should have the disposal of their time, and teachers in schools should not. The power to dispose of time is not the right to waste it, but an opportunity to use it and not be used by it. I feel this the more strongly because bad scholastic habits tend to spread to the universities. This, however, is another story.

Now I leave the schools and turn to other forms of discomfort; and first to what I will call the discomfort of the historic generalization.

Until the last fifty years I doubt if the problem of the historical generalization caused much discomfort. It created some confusion, but not discomfort. The confusion was due to the fact that while some thinkers generalized in the light of wider conceptions about the place and behaviour of man in the universe, others generalized from the evidence at their disposal, and others, probably the majority, from a mixture of both. For reasons into which I need not enter here, the great Greek historians, notably Thucydides, had steeped themselves in cosmological, moral and psychological reflection, so that their acute and often profound generalizations were controlled, to a greater or less degree, by their philosophy of history. Thucydides, indeed, surpasses all his successors by the sheer intellectual ability with which he fuses generalizations drawn from close and direct observation with his deep convictions about the greater influences at work on man in history, whereas Polybius strikes a note more congenial to the modern mind in his pregnant observations about the ways in which man acts as a social being. It was not by chance that Thucydides opened Hobbes's eyes to the significance of history, while Polybius gives Mr. Toynbee so much material. It was not by chance that Plutarch influenced the contemporaries of Montaigne and Sir Francis Bacon. The deliberate and disiplined pursuit of historical generalizations which we find in the great Italians, in Voltaire and in Gibbon, transmitted ways of thought derived from the pungent, direct, critical yet humane reflections upon human nature so common in the literature of their times, influenced as it was by ancient writers. The difference between this deliberate comment upon history and the more discursive observations which were fashionable between the age of Æneas Sylvius and the age of Goethe lies in the fact that the historians, as acute men of the world, allowed their reflections to play upon a mass of historical material. The reputation of Gibbon as one of the two or three greatest historians who have ever lived is the measure of the delight and satisfaction of the cultivated man as he surrenders himself to the finest expression of a new kind of art. There had been nothing like it before and there can be nothing like it again. One reason for the pleasure which it gave and continues to give is its confidence; it seems to open the door to secrecies and at the same time to assure the reader that no more need be said. It suggests that history is written by scholars to be read by gentlemen. This quality in the older historians has helped later generations of scholars and readers to adjust themselves to the more scientific historical writing whose generalizations seek to reveal history to itself. I am thinking here of the kind of generalizations with which I was familiar as a boy and in my early manhood. I think of Guizot's lectures on European civilization, Maine's *Ancient Law,* Ranke's book on Latin and Teutonic peoples, Seeley's *Expansion of England,* Bagehot's *English Constitution,* Mahan's book on the influence of sea-power in history, Warde-Fowler's *City State of the Greeks and Romans,* W. P. Ker's *Epic and Romance,* Dicey's *Law and Public Opinion;* books which kept pace with historical knowledge and explained it to itself, and were comfortable to the mind. Nowadays books of this kind, numerous though they are, are not guides to history in the same way. Since Graham Wallas wrote *Human Nature and Politics,* they have tended to fall into a separate class. They relate historical investigation, as we have known it, more deliberately to the new learning in the social sciences and anthropology, and in the history of art, literature and thought. They do not ease a burden, but call attention to an infinite complexity. They raise all sorts of doubts in our minds. We tend both to rebel against the challenge which they throw out to us, and to lose our old sense of confidence. We are so busy, so harassed, yet so sure that our particular kind of history has its own validity, that we are inclined to resent the intrusion, while we have an uneasy feeling that we could learn much from the intruders. In a word, we have a sense of discomfort.

Fifty years ago the enlargement of history stimulated rather than perplexed its students. Since the eighteenth century they had welcomed Voltaire, Montesquieu, Adam Smith, Buckle, Lecky, Burckhardt—I mention only a few well-known names—and had been unruffled by or disregarded the philosophies of history. Only Karl Marx had succeeded in troubling the Gibbonian tradition, and he had annoyed, not disturbed, the historians. The emergence of history as a "subject" created a new situation. It gave poignancy to that venerable problem "Is history a science or an art?", and insistence to the demand for clear-cut statements of cause and effect. Moreover, the growth of political and social unrest in a contracting, troubled and mechanized world intensified the desire for certainty. If history is a science, how is it to be interpreted? If it is an art, what are its lessons? The cry arose "We do not want isolated facts or amusement or desultory reflection; we want to know what it is all about and how it can help us. If you can't tell us this, what use are you and your pretentious subject?" And how various the answers have been. Some scholars have retreated into their laboratories and repudiate any responsibility. Here are the facts, say they; make of them what you like. It is a delight to establish them, but what you do with them is not our concern. Others, especially in America, talk as though the incessant pursuit of historical information were in itself a solution of our problem. They try to lift themselves by their own shoulder-straps, and suppose that their pattern of cause and effect reflects the mind of the Creator, an illusion which has provoked one distinguished American scholar, Carl Becker, to the caustic comment, "Hoping to find something without looking for it, expecting to obtain final answers to life's riddle by resolutely refusing to ask questions—it was surely the most romantic species of realism yet invented, the oddest attempt ever made to get something for nothing." Some, like the late Flinders Petrie, go to the other extreme and deny that the concerns of man are any measure of the real value of a subject.

"Government is of great concern, but of little import." Some refuse to admit that history reveals any patterns at all; there is neither concern nor import, neither cause nor effect. Tolstoi and the logical positivists join hands. There are no lessons of history. Some, on the contrary, insist that only the lessons of history matter, but do not agree about the lessons. One says that history is material for the ethnologist, the psychologist, the statistician—they will teach its lessons in the form of laws of human behaviour; another says that history provides its own lessons in the rise and fall of peoples and civilizations and in the lives of great men.

I wish to suggest that the Historical Association might do something to allay the discomfort which I have tried to analyse. Much of it is unreal, due to overstrain, professional seriousness and the wrong kind of specialization. After all has been said, we are still quite safe. Nobody can abolish the past. No power on earth can stop man being interested in himself and his forbears. More leisure for quiet study and reflection, a frank and humble admission that all historical generalization is an aid to the further pursuit of truth, not the knowledge acquired by a learned class, study of the past in the light of the wider experience of mankind, would make a lot of difference. If you say that these are commonplaces, I gladly agree, but add that my repetition of them is provoked by a tendency to overtax both teachers and pupils, an implication that history is so much lore to be displayed, and a belief that the study of a special theme can solve its own mysteries. The Association, in my view, should set itself resolutely against every illusion of the kind. It should do much more than this. Resisting all temptation to apologetic self-assertion, it should range itself beside every interest similar to its own. It should believe in the highest traditions of its subject, as science, art and craft. The best, the only profitable way to study history for its own sake—and who does not, if he loves history?—is to choose the significant things as objects of study. We can best maintain the validity of our own modes of thought, political, ecclesiastical, economic, social, military, by free and unhurried recognition of the help which others, who regard humanity from other points of view, can give. Our generalizations clear the way to thought, they are not ultimatums; they are provisional bases for discussion in which anybody can join. The greatest enemy of truth is the self-contained category of thought. In this sense Tolstoi was right when he said "Once admit that human life can be guided by reason, and all possibility of life is annihilated." I wish that this Association would organize learned conferences on great themes and, in doing so, associate with itself the scholars who are best able to advance our comprehension of them, whether they are historians in our sense or not. The new regius professor at Cambridge[1] once wrote a little book with the title *Science and Social Welfare in the Age of Newton*. Since I began to study history, themes of this kind have acquired reality. Attention to them would do far more to stimulate and encourage us as students and teachers than all our discussions on curricula, methods of teaching, and the like.

There is one last cause of discomfort—the most insidious of all. It is the perverted realism which can be fostered, especially among city-dwellers, by devotion to facts and generalizations from facts. This can make the study of man inhuman. It can divide us from the very thing which makes our study worth while, and turn the lessons of history into a dreary code. "Two things fill the mind with ever-increasing admiration and awe ... the starry heavens above and the moral law within." These well-known words point to the deepest and most ineradicable experiences of man throughout the ages, his joys and his sorrows, his failures and his success. And nobody can forget them more easily than the historian, as he plays with his puppets and his statistics. I do not wish to say more; but I will close this address by recalling to your minds the early experiences of a great Englishwoman of our time.

In 1885 a young woman, twenty-five years of age, was making up her mind about the great issues of life and the way in which she should direct her own life. She had lived in London society, and had no academic ties whatsoever, but she had worked out for herself the relation between history and contemporary social problems. She had broken away from the

[1] Now Sir George Clark, Provost of Oriel College, Oxford.

influence of her friend Herbert Spencer. "He irritates me", so Beatrice Potter wrote in her diary, "by trying to palm off illustrations as data; by transcribing biological laws into the terms of social facts, and then reasoning from them as social laws. . . . I will keep my own mind from theorizing about society. . . . One needs more knowledge of antecedent facts. . . . For instance, a general knowledge of English history, with a due proportion of 'setting' from other contemporary history; a special knowledge of the state of the working man in the different periods of our history, and of the laws regulating commerce and industry; the growth of industrial organization and of its rival organization; influence of religion in determining political and social action; rise and fall of various religious sects with the peculiar activities belonging to them; the difference of race in the working-class communities; the growth of towns and the occupations necessitated by these, and the reaction of these occupations on the minds and bodies of the people; the formation and dissolution of classes, with their peculiar habits of body and mind. There is a study for a lifetime."[1] I may add that it is a very fair forecast of the development of historical work in *my* lifetime, in ancient, medieval and modern social history alike. And here are Mrs. Webb's matured reflections upon the attitude of the historian to life:

"How things happen!" mocks the Ego that denies, "but that does not settle what *ought* to happen."

"I thought I told you long ago," calmly answers the Ego that affirms," that with regard to the purpose of life, science is and must remain bankrupt; and the men of science of today know it. . . . How each of us determines our scale of value no one knows. For my own part, I find it best to live 'as if' the soul of man were in communion with a superhuman force which makes for righteousness. Like our understanding of nature through observation and reasoning, this communion with the spirit of love at work in the universe will be intermittent and incomplete and it will frequently fail us. But a failure to know, and the fall from grace, is the way of all flesh."

I leave these words with you as a New Year's message.

[1] Beatrice Webb, *My Apprenticeship* (1926), pp. 270-1.

CHAPTER XIX

THE ECONOMIC MOTIVE IN POLITICS[1]

My object is to call attention to a common, indeed a general, difficulty in the experience of the historical student. I may define it as a sense of contrast between the strength of the economic motive which the student uses as an explanation of a particular historical process and its elusive behaviour. In his desire to make sense of his subject the historian, if he is honest, must often feel that he is making nonsense of the evidence upon which he has to rely. The golden key turns in his hands into a slippery eel.

The need for food and clothing is so quickly felt that the economic motive has been active in man at all times, and, strange though this would seem to be to its exponents, it has always been known to man. As soon as he had been driven from Eden, he had to make his living by the sweat of his brow. Yet man, as far back as we can have knowledge of him, has always refused to regard this motive as the clue to his way of life. We can see this in the *Odyssey*. Over and over again in this great story, the pangs of hunger and thirst and the dangerous discomforts of cold are violently stressed, so regularly, indeed, that their removal is described in set forms of words. The housekeeper sets a table and puts bread and whatever she has upon it. Wine is mixed and poured out. A cloak is provided. In cold weather a fire is also provided. Nothing else must be done until hunger and thirst and cold are relieved; yet even during this time, respect is paid to the amenities in the grace of hospitality. Hot water is poured out for a bath, oil is rubbed on tired limbs, a ritual of washing the fingers is observed. And then, the eagerly awaited conversation, the questions and answers, the traveller's tale, the real business of social happi-

[1] Reprinted from *The Economic History Review*, xvi (1946), 85-92. This article contains the substance of a paper read to the Anglo-French conference of historians in Paris, September, 1946.

ness begin. The economic motive is transcended, even by the suitors of Ithaca, although these are the Homeric caricature of the economic man, who turns the gracious customs of hospitality into a disgraceful game of grab.

A short-sighted indifference to the dialectic of materialism has afflicted mankind throughout his long experience. Man will insist on turning the material things of life into symbols, into means of grace. Take, for example, the parables in the Gospels. They are about everyday incidents familiar to their hearers. The elder brother of the prodigal, honest hardworking worthy fellow though he was, would instinctively have been repudiated by them; he had not used his position in society to cultivate the graces of life. What are the causes of this disregard for the compulsive forces in the historical process? One cause, no doubt, is the shortness of life. Let us eat, yes, but also be merry, for tomorrow we die. Put in another and deeper way, this sense of the fugitive in life makes man reluctant to devote himself entirely to the furtherance of what, if the dialectic is right, must happen anyhow. Even the sufferers feel the need for a rest from strife, or are slow to cut short pleasant relations with the enemy, or prefer irrelevant vendettas of their own. The more thoroughgoing champions, whether they are capitalists or neo-Marxists, like, in their turn, to anticipate and enjoy the social amenities available to them, and to remind themselves that when free enterprise has had full play or the proletariate has ceased to be, there will be a good time for all. This is not so strange as it may seem, for the idealists are just the same. Immanuel Kant was tempted to deplore the necessity of progress through strife, for he saw so much that would be agreeable in a state of stagnation.

Hence the difficulty of discussing the "reaction between politics and economics". Mankind has been reluctant to distinguish between its social impulses. It has sought to transcend material considerations, not only as an ideal or in times of conscious conflict, but day by day, in the adoption of ways of life. This raises the question: Can the movements or tendencies in human behaviour be independent of the instincts and even the will of man? Is it possible, not by imposing a law of development from without, but by historical analysis, to discover a process in history of which man is unconscious or only reluctantly conscious? I cannot think so. In the world of today, where we seem to be thwarted at every turn by incalculable forces, we do not need to be reminded that "what happens in history need not happen through anyone's deliberately wishing it to happen"; but it has always seemed to me perverse to conclude that there is any one explanation or two or three rival explanations of this incoherence. I am more inclined to agree with Professor Butterfield that "the great prizes in life seem much rather to have been the co-operative achievement of the human race. The things which matter most . . . are products so to speak of history itself." Professor Butterfield is fortified in this view by the results achieved "in an endless number of detailed microscopic investigations on the quiet and apparently less eventful periods" that lie between the cataclysmic events. Personally, I would go a step further, and add that the cataclysms, as also the indubitable influence of outstanding men, good and bad, confirm in a large and dramatic way the truth which minute investigations into quieter and more persistent processes suggest to us—the truth that there is no single impulse in man so compelling or so consistent that concentration on it can "make sense" of history or give us a sure criterion by which the strength of human motives can be judged. We can only say, for example, that the motive of gain was more general at particular times or in particular persons or groups of persons or under particular circumstances than it was in other times or circumstances or in other persons.

In the light of these considerations, I would suggest that historical students should concentrate more closely than they have been wont to do hitherto upon the interplay of economic and other motives in political life. The first need here is to distinguish between the conditions under which the economic motive, in its cruder and simpler expression, is, so to speak, taken for granted, and those conditions under which its operations are subject to conscious reflection. Nowadays we live continuously and anxiously under the latter conditions. Nearly all our political action is influenced by our conceptions of economic forces, by our understanding or misunderstanding of what we call economic law; but this has not been the case throughout the history of the past, and, until recently, human anxiety of this kind has not been general. We used to be told that the wanderings of peoples were due to the pressure exerted by hungry tribes, that the conquests of the Arabs can be explained by the desiccation of Arabia, that the crusades were in fact the outcome of economic causes, that piracy throughout the ages has been a gesture of desperation by the unfortunate. When we think of the dreadful problems created by the displacements, the starvation, the over-population in so many parts of the world today, we are not likely to overlook the measure of truth in such generalizations; yet it is remarkable how quickly the stark struggle for existence gives way to other influences in the history of communities. Political life, indeed, seems to begin as the struggle abates, as movement is succeeded by settlement, and settlement finds room for wider interests. The satisfaction of material needs remains as the basis and condition of social order; it shapes the social pattern, so that the state can never be separated from what von Below calls its economic presuppositions; but it is transcended in the activities and interests of every day. In the more lawless spirits, the craving for the means of subsistence becomes a desire for loot, a piratical profession which gets in the way even of the economic motive, and has to be suppressed if it cannot be disciplined. The depressed classes themselves develop ways of life in which their misery is transcended. Christianity, in the days of the early Church, has been described as a new civilization of the proletariate. Social workers soon become aware of a peculiar culture of the slums, like life in Bleeding Heart Yard, or the social system of the debtors' prison, described by Dickens in *Little Dorrit*. With a surer effect, prosperity, both in the Ancient World and in its successor, transcended the motives which created it and found a justification of its own. The Greeks, it has been said, regarded beauty as a spiritual power that could influence politics. Riches, said Bacon, "are for spending and spending for honour and good actions". Just as the pressure was relaxed at one end of the scale, so a limit was imposed upon the desire to accumulate wealth for its own sake at the other end. This desire gave way to a sense of mental and spiritual freedom. Hence came the cathedrals, the great country houses, the graces of towns and villages, the splendours of public life in Italian and Flemish cities, which so long survived their own decadence. Hence came the apology for riches, that the poor man in a well-ordered society is indebted to the toil of the rich for his livelihood, or, it may be, for his luxuries; and hence, again, the indignant repudiation of arguments of this kind.

Here we come to the influence of reflection upon the relations between economic and political factors in social history. This, it is needless to say, has rarely been entirely dormant, but it has grown with the complexity of society and the consequent realization of the necessity to understand the nature of the social organism and to take longer views in politics. The history of usury provides a good illustration of this point. So far as I can understand the matter, the medieval attitude to usury was more sensible that it is usually supposed to have been. The objection was not to what we call interest or the costs of accommodation (*interesse*) but to usury, the levying of rates or rent on things which were both spent or consumed and at the same time could be returned—cash, grain and the like. There was no objection to a charge for the usage of land and things which are not consumed and in a sense remain the property of the lender. There was no objection to the profits of labour. A man was free to increase the value of parchment by writing a book, or to breed chickens for the sale of eggs. Moreover, the cases in which something might be received in excess of the principal were so numerous that they comprised a large area of the field of transactions in a feudal society. This charge is not usury, but damages, reasonable in itself and approved by the canonists. The discussions by the canonists of the problems created by rent charges and annuities reveal an understanding of social conditions which would be creditable in any body of men in any age. The test of legality was not a pedantic adherence to the definition of usury but the observance of equity. Similarly, all agreed that a borrower of money *need* not be guilty of connivance with usury, for, though the lender might be guilty, necessity or the public welfare might exonerate the borrower; and, the casuist would sometimes add, the usurer would have lent his money anyhow and was not in any way seduced into sin. Nor was there anything wrong in the exaction of a penalty if the money borrowed was not returned on a certain date—what was wrong was to speculate on the probability that the debtor could not pay on that date and to hope that he would not. All this means that the medieval thinkers were quite aware of the complicated nature of economic transactions and were concerned, just as law-makers today are concerned, to put obstacles in the way of the cheat, the forestaller and regrater, the man who takes an unscrupulous advantage of his neighbour and so on. Their traditional conception of the nature of money was false and put them in constant embarrassment, but, so far as I can see, they tried to play fair, not as sophists, but as shrewd men of the world. The time came when it was no longer possible to impose ecclesiastical, still less civil, penalties. The whole business of trade and the instruments of credit was so complicated that moralists could rely only upon general exhortations to probity, as when our English archbishop Tillotson (d. 1694) wrote that the problem of exact righteousness in contracts is "to be handled very modestly by such as acknowledge themselves unacquainted with the affairs of the world and the necessities of things and hidden reasons of some kind of dealings"; yet, none the less, I think a strong case could be made out for the continuity of common sense in the criticism of the economic motive in man, and in the discussion how best both to recognize its necessity and to transcend it in the public interest.

As the late Marc Bloch once remarked, the date when an economic movement is first perceived has a peculiar significance. It tells us when deliberate economic motives can find expression, although the expression may be limited and may not directly affect general policy. Marc Bloch had in mind a passage written by Alain Chartier in 1422. Chartier was referring to the French peasantry. "The common folk (*populaires*) have this advantage, that their purses are like a cistern which has gathered and continues to gather water and drops from all the riches of the kingdom. The rise in prices has reduced the value of their rents and services and their outrageous charges for food stocks and labour daily increase their wealth." The result was a struggle between the tenants and their lords in which at first the tenants were successful, for, during the next four centuries, the tenants won recognition from the civilians of their right to regard their tenements as their property, while their lords, in spite of the growth among them of a capitalist element derived from the trading class, were not able to reassert themselves at once, and, whatever progress they made in the precise definition of legal claims and in the reformation of their domain lands, were never able to win the victory which, for various reasons, came to the English landlord and the Prussian junker. Now here we have an economic conflict which doubtless helped to shape the social system of France and to give a peculiar quality to French politics; but it was not merely an economic struggle. We may be sure that it was, during long periods, a dormant problem, underlying social adjustments and loyalties and softened by social amenities or embittered by local passions. Moreover, it was not purely economic in character. Legal and political movements influenced its course. It was entangled in the larger process between the crown and the local parliaments. It could not, so to speak, emerge into the open and have free play until the deadlock between the central power and those intermediate powers so dear to the constitutional thinkers had been resolved. In short, it was but one expression of the social *impasse* which, until the Revolution, so often doomed a clear-cut economic policy in France to frustration. To see an issue is one thing, to find a solution, except by those ways of transcendence which we call compromise and the method of trial and error, is another thing. I can see little trace of *pure* economic motives in *free* play throughout the course of French or any other history. Other considerations, like the cheerfulness of the pessimist, will persist in breaking in. An economic policy seems to have most chance of success when its promoters have wider and more humane views than its subject matter seems to suggest. The commercial treaty between France and England in 1860 is a case in point. Both Cobden and Napoleon III agreed that a dangerous state of tension must be eased. And it is significant that it was in this connexion that Cobden made his remark about Gladstone, his temporary ally, that Gladstone was the only cabinet minister in England who allowed his heart to get a little the better of his head.

However this may be, the growth in understanding of the nature and bearings of economic conditions has given national life, in increasing measure, the benefits and also the perplexities of self-conscious movement. It has made social activity more intense and more poignant than political and even artistic consciousness can make it, for its penetration has been more wide and deep. In our modern world it has taken the place once held by religion; but it has not given any more coherence; rather, its emphasis on the particular interests of persons and groups tends to incoherence. Indeed, it can only acquire coherence and give additional purpose to politics in the course of a long discipline in which it is enlarged by a wider comprehension and submits to what I have called transcendence. A book which I like to take up from time to time is Professor Notestein's great edition of the diaries and memorials of the English parliament of 1621, in the reign of our James I. About half of this record is concerned with the discussion of economic interests and economic problems, and, regarded as a whole, its incoherence becomes a nightmare. I suppose that most people in England were going about their daily avocations in a quiet, steady and purposive way, but their state, as reflected in the discussions of their representatives in the House of Commons, who at this time were beginning to insist on what Professor Notestein has called the right of initiative, is like a picture in a distorting mirror. Yet English parliamentary government, which, so far, is the most stable form of government in the world, has grown out of all this, and its strength mainly lies in its capacity to deal with our economic life as part of the life of the community. Just as in the fourteenth century the English parliament refused to allow the relations between the crown and the merchants to be conducted apart from itself, so in later times our economic problems, conflicts, and interests have been subjected to the scrutiny of parliament. They have been comprehended in a larger setting and have been forced to contribute to the common welfare. As an illustration of what I mean I will quote a passage (with slight adaptations) from Mr. and Mrs. Hammond's little book, *The Bleak Age,* about the Ten Hours Act of 1847:

> The Bill won its way against the prestige and power of the ablest and most experienced statesmen in public life. Peel, like Cobden, believed that to pass the Ten Hours Bill was to run the risk of industrial disaster. Nobody who heard his speeches could think the danger illusory. He enjoyed greater credit than any other man in public life. He had been familiar from childhood with industrial problems. He had shown that he had larger views than the capitalists and larger views than the landlords.
>
> The House of Commons in 1847 decided to take the risk that Peel thought so menacing. And for what? To banish from English life a terrible formula, the phrase so long remembered in the mills of Lancashire, that the workman's life was eating, drinking, working and sleeping. . . . The English people decided that they would risk the loss of their proud place in the world rather than let that formula oppress their civilization any longer. It was a momentous choice, and the future of England turned on the answer. . . . Every step taken towards civilizing town life meant only another contrast between rich and poor, if the workman was to be shut up in the mill while the well-to-do enjoyed themselves in the park and the library. The Ten Hours Bill was in this sense the most important event of the first half of the century.

In quoting this passage I do not imply that the deliberate discipline of powerful interests has been the normal way of transcending economic motives. My point rather is the capacity of man to control the economic motive whether by resolving its incoherence in the pauses and adjustments of everyday life or by transcending a dominant impulse. In the course of three centuries English politics came under the control of three great economic forces, the landed interest, the chartered companies for foreign trade and plantations, and the manufacturers. These were sometimes in acute competition with each other, but they also became closely interlocked with each other, especially as trade and industry brought capital to the land, and the profits of trading companies in India and the Indies, East and West, and the American colonies gave impetus to the industrial revolution. The outcome, in spite of the evils which give to this long period its tragic element, was one of the most spacious, vigorous and cultivated civilizations in history. The variety of social interests and the geographical security of the British Isles gave them an advantage over the power which at one time had showed a more single-minded concern for economic developments. All proposals "of alliances of common and mutual defence", declared Thurloe, "wherein provision was to be made for the good of the Protestant religion" failed for one and the same reason: "in respect the United Provinces always found it necessary for them to mingle therewith the considerations of trade". And again: "The Hollanders had rather His Highness [Oliver Cromwell, June 1656] be alone in it than that they should lose a tun of sack or a frail of raisins." The position of affairs on both sides of the Channel was much more intricate than these generalizations would admit, but I think it is true to say that at the height of their power the United Provinces, notwithstanding their religious and artistic and learned preoccupations, were not so free to transcend economic motives as England was, and continued to be. As Professor Clark has said, thinking of Robert Boyle's religious interest in the East India Company: "When seventeenth-century writers profess religious motives, they are to be believed unless there is evidence to the contrary." And one of the most glorious episodes in the history of the British in India is the disinterested administration of the Punjab by Henry and John Lawrence and their colleagues in the years before the Indian Mutiny. There is no evidence to the contrary to cloud belief in their single-mindedness.

The outstanding instance, in modern British history, of a

carefully pursued economic policy is that which led to the war for American Independence. In the view of Adam Smith, whose *Wealth of Nations* appeared early in 1776, only a year after the outbreak of hostilities, this policy was purely economic in aim and character. Smith must have written his chapters on the mercantile system before the crisis had begun and he makes no reference to it. Here is the well-known passage:

> In the system of laws which has been established for the management of our American and West Indian colonies, the interest of the home consumer has been sacrificed to that of the producer, with a more extravagant profusion than in all our other commercial regulations. A great empire has been established for the sole purpose of raising up a nation of customers, who should be obliged to buy, from the shops of our different producers, all the goods with which these could supply them. For the sake of that little enhancement of price which this monopoly might afford our producers, the home consumers have been burdened with the whole expense of maintaining and defending that empire. For this purpose, and for this purpose only, in the last two wars, more than two hundred millions have been spent, etc.

This is a precise statement. It says, and with some truth, that the energies of a great nation had been focused on an economic policy, for purely material ends, in the interests of a powerful section of the community. Yet careful scrutiny does not leave it untouched. The suggestion that an empire was deliberately planned and maintained for a definite purpose is a half-truth. While it points to a policy of plantations which certainly was expressed, it neglects both the political traditions, the influence of historical analogies and the sheer spirit of adventure which contributed to these projects of empire, and also the non-economic motives which, from the voyage of the Pilgrim Fathers onwards, did so much to make them a success and to give a peculiar direction to life and institutions in the new settlements. Moreover, Adam Smith elsewhere in his book pays a tribute to the forbearance with which the mother country had encouraged the colonists to establish a tradition of freedom such as existed in no rival empire. It may also be observed that the two greatest critics of the British government, Chatham and Burke, shared, as political thinkers and statesmen, the view denounced by the famous economist, that colonial trade and industry should be restrained in order to bring wealth to the mother country, and would appear not to have realized that this policy was the main cause of American discontent. Here, as in the case of Ireland, the barbed shaft of economic motive had behind it a political momentum, and in the American colonies, more fortunate than Ireland, the poison had not been without its antidotes. And, finally, the very fact that, in this leading instance, economic interests and political theory coincided, was to make their transcendence in the British colonial policy of the future all the more impressive and complete.

My remarks have been too slight and desultory. I wish I could take to myself Dr. Johnson's defence of Adam Smith: "A man who has never been engaged in trade himself may undoubtedly write well on trade; and there is nothing which requires more to be illustrated by philosophy than trade does. To write a good book upon it one must have extensive views." But what I can and do plead for is the belief in history as it is revealed to us in contemporary everyday evidence and less belief in the one-sided generalizations out of which the historian is tempted to try to make sense of his subject. There is a sort of dullness so intense that it must be false. It gives the lie to everything that makes the study of history worth while.

INDEX

ACADEMIES, Union of; see Union Académique
Acton, Lord, 17, 56, 128, 131, 161, 201-2
Allen, Hope E., 189-90 and note
Allen, J. W., 47, 48
Allen, P. S., 85, 168
America, Medieval Academy of, 199
American Historical Association, 109, 110, 162
Anson, Sir William, 49
Armstrong, Edward, 132, 165
Arnold, W., 100
Ashley, Sir William, 24
Aspinall, A., 124
Aulard, 161

BACON, Francis, 243
Ballard, A., 65-6
Balliol, derivation of family of, 57-8
Balliol College, Oxford, 22-4, 90, 121, 165
Barker, Sir Ernest, 166
Baronius, 201
Bateson, Mary, 62, 66, 67, 129, 167
Beazley, Sir Raymond, 48
Becker, Carl, 236
Bédier, J., 114, 186
Below, G. von, 100, 243
Bémont, Charles, 13, 38, 57, 112, 114, 148-9
Bloch, Marc, 245
Bollandists, the Society of the, 185, 195
Boyle, Robert, 249
Bracton, 10, 12
Bradshaw, Henry, 9-10, 129, 131, 136
Bréquigny, L. de, 147
Bresslau, H., 98, 186, 188
Bright, J. F., 22
British National Committee, 197, 210, 214
British Records Association, 198, 209-10
Brooke, Z. N., 127, 128-9, 130-6 *passim*
Brunner, H., 9
Brussels, International Historical Congress at (1923), 18, 39, 106
Bryce, James, Lord, 19, 167
Burdach, Konrad, 184

Burdon-Sanderson, Sir J. S., 79
Burke, Edmund, 251
Burkitt, F. C., 136
Bury, J. B., 131, 132, 136, 191 note
Butterfield, H., 242

CAM, Helen, 130, 217
Cambridge, University of, historical study in, 129-32, 135-6
Cambridge Histories, the, 201-2; *Cambridge Medieval History*, 131-4 *passim*
Canterbury and York Society, the, 195
Carlyle, A. J., 169
Carlyle, Thomas, 225
Carte, Thomas, 147
Centuriators of Magdeburg, the, 201
Chadwick, H. M., 136, 186
Champollion-Figeac, J. J., 146, 147 note
Chartier, Alain, 245
Chaytor, H., 136
Chetham Society, the, 63 and note, 68; James Tait and, 63-4, 195
Christie, R. C., 19, 21, 28 and note, 47, 52, 63
Clapham, Sir J. H., 131
Clark, Sir G. N., 132, 238, 249
Clark, J. W., 129, 131
Clarke, Maude, 207, 217
Clay, Charles, 61 note
Clery, Gregory, 93
Cobden, Richard, 247
Collingwood, R. G., 191 note
Complete Peerage, The, 208
Corbett, W. J., 130
Coulton, G. G., 75, 90, 127-8, 136-41; his pupils, 140
Coville, A., 214
Craster, Sir Edmund, 170
Creighton, Mandell, 131
Crossley, James, 63, 68
Crum, W. E., 48
Crump, G. C., 156
Cunningham, William, 131

DARESTE, R., 13
Davidssohn, R., 186
Davis, H. W. C., 31, 32, 82 note, 118-26, 164-5, 166

INDEX

Delisle, Léopold, 112, 117, 142-9, 154
Delorme, Ferdinand M., 86
Delpit, J., 146, 147
Dempf, Alois, 191
Denifle, H., 186
Déprez, E., 33
Dickens, Charles, 243
Dictionary of National Biography, The, and historical scholarship, 25-6, 53, 54, 56, 59, 82, 124-5, 170, 171
Domesday Book, the study of, 15, 54-7, 64, 72, 75, 77, 112
Dopsch, A., 104, 186, 191
Doucet, V., 139
Doughty, Sir Arthur C., 207
Ducange, 196, 197
Duhem, Pierre, 86, 186
Dunlop, Robert, 47

EARWAKER, J. P., 61
Edwards, J. G., 70
Edwards, Owen, 47, 165
Espinas, G., 102
Estates, the Commission on, formed by the International Historical Committee, 214; paper read to at Zurich, 217-24
Eyton, Robert, 60

FAIRBAIRN, A. M., 48
Farrer, William, 56, 58, 59-64 *passim*
Firth, Sir Charles, 23, 24, 34, 49, 50, 59, 150-3, 165, 169, 207, 225
Fisher, H. A. L., 10, 132, 166
Flacius Illyricus, 185, 201
Fletcher, C. R. L., 165
Foster, C. W., 170, 195
Fournier, Paul, 186
Fowler, G. H., 195
Francis, St., and the Franciscans, A. G. Little's work on, 78 and note, 82, 83-92 *passim*, 139
Fransiscan Studies, British Society of, 87-8, 195
Frederick, the Emperor, accession of (1888), 77-8
Frédéricq, Paul, 97 and note
Freeman, E. A., 42, 47, 48, 71, 146, 167, 170, 180, 225; his library, 20, 31, 52-3, 165
Froude, J. A., 167

GALBRAITH, V. H., 69 and note, 70, 72, 188 note
Ganshof, F. L., 101 note, 102
Gardiner, S. R., 47, 225

Gerville, Charles de, 146
Gibbon, E., 200, 201, 202, 234-5
Gierke, O. von, 100
Giesebrecht, W., 189
Giry, Arthur, 98
Gladstone, W. E., 247; in Oxford (1890), 78-9
Grabmann, M., 186
Graham, Rose, 195
Grant, A. J., 225
Green, J. R., 170; on the Norse settlements in the Wirral, 57 note
Green, T. H., 23, 75, 167
Gross, Charles, 66, 67, 115, 116
Guérard, B., 146
Guizot, 180, 235
Gwatkin, H., 131, 132

HALL, Hubert, 57, 199, 214
Hallam, Henry, 19
Hammond, J. L. and Barbara, 248
Hardy, T. Duffus, 147, 148
Haskins, C. H., 38, 109-17, 149 note, 186, 188
Hassall, A., 165
Hauréau, B., 188
Haworth, Philip, library in memory of, 31
Hearne, Thomas, 186
Henson, Hensley, 49
Historical Association, the, 83, 85, 208, 210, 225, 237-8; address to (1944), 225-39
Historical Manuscripts Commission, the, 170
History, study and writing of, 227-39; about the year 1900, 166-7, 225-6; more recent developments, 168-71, 208-10. *See* International Historical Congress; *also*, Cambridge, London, Manchester, Oxford
Hopkinson, Sir Alfred, Principal and Vice-Chancellor of the University of Manchester, 30
Hovell, Mark, 35-6
Howlett, Richard, 143
Huntington Library, San Marino, California, 40 and note
Hutton, W. H., 49, 165

IHERING, 11, 16 and note, 18
Institute of Historical Research, the, *see* London, University of
International Historical Congress and the International Historical Committee, 106, 196, 214; its

253

INDEX

International Bibliography, 210.
  See British National Committee;
  Estates, commission on; *also*
  Brussels, London, Oslo, Zurich
Irvine, Fergusson, 63

JACOB, E. F., 63 note, 70
James, Henry, 182
James, M. R., 129, 131
Jayne, F. J., 25, 27
Jeffrey, R. W., 190
Jenkinson, Sir Hilary, 195
Jevons, W. S., 19
Johnson, Andrew, 22
Johnson, Arthur, 165
Johnson, Charles, 156, 197
Johnson, Samuel, 251
Johnstone, Hilda, 33, 41
Johnstone, Mary (Mrs. Tout), 40, 41
Jowett, Benjamin, 49

KANT, Immanuel, 241
Kehr, Paul, 187-8
Ker, W. P., 90 note, 166
Kobeleff, General P., 9
Kurth, Godefroid, 97

LAGARDE, G. de, 224
Lampeter, and St. David's College, 24-7
Lamprecht, Karl, 53, 101 note
Langlois, C. -V., 38 and note, 109, 112, 154, 186
Lappenberg, J. M., 145
Lapsley, Gaillard, 130, 217
Lawrence, Henry and John, 249
Lea, Henry Charles, 115, 116, 186
Lee, Sir Sidney, 51, 53
Leicht, P. S., 214
Le Prévost, A., 146
Liebermann, F., 38
Lightfoot, J. B., 128
Little, Andrew George, 21, 31, 73-95, 128, 139, 171, 195; his wife, Alice Hart, 79
  David, 73-4; his wife, 74 and note, 76, 78
  Dora, 74
  Frank, 74
  Thomas, 73; his wife, Ann Wright, 73
Lloyd George, David, 27
Lodge, Sir Richard, 24, 47, 132, 165, 207, 211
London, International Historical Congress at (1913), 39, 82
London University, Institute of Historical Research, 171, 198, 208-10
Lord, Robert Howard, 115
Lot, Ferdinand, 105, 187
Lousse, E., 217, 219
Lowe, E., 195
Luard, H. E., 129, 136

MACAULAY, Lord, 166, 225, 226
Madox, Thomas, 44
Mahan, Admiral, 161
Maine, Sir Henry, 128, 167, 181
Maitland, F. W., 9-11, 15, 33, 41, 54-6, 66, 84, 128, 129, 130, 131, 136, 144, 145, 165, 186, 218, 220, 221, 225
Manchester, The Owens College, later the University, 30, 69-70; history school of, 19-21, 28-33, 47, 50-3, 69, 81, 88, 121, 123-4, 165; Manchester University Press, 21, 30, 31, 70, 88
Manchester, the John Rylands Library in, 21, 30, 31, 60 note, 70, 165
Mandonnet, P., 186
Manning, Bernard, 130, 134
Martin, Olivier, 186, 214
Marx, Karl, 229, 236
Mas-Latrie, L., 197
Maurenbrecher, 161
Mawer, Sir Allen, Provost of University College, London, 65, 195
Medley, D. J., 165
Merewether and Stephens and their effect on the study of the English borough, 66
Meyer, Paul, 90 note, 186
Michel, Francisque, 146 and note, 149
Mill, John Stuart, 226
Mitteis, H., 224
Mommsen, T., 9
Monod, Gabriel, 98
Montague, F. C., 24
Moor, Miss M. F., 17
Moorman, J. R. H., 91 note, 92, 93
Morris, J. E., 233
Moscow, University of, 9, 11-3
Muir, Ramsay, 32
Mullinger, J. B., 129

NITZSCH, K. W., 100
Normandy, development of study of early history of, and of Anglo-French historical studies, 145-9 *passim*
Notestein, Wallace, 247

254

INDEX

OLIGER, Livarius, 85, 89
Oman, Sir Charles, 132, 165, 168
Oslo, International Historical Congress at (1928), 106
Owen, John, later bishop of St. David's, 25, 27
Oxford University, the office of proctor in, 51 note; school of history and jurisprudence, 19; school of modern history, 22-3, 165-74 *passim*; historical seminar, 49, 50; Vinogradoff and, 10, 13-4, 16-7; Firth and, 152; R. L. Poole and, 154

PAGE, William, 196, 207
Palgrave, Sir Francis, 145, 146, 180
Paris, Gaston, 186
Paris, peace negotiations in (1919), 114-5
Parker, Matthew, 129
Parliament, the early history of the English, 217-24
Parsloe, G., 209
Pattison, Mark, 19
Pelster, F., 89
Penson, Sir T. H., 122
Petrie, Flinders, 236-7
Pipe Roll Society, 195
Pirenne, H., 38, 39, 67, 96-108; some of his pupils, 101-2
Pitt, William, Earl of Chatham, 251
Place-Name Society, the English, 65, 195
Plutarch, 234
Pollard, A. F., 38, 171, 225
Pollock, Sir F., 9, 13
Polybius, 234
Poole, R. L., 23, 24, 38, 51, 54, 57, 58, 68, 127, 132, 142 note, 154-5, 165, 169, 186
Porter, A. Kingsley, 114
Potter, Beatrice (Mrs. Sidney Webb), 238-9
Powell, Thomas, 187
Previte-Orton, C. W., 127, 128-9, 130-6 *passim*
Prothero, Sir George, 207, 212, 213; Lady, 207
Prothero, R. E., 49
Prou, Maurice, 189
Prynne, William, 44
Public Record Office, Maitland's visits to, 10 note; Tout and, 34, 43; Willard and, 156-7. *See* Records

RAND, E. K., 117
Ranke, L. von, and his pupils, 161, 165, 167
Rashdall, Hastings, 127, 169
Records, Royal Commission on Public (1912-19), 151. *See* British Record Association, Public Record Office
Renan, E., 128, 167
Richardson, H. G., 214
Riley, H. T., 188
Robertson, Sir C. G., 166
Rose, J. Holland, 47
Rostovtzeff, M., 18
Round, J. H., 23, 56-9, 121, 144, 186
Royal Historical Society, 38-9, 196-9, 206-7, 211-6; former Fellows of (1937), 207
Russia, political developments in, 11-3

SABATIER, Paul, 83, 84, 85, 87, 91-2
Saint-Maur, Benedictine Congregation of, 185, 203
Salter, H. E., 154, 170, 195
Savigny, 11, 16 note, 18, 167
Schmoller, G. von, 97-8
Seccombe, Thomas, 48, 51, 53
Seebohm, F., 9
Seeley, Sir John, 23, 131, 161
Selden, John, 144, 151
Seton, Walter, 87
Sharp, Margaret (née Tout), 41
Shaw, William Arthur, 47
Sickel, W., 188
Sikes, J. G., 134
Simpkin, Sir O. R. A., 123
Smith, Adam, 250, 251
Smith, A. L., 47, 48, 78, 165
Smith, G. Gregory, 48, 50, 51
Sohm, R., 100
Spelman, Sir Henry, 12, 44, 144
Spencer, Herbert, 239
Stapleton, Thomas, 145, 147, 148, 149
Steele, R. R., 86 and note
Stenton, Doris (Lady), 195
Stenton, Sir Frank, 15, 62, 65, 170-1, 195
Stephen, Leslie, 26
Stephenson, Carl, 66-7, 101
Stevenson, W. H., 166, 170
Stewart-Brown, R., 63
Stuart-Jones, Sir H., 49
Stubbs, William, 22-3, 41, 75, 145, 165, 166, 167, 181, 189, 220, 225

TAIT, Beatrice, 70-1
Tait, James, 20-1, 28, 30, 31 note, 32, 37, 44-73, 81, 170, 195

255

INDEX

Tait, Robert, 45, 47
Tanner, J. R., 132
Taylor, C. H., 223
Temperley, H. W., 131
Thévenin, M., 98
Thierry, A., 146
Thomson, S. Harrison, 156
Thucydides, 226, 234
Thurloe, John, 249
Tillotson, John, 245
Tocqueville, A. de, 181
Tout, Margaret, *see* Sharp
Tout, Mary, *see* Johnstone
Tout, Thomas Frederick, 19-43, 47, 51, 52, 69, 81, 82, 124, 127, 156, 171, 186, 219, 225; his parents, 21-2
Toynbee, Arnold (d. 1883), 24
Toynbee, A. J., 234
Troeltsch, E., 17
Tupling, G. H., 63 note

UNION Academique, 107, 195, 196
Unwin, George, 21, 32, 171

VACARIUS, Master, 9
Vattasso, M., 94
Vaughan, C. E., 24, 74-5, 77, 80-1, 82
Victoria County Histories, 56-7, 60-4, 82, 170, 195, 207, 209
Vinogradoff, Sir Paul, 9-18, 31, 39, 56, 96, 101 note, 165, 167

Viollet, Paul, 13, 33
Voltaire, 234, 236

WAKE, Joan, 195
Walker, Professor Hugh, 25, 27
Walker, Thomas Alfred, 47
Wallas, Graham, 235
War Trade Intelligence Department, the (1915-19), 82 and note, 122-3
Ward, Sir A. W., 19-20, 21, 28 and note, 44-6, 51, 52, 63, 131
Warren, T. H., 49
Weaver, J. R. H., 124-5
Webb, C. C. J., 154, 169
Webb, Mrs. Sidney, *see* Potter, Beatrice
Webster, Sir Charles, 205 note
Weiland, Ludwig, 75, 76, 77
Whitney, J. P., 47, 131, 132
Whitwell, R. J., 121
Wilde, W. E., 100
Wilkinson, Spenser, 33, 47
Willard, J. F., 156-8
William I, Emperor, 77
Willis, Robert, 129
Wood, George Arnold, 47, 48, 50, 51
Woolf, L. S., 163

YORK POWELL, F., 9, 47, 49, 56, 151, 165, 166, 168-9, 175

ZURICH, International Historical Congress at (1938), 217 note